PRESIDENTS AND
Political Thought

T0307648

PRESIDENTS AND
Political Thought

David J. Siemers

UNIVERSITY OF MISSOURI PRESS
COLUMBIA AND LONDON

Library of Congress Cataloging-in-Publication Data

Siemers, David J.
  Presidents and political thought / David J. Siemers.
      p. cm.
  Includes bibliographical references and index.
    ISBN 978-0-8262-1866-7 (hardcover : alk. paper) — ISBN 978-0-8262-1878-0
(pbk. : alk. paper)
  1. Presidents—United States. 2. United States—Politics and government. 3. Political
science—United States—History. I. Title.
  JK516.S54 2009
  320.092′273—dc22

                                                2009032145

Composition and design: Aaron Lueders
Printing and binding: Integrated Book Technologies, Inc.
Typefaces: Palatino, Nimbus Roman No9, Poppi-Exquisit

Contents

Preface

WHAT WE REALLY SHOULD KNOW ABOUT BARACK OBAMA

"We hold these truths to be self-evident, that all men are created equal, that they are endowed by their Creator with certain inalienable Rights, that among these are Life, Liberty, and the pursuit of Happiness." Those simple words are our starting point as Americans; they describe not only the foundation of our government but the substance of our common creed. Not every American may be able to recite them; few, if asked, could trace the genesis of the Declaration of Independence to its roots in eighteenth-century liberal and republican thought. But the essential idea behind the Declaration . . . orients us, sets our course, each and every day.
> —Barack Obama, *The Audacity of Hope*

It is mistaken to say that America has got along nicely without political philosophizing. . . . this nation, more than any other, is a work of political philosophy.
> —George F. Will, *Statecraft as Soulcraft*

The long presidential campaign of 2008 allowed the American people to get acquainted with Barack Obama—at least in a certain sense. We discovered that, as with any human being, many different things have contributed to making Barack Obama who he is. His experience with multiple ethnicities and cultures, in Hawaii and in Indonesia, seemed to have a profound effect on him. So too did his anthropologist mother, who taught her son that there is value in each culture and religion.[1] As described in Obama's autobiographical account *Dreams from My Father*, a quest to discover more about his absent father's life and to connect with his African relatives animated his early adulthood. His discovery that churches are the social and spiritual glue of the black community in Chicago transformed his life. In 2008 we got to know these things and with them to know Obama the person, quite well.

Additionally, the media paid a great deal of attention to his positions on issues. Like every other recent presidential-campaign organization, the Obama camp offered up a blizzard of proposals, covering almost every subject about which Americans are concerned. The opposing candidates criticized these proposals, the media scrutinized them, and the American public judged between his suggestions and what the other contenders offered. All this is as it should be. Understanding the candidates' personal backgrounds and policy positions are vital to casting an informed vote.

But there is another matter which voters should consider. It is one about which we typically have almost no information. Citizens should know the theories about politics, if any, that a president carries with him or her into the White House. We routinely fail to consider the ideas which unify a candidate's thinking. This is like hiring a teacher by looking over lesson plans and a résumé but not bothering to ask about her teaching philosophy. This is akin to a church hiring a pastor on the basis of old sermons and testimony about the spiritual milestones in his or her life but not inquiring about theology. It is like hiring a football coach by looking at game tapes and finding who he coached under but failing to ask about the "West Coast offense" or other ideas about how to be successful in the sport.

In the vast academic literature on the presidency there is almost nothing about how, in general, presidents' ideas have shaped their policies and strategies. There is a literature on presidential personality, on the constraints presidents work under in implementing their agendas, on the bargaining situations they face with Congress and the courts, on how the ebb and flow of political cycles affect their success, on how public opinion impacts the presidency, and on many other subjects. These are worthy lines of inquiry. However, we shy away from discussing a president's views about politics and how these ideas or theories contribute to what the president proposes and does.

Consider how little we know about Barack Obama's theoretical approach to politics. Obama went to Harvard Law School, but rather than the substance of what he learned there, what we know about those three years is that he became the first African American president of the *Harvard Law Review*. He was an undergraduate at Occidental College and Columbia University, where he took political science classes. Even attentive students of Obama's life have heard next to nothing about the courses he took as an undergraduate. Did he apply any of the lessons he learned in the halls of higher learning to the jobs that he has subsequently occupied?

Obviously learning about politics is not something that happens only in universities. Have Obama's life experiences given him an understanding of how politics works? Has he been reading about politics in the last twenty-five years? If so, what? Has he been reading books on political theory, a discipline which offers up visions about how politics works—and about how it *should* work? If so, what has Obama agreed with and what has he disagreed with in this field?

Has Obama thought about how human nature shapes politics? Has he pondered how government institutions should be arranged to help democracy work? What is his attitude about theories of politics themselves? Among all the ink used to explain Barack Obama, only a tiny portion of it has been devoted to examining these matters. Yet Obama's intellectual understandings and his theoretical commitments are arguably more important to know than any particular policy position, because he might bring theory to bear across many issues. Theories may go beyond inspiring policy stances to influence how he understands the president's role in the constitutional system, and they might frame his approach to the rule of law. In the writings of political theorists he may find ideas and phrases to use in public speeches.

What happened in the 2008 campaign is a microcosm of American presidential history. We have known far less about the intellectual lives and theoretical views of our presidents than we should. A president's personality, background, and policy preferences are important things to know, but his or her theoretical approach to politics is important to know too. If a presidential candidate has a general orientation toward politics, voters should be aware of what it is. If the candidate lacks any theories about politics, voters should know that as well. Candidates can be asked to explain and justify why they believe in certain theories. If a candidate claims not to have theoretical commitments, the candidate should be asked to explain why it is unimportant or even problematic to have them.

The passage from Obama's book quoted above indicates that he knows something about political theory. He cites the Declaration of Independence's opening words, authored by Thomas Jefferson. He knows that these words were directly inspired by a political philosopher—John Locke—and his book *The Second Treatise on Civil Government*. Locke's and Jefferson's words assert that every human being possesses rights by virtue of his or her humanity. Both men used the assertion to argue that governments must work in certain ways: governments must respect rights; they must protect property, safeguard citizens' lives, and generally respect their autonomy; when a government does not do these things, then a new government which does protect rights can be implemented.

Not only does Obama acknowledge this theory, he stresses its importance. Jefferson's language and the ideas behind it are the United States' political spine, according to Obama. He waxes poetic about the profound influence that these ideas have had on the lives of Americans, even though most do not know that they were conceived by Enlightenment political philosophers over two centuries ago. He says that these ideas "orient" us and "set our course."

A careful reading of *The Audacity of Hope* demonstrates that this stance is more than high-flown rhetoric. Barack Obama has read political theory. He has incorporated some of its ideas into his worldview. He has pondered it seriously enough to develop an attitude about the utility of theories of politics. And he has embraced ideas which have significant real-world implications both in the policy arena and in how he conceives of his job as president.

Obama mentions several political philosophers in *The Audacity of Hope*. He references John Locke and Thomas Hobbes as among those who helped inspire Americans to conceive of proper citizen-government relations as a contract, where rights are safeguarded in exchange for allegiance.[2] A number of modern professors and politicians have updated the idea of the "social contract," using the phrase to refer to the social safety net of the modern welfare state. Obama has explicitly adopted this language, typically employing the phrase "social compact."[3] Endorsing this idea means that he wants to place special emphasis on what American citizens owe to each other—a decent education, a living wage for those who work, Social Security for the aged and disabled, and something approaching universal health care. This theory about politics—the social compact—helps to explain Obama's domestic-policy commitments.

The *Los Angeles Times* reported in January 2007 that as an undergraduate Obama took courses in political theory from Occidental College's Roger Boesche. The *Times* mentioned that in Boesche's classes he read the writings of a number of unspecified American political theorists, as well as works by Friedrich Nietzsche and Max Weber.[4] Obama seems to have put these lessons to some use. He relates that "in my teens, I became fascinated with the Dionysian, up-for-grabs quality of the era [the 1960s]." This may be a reference to Nietzsche's book *The Birth of Tragedy*, where Nietzsche used the term "Dionysian," after the Greek god of wine, to refer to a raucous, self-centered lifestyle, or to Allan Bloom's adoption of the term to describe the 1960s in *The Closing of the American Mind*.[5] By his own admission, Obama was focused on selfish matters in his young adulthood. Though he does not say so explicitly, there is the suggestion that he was influenced by Nietzsche's antiestablishment "will to power."

Yet Obama takes pains to tell readers that he came to reject that way of life. In his more sober moments in college, Obama realized that a "Dionysian" worldview held in contempt the values he was taught by his grandparents. Nietzsche disdained responsibility, respectability, and faith. Obama's renewed embrace of these values imparted a healthy skepticism about political theory. He knows that political theory can advocate things that are very harmful—destructive of the kind of social cohesion upon which the social contract depends. Thus he begins *The Audacity of Hope* by deliberately acknowledging, "I offer no unifying theory of American government" but "something more modest," and he calls himself a "skeptic."[6]

How can the person who has inspired so many possibly call himself a skeptic? Obama's skepticism is about political theory and its ability to effect fundamental transformations of the world. *The Audacity of Hope* suggests that only by reemphasizing common core values can Americans make their politics better. The subtext—only briefly hinted at—is that reemphasizing values requires abandoning neat theories about politics and economics which purport to have the truth, but which are destructive in practice.

In April 2007, *New York Times* columnist David Brooks reported that he was conducting a rather lackluster phone interview with Obama in which they were discussing foreign aid. Realizing that, as it was going, the interview would not help him write a good column, Brooks turned on a dime and asked Obama if he had ever read the Christian realist theologian Reinhold Niebuhr. "Obama's tone changed," Brooks noted; the presidential candidate answered, "'I love him. He's one of my favorite philosophers.'" Brooks asked, "What do you take away from him?" and "Obama answered in a rush of words, 'the compelling idea that there's serious evil in the world, and hardship and pain. And we should be humble and modest in our belief that we can eliminate those things. But we shouldn't use that as an excuse for cynicism and inaction.' "[7] Brooks had just experienced a revelation about Obama's worldview. In the following day's editorial he pointed out that this position does not offer foolproof answers about what to do. However, it is not meaningless either. It points to such things as a more realistic and muscular foreign policy than many liberals advocate and also a skepticism about "the grand Bushian rhetoric about ridding the world of evil and tyranny and transforming the Middle East." Obama is a Christian realist, like Niebuhr, whose chastened take on democracy was that "man's capacity for justice makes democracy possible, but man's inclination to injustice makes democracy necessary."[8]

There is nothing out of the ordinary in the values which Obama finds praiseworthy. They include personal responsibility, hard work, self-improvement, drive, risk taking, and self-reliance, leavened with a healthy dose of "social solidarity." Emphasizing these values *over* theory is important to Obama because "values are faithfully applied to the facts before us, while ideology overrides whatever facts call theory into question."[9] This

sentence from *The Audacity of Hope* deserves some unpacking. It says that
those who possess an ideology or theory stick to it rigidly, regardless of
the presence of evidence which would disconfirm the theory. Ideologues
move through the world with blinders on. By contrast, values deal "faithfully" with facts. Those who lead with their values rather than a theory
do not warp the world to see it as they wish to see it. They can react to the
world as it is, applying their values situationally, to beneficial effect. Values
trump theories. Or, to put it more precisely, values *should* trump theories.

This means that Obama thinks that values do not necessarily win out.
Enter his critique of the Republican Party. Obama suggests that the main
problem with the current Republican Party is that it has "absolutist" tendencies—in its approach to taxes, free markets, and religion. Rather than
developing a platform based on probing the needs of the American people, or applying basic values to politics, the party offers up an ideology
driven by the law of supply and demand and a variant of Christianity that
is impermeable to lived experience. By contrast, Obama praises the American founders for doing precisely the opposite. They "were suspicious of
abstraction and liked asking questions, which is why at every turn in our
early history *theory yielded to fact and necessity.*" He singles out the authors
of *The Federalist* for their practicality. Obama notes that they discovered
that a popular government is more likely to work the larger the territory it
encompasses—a clear reference to James Madison's argument in Federalist No. 10. This discovery is praised because it used observation to reverse
the theoretical orthodoxy of the day, which "assumed that such a system
could work only for a geographically compact and homogeneous political
community."[10] Thus to Obama the founders were not theorists. They were
more practical than that. They applied values to experience as a means of
solving particular problems. Whether these interpretations of the Republican Party and the American founders are true or not is eminently debatable. What is clear is that Barack Obama has developed a suspicion of
abstract theories and their ability to effectively solve real-world problems.
He suggests that to the extent that politicians are devoted to their theories
they are unrealistic and unhelpful.

Obama does not want to go too far, however. He praises "the Enlightenment spirit" as something which inspired the founders to be practical. Thus
his is not a blanket condemnation of political theory. It may be that he thinks
if a theory is self-aware, emphasizes practicality, and allows adherents to
learn from empirical reality and adjust to changing conditions, then it might
be useful. His words about Locke and Jefferson imply that political theory
can have value to the extent that its ideas become widely shared cultural
norms. In other words, what Jefferson wrote is no longer a theory so much

as it is a shared value—and that makes a great deal of difference. Someone like this, who is a political-theory skeptic, is likely to approach the discipline with caution, chafing at its many hard edges. But there is also a long tradition of practical or "empirical" political theory, which emphasizes real-world solutions. Obama is the latest in a line of presidents who have rummaged through political philosophy, discarding most of it as impractical or extreme, but finding value in certain key ideas, thinkers, and concepts.

Obama's theoretical approach and commitments help us to make sense of his policy choices. He believes that it is worth sitting down with the governments of nations from whom we are estranged, in part because there may be a convergence of human values which extend to cultures where tyrants reign and in part to effect a pragmatic truce. His attempts to reach across the aisle and forge a post-partisan politics are built around the premise that if we move our national discourse away from ideology and toward values we can find some common ground. His proposals to update and strengthen the social safety net fit with his conception of government as a meaningful social compact of mutual benefit. He has confidence that he will be supported by the American people in this shift toward values because they "recognize the difference between dogma and common sense."[11] But he also understands that there are strict limits to the positive change he or government can bring.

A president who approaches politics with ideas about theory in mind has an anchor which can provide a good deal of guidance and confidence. This is not to say that having such an outlook prefigures success. This is one of the lessons to be found in this book. Theories must be interpreted. They are not ready-made blueprints. And when theories are applied to practice there are always challenges. Obama's plan to forge a bipartisan consensus by de-emphasizing theory in favor of values cannot change the stark fact that the two parties are now highly polarized. It remains to be seen how frequently he uses terms like "social contract" and "social compact" and how much these terms resonate with the public. He is not the first president to employ them, after all. How successful he will be in promoting policies which promise collective benefits is an open question in a nation founded on individualistic principles. Promised collective benefits also butt up against the reality of the need for more public revenue in a time of fiscal crisis. His emphasis of Niebuhrian realism over theory suggests that incrementalism and workability will be stressed more heavily than policy coherency. If this is the case, one of President Obama's key challenges will be to justify a set of choices that will seem ad hoc and unconnected. There may be a method behind this approach, but such pragmatism is not as neatly explained as other, competing views about government.

In short, we cannot fully understand President Obama without knowing something about his theoretical approach to politics. This is essentially true of every president and every candidate for the presidency. This brief commentary on Barack Obama offers a preview of things to come. In this book I will conduct an in-depth examination of six presidents' theoretical approaches to politics. I do so for three reasons. First, as a political theorist, I am interested in knowing whether and how political theory has had an impact on the "real world." Second, I want to discern whether there are patterns that emerge when theories about politics and political practice interact. Third, in the course of doing research I learned how little we know about the ideas of many presidents. I want to set the record straight about them, as best I can, and to reemphasize to my fellow citizens that we should be taking the ideas of presidents more seriously. Paying greater attention to the ideas of presidents will not enable us to predict with certainty what they will do. However, this book demonstrates that we cannot ignore the connection between presidents and their ideas if we hope to understand the presidency and to explain the actions of those who are the office's temporary stewards.

Acknowledgments

This book would not have been possible without those who have diligently researched individual presidents' intellectual lives. Ralph Ketcham's *James Madison: A Biography* is the gold standard of this kind of research. C. Bradley Thompson's *John Adams and the Spirit of Liberty* and Niels Aage Thorsen's *Political Thought of Woodrow Wilson* deserve special mention as excellent contributions within the discipline. These and many other scholars writing in this vein provide metaphorical shoulders for me to stand upon. There are a number of journalists who do good work in this area as well. David Maraniss and David Brooks are easily two of the best. For each president I have developed my own understanding and interpretation, but previous research has made this easier with some of the figures I discuss here.

Equally vital in facilitating this work are the documentary compilations of presidents' writings and speeches. Compiling and publishing the papers from a well-known life is a monumental task. From *The Papers of John Adams* to *The Papers of Woodrow Wilson*, these compilations have provided critical source material. Some may doubt the merit of printing every extant written fragment of a president's life, but important pieces of my puzzle were found in documents which almost surely would not have been included in briefer compilations. Thanks go to the editors of these collections, from Charles Francis Adams to Julian P. Boyd and Arthur Link. They, their associates, and the publishing houses which saw fit to bring this information to light have done the American people a great service. Collecting and disseminating the papers and writings of presidents is a tradition which must continue, though it is threatened by the twin challenges of "executive privilege" and the decreasing economic viability of academic publishing.

Those who have read this manuscript through offered many important suggestions which helped to improve the book a great deal. James H. Read understands American political thought as well as anyone I know, and he has been consistently willing to donate his time and share his expertise. Paul Schumaker urged me to see even more value in this work than I claimed for it by helping me to bring the book into the present era. Robert Booth Fowler continues to be a valued mentor and an important intellectual resource. Brian Dahlstrom demonstrates that the best student-teacher relationships never end with his continuing interest in what I have written and his valuable suggestions, though our brief classroom experience ended long ago.

Discussants at several conferences helped me to clarify my arguments and to more clearly conceptualize the book as a whole. They include Edward Heck, Evan Oxman, Robyn Marasco, Eric Beerbohm, Shirley Anne Warshaw, and Sean J. Savage. I also received valuable advice and assistance from Charles O. Jones, George C. Edwards III, Andrew Jackson O'Shaughnessy, John Bachman, William A. Galston, C. Bradley Thompson, and John P. Kaminski.

This project would not have been finished expeditiously without the assistance of the University of Wisconsin Oshkosh's Faculty Development Program, under the able direction of Linda Freed. Research on Presidents Madison and Clinton was completed with the aid of faculty-development grants. A one-year sabbatical in 2007–2008 offered me the opportunity to conduct further research and time to write the manuscript. I am proud to be at a school which supports scholarship as a means of increasing the expertise of its faculty and the vitality of their teaching. Fortuitous hires in recent years have helped the political science department at the University of Wisconsin Oshkosh grow into a highly professional, collegial, and supportive environment. I look forward to sharing experiences, professional and otherwise, with my colleagues for many years to come.

A Beeke-Levy Research Fellowship enabled me to conduct research at the Franklin Delano Roosevelt Presidential Library in Hyde Park, New York. I thank the Franklin and Eleanor Roosevelt Institute for its support and the staff of the Library for their assistance. Thanks go to the University of Missouri Press for enthusiastically supporting the book.

Finally, special thanks to my family. It is a blessing to have parents who value learning and who encouraged me to pursue it as far as I was able. Roger and Janice Siemers know that I am still at it. My brother, Jeff, a reference librarian, assisted me in tracking down some key sources and helps to distract me from political theory with canoeing and other fun pastimes. I want to dedicate this book to the memory of my grandparents, Arnold and Margaret Siemers and Leonard and Frieda Roecker. Their lives spanned the presidencies from William McKinley to Bill Clinton. Just by being who they were, they helped me to love history.

PRESIDENTS AND
Political Thought

Chapter 1

ON PRESIDENTS AND IDEAS

The President has a position of immense dignity, an unrivalled platform from which to impress his ideas (if he has any) upon the people.
—James Bryce, *The American Commonwealth*

Even with the power of the presidency just emerging from its low ebb, Oxford University professor James Bryce found the office to be a focal point in the American system of government. In 1893, Bryce, a future ambassador to the United States, stressed that a president might persuade the public to see the value of his ideas. But Bryce also took pains to suggest that presidents do not necessarily *have* any ideas, worthy or otherwise. As he wrote what would become the late nineteenth century's definitive text about American politics, Bryce was struck by how much the presidency had changed in its first century. A change he chose to highlight was the intellectual training of the office's occupants.

Initially, the presidency was occupied by some of the nation's best-educated men. Their ideas helped chart the early republic's course. However, the presidency became an office filled by unremarkable party hacks—Bryce called them "intellectual pigmies."[1] These partisans were adept at doling out patronage and placating rival factions of their parties, but they were not "men of ideas." To Bryce, many of them did not have *any* ideas worth mentioning. Once in office, these presidents did not substitute what got them elected—the politics of patronage and sloganeering—with a vision for government. Most of them were incapable of doing so.

Bryce thought that ideas might still have their place in politics, but that a chief executive brimming with ideas was not normally in demand. Only at a critically dangerous juncture like the Civil War had a recent president provided significant leadership. "In quiet times the power of the President is not great. He is hampered at every turn by the necessity of humoring his party."[2] The presidency, concluded Bryce, is flexible enough to allow

1

a president with worthy ideas to lead—if the president has any worthy ideas in the first place. If he does not, the intellectually bereft party hack would probably not do irreparable harm.

Bryce segregated the presidents from George Washington to John Quincy Adams from later presidents. He characterized this earliest group as "statesmen in the European sense of the word, [and] men of education," implying that they developed an approach to politics partly from the study of politics in school and from books. Bryce had this experience himself. The professor was highly educated and had been a member of Parliament for nearly three decades. He felt that his own education had been an indispensable preparation for elective office. In comparison, the American presidents after John Quincy Adams lacked formal education in politics. They may have gone to college and they were certainly knowledgeable about politics because of their experience, but they had not undergone the kind of training the others had. To be clear, there *were* "statesmen in the European sense of the word" and "men of education" residing in the United States during this later period—but they did not become president.[3]

The presidency of today is not the presidency of Bryce's time. Nor is it the presidency of the early republic. With a public now accustomed to active campaigns and vigorous presidential leadership, no presidential candidate could possibly be without ideas and expect to win. All presidents after Harry Truman have graduated from college. In the typical modern campaign every viable candidate is a college graduate and many have earned advanced degrees. But the possession of a sheepskin does not capture Bryce's meaning. When he used the term "men of education" and the phrase "statesmen in the European sense of the word" he was not suggesting that early presidents were advantaged because they had diplomas. George Washington did not have one, after all. Nor was Bryce suggesting that the early presidents possessed well-reasoned positions on every issue of the day. He was claiming that their approach to government was aided by an education which induced them to think of politics in a different way than those who were schooled only by political practice. The earliest presidents knew something about political theory. This helped them to visualize politics as more than the satisfaction of interests and the skillful doling out of patronage. They could not have founded the country they did without this broader perspective. Their presidencies were governed by principles as much as interest—principles characteristic of "men of education."

In the presidency of his day, Bryce mused that an educated officeholder might be very frustrated. "The present system makes a wire-puller of [the president]. It throws work on him unworthy of a fine intellect, and for which a man of fine intellect may be ill qualified."[4] In the transformation of the presidency during the nineteenth century, Bryce believed that something important—a style of leadership which emphasized an informed, principled approach taught through advanced education—had been lost.

The matters at issue in this book are approached, if somewhat obliquely, by Bryce: Which presidents knew something about political theory? What did they know? In what ways did political theory affect the presidencies of these "men of education"? Was political theory useful or harmful to the presidents who knew something about it? How did the presidents who knew something about political philosophy implement their understanding of it in practical politics? What were their attitudes about political theory? Studying the intersection between the presidency and political thought through in-depth examinations of six presidents has helped me to answer these questions. These six presidents are John Adams, Thomas Jefferson, James Madison, Woodrow Wilson, Franklin Delano Roosevelt, and Bill Clinton.

Jesus, Burke, and Machiavelli

During the 2000 presidential campaign, the leading Republican candidates were asked at a debate in Iowa, "What political philosopher or thinker do you most identify with?" The question, submitted from the audience, seems to presume that presidential candidates *should* develop a theoretical knowledge of politics and apply that theory to practice. Why else would it matter which political philosopher or thinker they identify with? Candidates were not asked to tell about the specific ideas they had internalized, but the questioner likely hoped to elicit that information too.

This question may have been posed as a deliberate test of the Republican front-runner, George W. Bush. Already during the primary season it was clear that Bush had spent much more of his life partying than reading. For a modern presidential candidate he was unusual in that his life seemed to have gained serious purpose only after his fortieth birthday, when he quit drinking and embraced Christianity with renewed fervor. Earlier in the campaign he had been quizzed about foreign leaders and had failed to produce the names of several leaders he would have to deal with as president. If Bush fumbled the answer to this question, the concerns about his intellectual qualifications might deepen.

Bush had sixty seconds to answer. The political philosopher or thinker that Bush identified with the most was "Christ, because he changed my heart." Taken aback by the candidate's brevity (the quote in the preceding sentence was his full answer), Des Moines television news anchor John

Bachman pressed Bush to elaborate, saying, "I think the viewer would like to know more on how he's changed your heart." Bush responded, "Well, if they don't know, it's going to be hard to explain. When you turn your heart and life over to Christ, when you accept Christ as the savior, it changes your heart. It changes your life. And that's what happened to me."[5]

This answer was exceedingly vague, probably frustrating the intent of the audience member who posed it. In a classroom, such an answer might be thought inadequate, but this was no classroom—it was an auditorium full of Republicans from Iowa. Bush's answer fit the situation and it was politically astute—it signaled that he was a man of faith without getting into any divisive specifics about how his faith impacted his politics.

Some subsequently ridiculed Bush for suggesting that Jesus was a political philosopher. This criticism was unfair, because the question asked what philosopher *or thinker* the candidate identified with. Virtually anyone who has uttered words relating to politics can be considered a political thinker, including Jesus. Among the statements of Jesus which might lead us to consider him a political thinker is the line from Romans 13 "Render unto Caesar what is Caesar's. Render unto God what is God's." What this meant in Jesus's own time is a controversial matter. What it means today, in a context vastly different from the one Jesus lived in, is even more difficult to discern.

Therefore, a more valid criticism is that the answer gave the American public no clue about how Bush's identification with Jesus affected his policy commitments or how it would impact his decision making in office.[6] Bush was narrowly elected in 2000 and he served two full terms. His answer to this debate question demonstrates that knowledge of political philosophy is not a prerequisite for the job. Iowa Republicans did not demand it in 2000, nor did the American people more generally. When given the chance to polish his intellectual credentials for the office, Bush made a point of declining the offer.

Meanwhile, candidate Steve Forbes cited John Locke as his favored political philosopher. Forbes's mention of someone academics readily accept as a political philosopher did not help his standing in the polls. The audience was not looking for an academically inclined president, and the media did not report Forbes's answer. But what if the audience *had* been looking for such a candidate? Would it have been helpful to a President Forbes that he knew something about and admired John Locke?

Consider a hypothetical scenario: what if, instead of describing Jesus as his favorite political thinker, George W. Bush had named the seminal conservative thinker Edmund Burke? Giving the latter answer would almost surely have meant that Bush had read *Reflections on the Revolution in France.* If Burke were Bush's favorite thinker, the president would have had great respect for Burke's distinctive contributions to political thought. This would almost surely have included the observation that attempts to tear down long-established governments and replace them with regimes not reflective of a nation's indigenous traditions are bound to fail.

Identifying with Burke would produce a deep and abiding antipathy toward nation-building. The Burkean president would understand that any attempt to fundamentally restructure a nation's government is likely to be the result of the foolish overconfidence of those who advocate radical change.[7] Regardless of the veracity of Burke's claims, if Bush had read and accepted his ideas, it is almost unthinkable that Bush would have ordered the invasion of Iraq in 2003. At the very least he would not have so underestimated the difficulties of a foreign occupation and an imposed turn toward democracy.

Of course this is just a hypothetical scenario. A theoretically informed politician could be an adherent of any political philosopher, or any combination of them, and these commitments would not necessarily be beneficial. Identification with the ideas of a political philosopher could do massive harm. Consider the rumor that Joseph Stalin was a devoted reader of *The Prince,* by Niccolo Machiavelli. It may be true that Machiavelli himself favored the least amount of violence to produce a stable regime, as Sheldon Wolin argues, but in the hands of a paranoid or sadistic leader like Stalin it is a short distance from being "wholly bad" *to induce stability,* as Machiavelli counsels a leader must sometimes be, to ordering the indiscriminate slaughter of innocent people for reasons of state.[8] Luckily, Americans seem not yet to have elected a Machiavellian sadist to the presidency.

A Burkean president and a Machiavellian president would do vastly different things, even if both took their commitments to political theory very seriously. But these possibilities suggest that presidential political theory may have a profound impact on politics. And it has. A number of American presidents have had at least some acquaintance with political theory. This book examines six of them. While each dealt with it differently, political theory affected their commitments, contributed to their understanding of politics, sharpened their views, and influenced their practical choices.

The subject matter of this book, then, is rather easily described. Political theory is the input; the conceptions and behaviors of six presidents who had some knowledge of political theory are the outputs. The six cases treated in the subsequent chapters are quite different, demonstrating that no two people approach political philosophy in precisely the same way.

These six presidents read different books. They learned in different ways. The breadth and depth of their knowledge varied widely. Their attitudes toward political theory as a body of writing differed too. The substantive commitments each internalized from it are unique, as are the ways each applied it to practice.

Partisans have predictably congratulated theoretically informed candidates for their intellect. Foes have engaged in the equally predictable behavior of deriding the theoretically oriented as bookish and unrealistic. These accolades and attacks are politically convenient, because they tap into widely held preconceptions which are readily understood. These assumptions include the idea that presidents should be intelligent, the view that theories are more intellectually rigorous than "everyday" thinking, and the belief that academic theories tend to be impractical. While there may be some truth to these preconceptions, they are also not fully compatible with each other. In the six case chapters which follow I will judge the relationship between presidents and political theory on the basis of evidence rather than on assumptions. The presidencies of the six men featured here suggest that such preconceptions fail to capture the complicated relationship between political theory and political practice as it plays out in the hands of presidents. Someone need not be unusually intelligent to read political theory or to apply it. Theories may be built around questionable assumptions and faulty logic. Presidents (and others) acquainted with political theory can strive mightily to be practical. Theories may be constructed with an eye to practical results.

Each of the six cases presented here is unique, but there are common threads running through them. First, political theory is available as a source for ideas which are often applicable in the real world. Approached judiciously, political theory may increase the range of options a president may consider and may help a president choose actions and consider alternatives. Second, presidents interested in political theory typically go to a lot of effort to distinguish good ideas from bad ones within the discipline. Thus it is of very little value to label a president "theoretical" or "atheoretical." What is far more important is specifically *how* someone was theoretical or atheoretical. It is critically important to explain how individuals approached various theories. Third, each of these presidents faced significant challenges in translating theoretical views to practice. Political theory rarely, if ever, provides a ready-made blueprint for the aspiring politician. Rather, politicians mediate and interpret theories as they attempt to apply them in practice. At the very least, it can be said of the six individuals described in this book that they did not come to the presidency bereft of ideas.

Case Selection

Forty-three people have been elected president. The intellectual background of each is an important story with its own unique impact on that person's presidency. Countless biographies have explored presidential backgrounds—even for those James Bryce thought of as "intellectual pigmies." But what is at issue here is a particular kind of intellectual background, which some presidents have had and others have not.

"Political theory" might be considered to be like a set of tools arrayed in a toolbox. Some presidents never once looked into this toolbox. Among these presidents was Warren Harding, and he felt himself overmatched by the job. To a friend he wrote these lines:

> John, I can't make a damn thing out of this tax problem. I listen to one side and they seem right, and then God! I talk to the other side and they seem just as right, and there I am where I started. I know somewhere there is a book that would give me the truth, but hell, I couldn't read the book. I know somewhere there is an economist that knows the truth, but I don't know where to find him and haven't the sense to trust him when I do find him. God, what a job.[9]

Harding found himself adrift in a sea of ideas, without any compass with which to navigate his way to a good decision. This kind of self-flagellation may be rare among presidents, who typically display much more confidence than Harding, but it is an indication that every president needs intellectual tools, regardless of where they are found, to have any chance of making competent decisions.

Some recent presidents may not have looked in the political-theory toolbox much longer than Harding did, but they almost inevitably have employed people who have. This may make even seemingly unfruitful subjects worthy of some attention. George W. Bush's intellect was the subject of sneers throughout his presidency. Much of this commentary was a by-product of partisan warfare. Bush staked his election in 2000 on presenting himself as a folksy, common sense–oriented individual whom voters would rather have a beer with than the supposedly aloof and intellectual Al Gore. The logical, if politically motivated, backlash emphasized Bush's lack of intelligence.

However, in the wake of the Iraq invasion, Bush justified his actions using language strikingly reminiscent of John Locke's *Second Treatise on Civil Government*: freedom is a gift from God to which all people have a right, which he stressed in his second inaugural address. Bush's aggressive projection of American power abroad has been attributed to the neo-Machiavellian historian and political theorist Michael Ledeen, and his obsession with secrecy has been attributed to the indirect influence of Leo Strauss.[10] At times the president's rhetoric about the Islamic world seems to be imported from Samuel Huntington's *Clash of Civilizations*.[11] Or from Bernard Lewis, the originator of the phrase "clash of civilizations." The president's vision of the unitary executive has been influenced by an interpretation of Alexander Hamilton's vision in Federalist No. 70 offered up by one-time political science graduate student Dick Cheney.[12] Bush may never have read a word of *The Federalist*, Locke, Machiavelli, Ledeen, Strauss, or Huntington. Some of those in the network around the president had, however, and these individuals, at the very least, made a great deal of difference in how President Bush spoke about what he was trying to accomplish. Bush seems to have internalized ideas reminiscent of various political theorists and chosen to publicly justify his policies through arguments with intellectual roots in the academy.

Among the presidents who have rummaged around in political theory's toolbox, some have had a much greater acquaintance with its tools than others. Some have favored a variety of tools, while others have seemed comfortable with just one tool. The tools themselves differ greatly, of course. Some are much more versatile than others. A number of tools may not *ever* be useful, or may inevitably do a great deal of harm when applied. Additionally, a potentially useful tool might be misapplied. Like a child using a chisel for a screwdriver, this may exacerbate the problem at hand.

A president can be a success or a failure regardless of whether he knows any political theory. There are a myriad of factors which contribute to presidential success, many of which are beyond the president's control. Yet if we are to take Bryce's observation seriously—that a president's ideas matter—the possession of tools provided by political theory must be considered as a factor in presidential performance. At least for those presidents who knew something about political theory and attempted to apply that knowledge to practice, we should analyze whether this knowledge tended to help or hurt them in their job. To this inquiry there is no simple answer. Political theory may enable a president to approach the presidency with the kind of intellectual confidence that Harding lacked, but it may simultaneously confuse many with whom the president works, including the voting public, which is not well versed in political theory.

The presidents who are the subjects of the subsequent chapters were not chosen at random. There would be little point to exploring this connection with Warren Harding. Nor is it appropriate to include someone who served a short time, like the ill-fated William Henry Harrison, even though Harrison's lengthy inaugural address contains several allusions to political theory. In that speech Harrison relates that it is the duty of public figures to "produce the greatest good to the greatest number," Jeremy Bentham's famed phrase describing his utilitarian philosophy. Harrison also echoes Locke, in saying that "we admit of no government by divine right, believing that so far as power is concerned the Beneficent Creator has made no distinction amongst men; that all are upon an equality, and that the only legitimate right to govern is an express grant of power from the governed."[13] Much of the remainder of the speech is a lesson in Whig theory—that there is a natural tendency in governments for power to concentrate in the executive office. Harrison pledged to resist this temptation and to advance curbs on executive aggrandizement. But Harrison simply did not have enough time in office to make a study of his approach to political theory compelling.

A number of presidents who connected political theory and practical politics are not included here. This is less a commentary on their worth as subjects than a reflection of my interest in presenting a broad cross section of such figures stretching into modern times. I have excluded John Quincy Adams, who was trained by his father to appreciate political philosophy from a very early age. James Buchanan, who delivered a commencement speech at his 1809 graduation from Dickinson College titled "The Utility of Philosophy," is not included here either.[14] I have also left out the avid reader and prolific author Theodore Roosevelt, who commented on political theory in several of his thirty-eight books and who quoted Edmund Burke in his 1905 Annual Address to Congress.[15] His theoretical insight is partially reflected in the words and actions of his fifth cousin Franklin Delano Roosevelt, the subject of Chapter 6. Herbert Hoover wrote what might be considered political theory in several books he authored, including 1923's *American Individualism*. James Monroe wrote a pamphlet opposing ratification of the Constitution in which he referenced several political philosophers, including Baron de Montesquieu, Locke, and Polybius. Richard Nixon quoted Machiavelli in a book on foreign policy.[16] We have not yet fully documented Ronald Reagan's intellectual influences, and someone must do so to gain a full measure of the man. These presidents might have made interesting subjects for this research.

Every reader of presidential history is transfixed by the office's most fascinating occupant, Abraham Lincoln. He is not the subject of a chapter in this book, mainly because he did not read a great deal of political philosophy. In fact, his law partner William Herndon was frustrated by Lincoln because Herndon read works of political theory and recommended them to his partner, only to be rebuffed. In the words of Herndon, Lincoln "read but little and that for an end. Politics were his Heaven, and his Hades metaphysics."[17] Nevertheless, Lincoln's intellectual approach to politics is of serious interest. Even if he did not read much political philosophy, he wrote a number of short, precise fragments which arguably describe a political theory. No one better defined the legitimate scope and purpose for government action in a sentence than Lincoln, when he wrote that "the legitimate object of government, is to do for a community of people, whatever they need to have done, but can not do, *at all*, or can not, *so well do*, for themselves—in their separate, and individual capacities." In his first message to Congress, on July 4, 1861, Lincoln posed one of the most important questions ever formulated: "Must a government, of necessity, be too *strong* for the liberties of its own people, or too *weak* to maintain its own existence?"[18] This single sentence captures Lincoln's understanding of what was at stake during his presidency. To him, the Civil War was a "great test," to see if popular government could actually work. Government has to be strong enough so that it will not be forced to split up whenever its citizens fundamentally disagree with each other. If governments split every time there were serious disputes, eventually there would be no government. To work, government needs to be coercive, but in being coercive, the critical question is whether it can still preserve freedom.

President Lincoln never gave a moment's consideration to doing what John Adams actually did: writing a book of political theory. Yet he did theorize. And he did forge a serious intellectual connection with key books, which he felt informed his political thought in very important ways. Lincoln learned Whig economics from Francis Wayland's *Elements of Political Economy*. He learned the law from William Blackstone's *Commentaries*. He may have had only a total of one year of formal schooling, but he read American political history, and he gained theoretical commitments from it. He revered Lockean principles because he was devoted to the version of them written into the Declaration of Independence. Lincoln's skill in rhetoric was due to his study of Shakespeare's works and the King James version of the Bible. To make his points, Lincoln was willing to engage in serious research. In the critical Cooper Union Address of February 27, 1860, Lincoln presented evidence about the signers of the Constitution. He documented that most of them, even most of the delegates from Southern states, objected to the extension of slavery into territories. Lincoln himself is the one who collected the evidence.

He also worked hard to apply logic to political practice. Lincoln studied Euclid to hone his skill in logic, an endeavor which he found useful, both as a lawyer and as a politician. Logic became a kind of homespun political theory to him. He used logic to denounce secession as "the essence of anarchy." In a broader sense he employed reasoning to "engage in continual, self-conscious assessments of political context to determine which of his core commitments to emphasize and which to de-emphasize at any given time." In another venue, I have argued that this ability is reminiscent of the counsel offered by Machiavelli.[19] Ordering and reordering one's commitments based on changes in context to pragmatically move toward goals is a key political skill that any president must have. Lincoln's acquaintance with Euclid helped him to develop that skill as well as any president has. So Abraham Lincoln's political thought is sufficiently interesting to warrant serious scholarly interest, but the same could be said of many presidents beyond the ones selected here. Lincoln also shows that theories of politics can be developed without political theory. This is an important point that I will revisit in the Conclusion. Regardless of whether presidents know political theory or not, they possess views about politics that are rightly called "theoretical."

Besides being a prominent president, each of the six subjects treated here made an important and recognizable connection with political theory. Simply put, I think theirs are the most interesting stories to be told about this connection. Collectively they help us to understand how theory and practice interact in the hands of a well-placed practitioner of politics. They also help highlight several important subtexts: massive changes in the field of political theory, stark alterations in higher education, and the evolution of the presidency itself.

Some of these presidents, particularly Jefferson and Madison, have had scores of books written about them which pertain to this subject in some way. Yet focusing in on how they approached political theory can deliver new insight. For others, this territory is much less complex or well trodden, as in the cases of Franklin Delano Roosevelt and Bill Clinton. In these cases I present previously unremarked evidence about what animated their thinking. Regardless of the individual, each chapter offers an interpretation of a president's relationship with political theory based on the evidence available. This study can also offer what individual biographies cannot: comparisons and generalizations across individuals which give us a better sense of how political theory and the practice of politics interact when the two come into juxtaposition.

This book would be unimaginable without the inclusion of three founders who became president in turn: John Adams, Thomas Jefferson, and James Madison. Adams was as devoted to reading and learning from classic and contemporary works of political theory as any politician has ever been. Because of his nearly obsessive reading in this field he felt that he had figured out politics in a way that almost none of his contemporaries had. He made few friends in applying his theory to practice, but taking positions which aggravated others gratified him. It showed him that others were driven by the whims of the day or their interests. His own decisions were made on the basis of (what he considered) the one true political theory, which was both principled and correct.

Thomas Jefferson was as uninterested in canonical texts of political theory as Adams was interested in them. At best he thought they chronicled the history of human oppression. At worst they provided false justifications for that oppression. Jefferson would not have been upset if the whole tradition of Western political theory from Plato through the Renaissance had been forgotten forever. His devotion was to the cutting-edge humanistic philosophy of the Enlightenment. Jefferson believed that Enlightenment thought was different from all that had preceded it because it aimed to use science to promote human happiness. The great discoveries which would advance happiness would come from outside government. With help from a wide array of contemporary theorists, Jefferson formulated his own unique philosophy of governmental minimalism, which would allow happiness to flourish. When he implemented these ideas the United States was left with very little in the way of a federal structure.

James Madison believed in the new Enlightenment philosophy too, but he was much more cautious about it than his political partner Jefferson. Where Jefferson was flippant about political theory, Madison was serious. Popular governments had never been stable in the past. A great many political theorists rejected popular rule because of this. Madison believed that these pessimists were mistaken and that mechanisms could be found to make popular regimes stable. He studied earlier republican philosophies to figure out where they had gone wrong. He emphasized that the Enlightenment needed to supplement its optimism about popular government with a hard-headed realism about what would make popular governments work. He proceeded to find the tools which he believed made stable popular governments possible in the dark corners of political theory's toolbox, applying these and other, more familiar tools during his presidency.

From Madison, I leap forward a century to consider Woodrow Wilson. Wilson was a professor of political science who was acquainted with the thinking of many political theorists because he read them in school and lectured on them prior to launching his political career. Before he was sidetracked by becoming president of Princeton University, governor of New Jersey, and president of the United States, he planned to write a master work of politics which he tentatively titled "The Philosophy of Politics." In general Wilson disliked theorists, dismissing them as impractical. However, he also found compatible minds among those who were theorists. Most notably he embraced Edmund Burke's idea that all nations are "organic" entities. Any proposed reforms had to be recognizable to the organism and compatible with its traditionally accepted practices. Yet Wilson's own ambition and the times that he was in seemed to challenge his commitment to Burkean gradualism. Wilson reconciled his theoretical views to the practice of politics in a very unusual way which is particularly noteworthy because of his own understanding of theories as impractical.

Franklin Delano Roosevelt also defined himself in reaction against political theories. His political path was made clear by the nearly global presence of two theories which seemed to dominate political discourse during his terms in office: laissez-faire capitalism descended from Adam Smith and Marxian socialism. FDR judged both of these views to be extremist and he was convinced that extremism in any form was the enemy of good politics. Roosevelt's thinking was reminiscent of that of Thomas Babington Macaulay, who suggested that mildly progressive compromisers were the real heroes of politics because they could blunt the potential damage done by extreme views while implementing incrementally beneficial policies. This was not exactly an inspirational message, so FDR rarely described it to others. In ways that were often exasperating to more ardent reformers, FDR happily trimmed between extremes, "reforming to preserve."

Finally, Bill Clinton learned about political theory as a Rhodes scholar during his two years at Oxford University. Clinton was well versed in the contractarian tradition of political theory and wrote papers applying the concept to various practical matters, including conscientious-objector status. He supplemented this knowledge with that of numerous academic acquaintances whom he consulted during his rise to the presidency and then while he was a resident in the White House. Though few recognized it, Clinton's so-called Third Way in politics drew on the extensive contractarian tradition of political philosophy. Clinton proposed to forge a "New Covenant" between the American people and their government, which would update the old social contract that he felt was concluded during the New Deal. In so doing he grafted a conception of political development gleaned from several academics onto a version of the social contract. Clinton referred to political theorists in his public speeches quite often, even if he used them more as intellectual window dressing than as a means of clarifying his own political thought.

Scope and Approach

To this point I have used the terms "political theory" and "political philosophy" rather loosely. I have provided no definition for either and have used them interchangeably. I will continue in the latter practice, seeing little reason to distinguish "theory" from "philosophy." However, some understanding of what these terms encompass is necessary, even though it must be squarely acknowledged that any definition of them is imperfect and that there is not a clear line demarcating what *is* political theory from what is not.

At some level it is easy to say with certainty that something is political theory or that it is not. Locke's *Second Treatise on Civil Government* is political theory as surely as a restaurant menu is not. A basic characteristic distinguishes the two: Locke's book is about politics and the menu is not. But most writing with political content is not political theory either. The newspaper article on the local politician's retirement is not political theory. What distinguishes it from Locke's *Second Treatise?* The article is much narrower in scope. It describes one piece of news from a specific time and place. Locke's subject matter is more encompassing and generalized. He attempts to define what makes for good government—a much larger subject—and he attempts to do so in a way that crosses boundaries of time and place. Additionally, Locke offers an argument, where the newspaper article does not. Locke wants to convince his readers of something, while the article's goal is merely to report a new fact.

Much that is written about politics offers an argument and aims to be convincing, but this does not make it political theory either. Books written by Ann Coulter and Al Franken, the *New York Times* editorial page, and the local blog all offer a perspective aimed at convincing readers. What distinguishes them from Locke's *Second Treatise* is the latter's breadth, its abstraction, and its perceived intellectual importance. In *Leviathan,* Thomas Hobbes presents an architectonic vision that moves logically from elementary definitions and an understanding about matter to a prescription for how authority should be distributed in a state. Not every thinker needs to be so all-encompassing as this, but a degree of thoroughness or a systematic aspect seems to be a necessary component of this discipline. Thus, political theory consists of a systematic, innovative argument about politics that purports to be broadly applicable across time and place.[20]

The boundary that this definition draws between political theory and other writings is far from absolute. There is no definitive list of books or articles that "count." But this boundary need not be wholly distinct for the concept to have meaning. Departments of Political Science and Philosophy offer courses on political theory without being paralyzed by this definitional conundrum. Scholars are properly uncomfortable with the idea that there is a "canon" of political theory. An imperfect but serviceable solution to this quandary is to give credence to the choices made by the individuals at hand. The presidents treated here define their own theoretical inspiration from among those who have written systematic arguments about politics that attempt to be broadly applicable across time and place. Among those whom presidents have admired are political theorists, their popularizers, and—in the case of the later presidents—academics.

Most presidents have found most of their ideas outside of political theory. However, a sizable percentage of presidents have used tools housed in the political-theory toolbox. In these cases it was not political theory itself that *caused* anything. Each president was fully responsible for his own actions. The research presented here demonstrates that some presidents have taken ideas from political theory quite seriously. They have felt they understood politics better because of an acquaintance with theory. They have sometimes explained themselves by referencing theorists, and they have taken positions which were reminiscent of those presented in theoretical works. Judging by their own actions and words, these presidents have found value in certain political theorists.

At the same time, it is unlikely that the theoretically informed politician will fully or frequently explain the intellectual origins of his or her ideas, since politicians in elective office must heed the popular will. Explaining the intellectual provenance or the nuances of one's ideas is typically tangential to soliciting votes or galvanizing support for favored policies. Rarely is a reference to a political theorist of benefit to the modern American politician, though anyone who reads the debates between the Federalists and the Antifederalists knows that this was not always the case. Nevertheless, in years of being president, few individuals could successfully conceal their sources of intellectual inspiration, particularly in modern times, when presidents face daily scrutiny and when so much of what they say is public record.

Some might dismiss an enthusiasm for political thought as a mere extension of an individual's personality. In this view it would be tempting to conclude that political theory did not have any *independent* effect on any of these six individuals. In other words, the behaviors I describe might be explained by the presidents' innate qualities, with political theory being a convenient post hoc explanation for their actions or a mediating variable. It is true that none of these individuals endorsed or pursued ideas from political theory which were incongruous with their personalities. However, that does not mean political theory had no independent impact on them. Instead, political theory often informed a course of action that they might not have envisioned without it. Even where theory did not suggest a specific direction, it deepened commitments and bolstered beliefs that an individual was doing the correct thing. The human mind is still too difficult for us to explain in many ways, but it seems fair to conclude that political theory interacted with the personalities of these presidents in ways that gave direction to their politics and provided critical reinforcement to their views.

Establishing connections between individual politicians and specific political theorists is important. But the chronicling of such connections does not fully treat the topic. Each individual subject's approach to political theory as a field of study is important too. Did the president read broadly in political theory? What did he think about political theory in general? What criteria did he employ in selecting or rejecting theories? Treating these questions will grant a holistic understanding of each individual president's political thought. Six individual presidencies take center stage as well. If there is a relevant connection between the historical presidency and political theory, then it must be reflected in actions. Therefore, I devote a section in each chapter to how the president applied theory to practice in the office.

Thus the book will proceed as follows: each of the six presidential cases will be presented in chronological order, beginning with John Adams and ending with Bill Clinton. After introducing an individual by discussing indicative quotes, I will examine his approach to political philosophy. Next, the specific thinkers and ideas the president valued will be described. Then I will show how the president applied these ideas in practice as president. Chapter conclusions comment on the positive and negative aspects of each president's approach and what we learn about the connection between political theory and practical politics from this individual. The Conclusion compares these presidents and provides an assessment of what happens when presidents use political theory.

My purpose is not necessarily to suggest that presidents *should* be influenced by political theory, even though in many cases I believe a judicious approach to political theory could have provided some guidance to a president in need of direction and could have cautioned against certain fateful, problematic decisions. For the time being, this subject can be approached without such preconceptions, letting facts yield their insights. Since past presidents have made a connection with political theory, future presidents (or their staffs) will too. We should simply have a better idea of how this connection has operated in practice so that we may better understand its potential pitfalls and possible advantages.

Conclusion

In addition to James Bryce, a number of scholars have presented views which imply a desired relationship between presidents and political theory. Treating the subject in a more systematic way may help us to discern whether these typically offhand observations have validity. In *Presidential Power and the Modern Presidents* Richard Neustadt maintains that the presidency "is not a scholar's job."[21] By this he means that the president who attempts to use reason to effect a rational plan will not be very successful. The reasoning president butts up against the fact that the authority of others is typically independent of his. Members of Congress are elected by constituents whom the president cannot control. These politicians understandably have their constituents' interests in mind when making decisions. The president's fellow Washingtonians, Neustadt notes, may respond to strategic bargaining or shifts in public opinion, but they will not respond to reason. Additionally, he stresses that the ability to "ride events," or to manage unexpected occurrences, is a much more valuable skill than is the ability to plan a course of action beforehand. Though he does not comment on political theory itself, Neustadt seems to suggest that a president who is in possession of a well-reasoned political theory would not be advantaged. This attribute would perhaps even hinder the ability to exercise the more pragmatic skills that Neustadt believes are required to succeed in the job.

Former librarian of Congress Daniel Boorstin would do much more than discourage presidential hopefuls from reading political theory. In *The Genius of American Politics* Boorstin observes that those who adhere to political philosophies are rigid in their thinking, and that because of this they pose a danger to the public because they will not compromise. The genius of American politics, according to Boorstin, is that Americans are pragmatic. Americans avoid political theory, which distinguishes them from Europeans. The great political theorists of Europe wrote treatises which purported to uncover immutable truths. These authors made converts in the Old World and these true believers convulsed Europe throughout the nineteenth and twentieth centuries with their ironclad convictions about politics. Thankfully, he observes, the United States has remained largely free of the reactionary strife prompted by competing philosophies. Written at the height of the Cold War, Boorstin's book is a cautionary tale about political fanaticism, which the author believed had its roots in political theory.

More recently, Garry Wills's study of James Madison's presidency approaches the fourth president's career as something of a puzzle: how did someone who was so accomplished in politics become such a poor commander in chief?[22] Wills's solution to this conundrum is that an acquaintance with political theory helped Madison to be an effective nation-builder and constitution writer, but was harmful when he was president. Madison was one delegate among fifty-five at the Constitutional Convention and one voice among scores of representatives in Congress. Wills suggests that in these two settings Madison's theoretically inspired ideas which were judged helpful by more practical minds could be adopted, while his more fanciful theoretically inspired ideas could be safely rejected. His executive pronouncements, however, could not be outvoted. The president's decisions inevitably determine the nation's course, and in Madison's case Wills stresses that this was to its detriment.[23] Without examining other presidents, it seems that Wills believes that a politician who has a theoretical streak may make a good representative or a valuable delegate at a constitutional convention, but will almost inevitably make a poor president.

Kenneth W. Thompson's *The President and the Public Philosophy* is an eloquent riposte to these skeptics. Thompson argues that politicians in a democracy cannot expect people to retain faith in government without the articulation of a public philosophy. Without that faith, democratic rule will inevitably devolve into a flaccid technocratic incrementalism. The increasingly shallow media have abdicated their responsibility to discuss the complex issues which define the modern political agenda. "For a government whose approach is not anchored in some enduring body of political thought," Thompson argues, "inconsistent and contradictory policies become inevitable. For the public, comprehension of the course its leaders are following is blurred."[24] Thompson believes that only the president is in a position to reconstruct public philosophy in the United States and that the president should consider the founding generation as a model of how to apply theory to practice.

For his part, James Bryce felt his resignation about the presidency's relationship with education and ideas turn to hopefulness twenty years after he wrote *The American Commonwealth.* In the election of 1912 Woodrow Wilson was elected to the presidency. Bryce, then the British ambassador to the United States, wrote Wilson a private letter congratulating him on his victory. The sentiments contained in the letter were not the official reaction of His Majesty's government, but the views of Wilson's personal friend and fellow political scientist, who happened to occupy a key diplomatic office. Bryce sent "sincere good wishes and earnest hopes to an old friend who, being a scholar and a man of learning has obtained a rare and splendid opportunity of showing in the amplest sphere of action what the possession of thought and learning may accomplish for the good of a nation in the field of practical statesmanship."[25] Bryce expected Wilson to be a better president than the "intellectual pigmies" he had referred to in *The American Commonwealth.*

The six presidencies examined here offer insight into whether the enthusiasms of Bryce and Thompson are more realistic than the pessimistic outlook of Wills, Neustadt, and Boorstin. The fact is that there have been successful and unsuccessful presidents with a penchant for political philosophy. Beneficial results have been accompanied by drawbacks. Above all, this book should help us move beyond simplistic views about what happens when theory meets practice. The next six chapters collectively show that the president who knows something about political theory is just as unlikely to be our savior as he is to be the death of us. The real stories of these individuals are far more interesting than the theories about theory which have been spun without much attention to the evidence. The connection between presidents and political theory has contributed significantly to American political development. Here begins that story.

Chapter 2

JOHN ADAMS: DEFENSE OF THE MIXED CONSTITUTION

It is true that I can say and have said nothing new on the Subject of Government. Yet I did say in my *Defence* and in my *Discourses on Davila,* though in an uncouth Style, what was new to Lock, to Harrington, to Milton, to Hume to Montesquieu to Reauseau, to Turgot, [to] Condorcet, to Rochefaucault, to Price to Franklin and to yourself; and at that time to almost all Europe and America. . . . Writings on Government had been not only neglected, but discountenanced and discouraged, through out all Europe, from the Restoration of Charles the Second in England, till the French Revolution commenced. . . . In this state of Things my poor, unprotected, unpatronised Books appeared.
　　　　　—John Adams, letter to Thomas Jefferson

My plain writings have been misunderstood by many, misrepresented by more, and vilified and anathematized by multitudes who never read them. They have, indeed, nothing to recommend them but stubborn facts . . .
　　　　　—John Adams, letter to Charles Holt

John Adams read more political theory and felt he learned more from it than any other prominent politician. His sense of worth was intimately wrapped up in his knowledge of political philosophy. As a young man he set out to gain a systematic understanding of politics. Well before he reached the presidency he felt that he had lived out his ideal by reconciling book learning and lived experience.

Adams would not have become president were it not for his facility with political theory. This was not because voters preferred to have the most well-read scholar of politics in the job. Rather, his elite colleagues bestowed positions of high responsibility on him partly because of his hard work and learned nature in the field and partly because they valued the substantive commitments he had found in theoretical works.

His theory-based understanding of the relationship between the British government and that of the colonies led him to be an early and forceful advocate for independence. His knowledge of institutional dynamics prompted the Massachusetts constitutional convention to let Adams write the state's new constitution virtually single-handedly. Partly due to his facility in international legal theory the Continental Congress appointed him as an envoy to France and to Holland. Later he was selected to be one of the peace negotiators with Great Britain. His work in these roles placed him among the nation's foremost leaders, and the renown he gained in them culminated in eight years as vice president and four years as president. In an age when political theory was valued—in large part for its role in justifying the Revolution—Adams's own obsession with this body of work helped him to become a national leader.

As indicated in the first quote above, Adams did not claim to be original. He did not think he advocated an innovative political philosophy. He judged that the essential truths of politics had already been discovered by others. His reputation was to be staked on being the champion and implementer of the correct understanding of politics. Doing so required him to refute mistaken understandings, which he found abundant among political philosophers and politicians. According to Adams, neither Franklin nor Rousseau, neither Condorcet nor Jefferson really understood politics, because they rejected theories which were empirically demonstrated to be correct. While Adams was devoted to reading all political philosophy, he discarded much of it as nonsense. Winnowing its valuable ideas from the chaff was so important to him that he developed a method of discerning how to do so. For the benefit of the public, and to refute mistaken ideas, he compiled two books in rapid succession during the late 1780s: his massive *Defence of the Constitutions of Government of the United States of America* and his *Discourses on Davila*. Through them he hoped to end the neglect of "Writings on Government."

It does surprisingly little violence to these books and to John Adams's political thought in general to say that they consist almost exclusively of pieces cobbled together from an array of political theorists. C. Bradley Thompson suggests that "the primary context within which Adams' political thought must be viewed . . . is his confrontation with the Western political and philosophical tradition."[1] This is not to say that Adams was always incisive or careful about political theory. He seemed to place an almost exclusive faith in it—as if all useful political wisdom could be reduced to general rules and that wisdom had already been elucidated by the Western tradition's greatest political theorists. Adams also had the utmost confidence that he was correct.

He intended the *Defence* as a master work of political science. Begun in 1787, it stretched to three volumes. Though rarely read today, the book is a compendium of wisdom about and historical experience with popular—or, as it was called in his time, "republican"—politics. Well over half of the work consists of extended quotations from theorists like Niccolo Machiavelli, Plato, James Harrington, and the Baron de Montesquieu. Adams insisted that his subsequent work, *Discourses on Davila,* was of a piece with the *Defence,* a fourth volume in his epic work. They, with his other writings, constitute as well-developed a theoretical vision of politics as a president ever had.[2] Adams's grandson, Charles Francis Adams, who compiled a ten-volume collection of his grandfather's political writings, observed that the *Defence* was "the author's contribution to science, upon which whatever may belong to him of name and fame must ultimately rest."[3] It is a stunning claim on behalf of a president that his contribution to the world rests more on his compilation of the wisdom within political theory than on his service in public office.

Though Adams gained much from his acquaintance with political theory, he was also keenly aware of how much it cost him. To his friend Thomas Jefferson he lamented, "Education! Oh Education! The greatest Grief of my heart, and the Greatest Affliction of my Life!"[4] His education in political affairs led to nearly ten years of diplomatic assignments in Europe, most of which was spent away from his beloved wife and their three youngest children. But Adams also felt afflicted because he was greatly misunderstood and even vilified for his superior understanding of politics. Very few people wished to understand politics theoretically. He felt he had offered the world a great gift in his political writings, and the world had spurned him. In fact, his writings on political theory were "misrepresented," "vilified," and "anathematized" by his opponents and turned into powerful ammunition against him.

Already in 1774, his theoretical writings were being denounced. His vigorous defense of the American colonies' right to make laws independent of Parliament written under the pen name "Novanglus" was rebuked for its scholarly nature. As "Massachusettensis," Tory Daniel Leonard dismissed the Novanglus letters as "nothing but 'a huge pile of learning.'"[5] Consulted by George Washington about who should become the first vice president, James Madison objected to Adams in part because he was "obnoxious to many . . . by the political principles avowed" in his recently published *Defence.*[6] If his acquaintance with political theory was partly responsible for Adams's political success, it was also a root cause of his troubles.

Adams believed that politics could be reduced to a science through systematic observation. Eternal laws built around the "stubborn facts" of human nature could be—and had been—discerned. These laws had to be publicized and applied just as surely as the fanciful notions of others who did not approach politics scientifically had to be refuted. The range of thinkers whom Adams borrowed from is astounding. Joseph Ellis reminds us that "he was, by the common consensus of his contemporaries, the best-read member of his remarkably literate generation."[7] No book was too obscure to escape his notice, and he might incorporate the views of anyone he thought correct, regardless of the thinker's reputation. Of course many political theorists borrowed from and built on the ideas of others. Adams read them all, and like many of them, his thinking reflects a widely ranging network of influences. While Adams could not aggressively pursue all of his theoretical commitments during his four years in the presidency, his actions in office are made more understandable when viewed in light of them. Adams hewed closely to his theoretical ideals as president. Unfortunately for him, this alienated his potential allies and prevented him from winning reelection.

"The Science of Government"

John Adams set a goal for himself early in his life: to apply the wisdom of humankind about politics to practice, for the benefit of all. Doing this required discerning what that wisdom was, gaining high political office, and applying that wisdom judiciously. By his own reckoning, Adams was remarkably successful in executing his plan. By conviction and by habit Adams scoured political theory. By his early adulthood he felt he had discerned its wisdom. He found that the political theorists who based their conclusions on observation and lived experience had almost all come to a similar conclusion about what was required to construct a stable government. The politicians who did not read these works—and they were many—turned away from that which could help them succeed. They were unlearned, and as a result they tended to be impetuous. Those unschooled in political theory might effectively tear down a government, but they could not build one up, because they were unaware of what doing so required.

In his early, fragmentary diary, written while he was a student at Harvard College, the unsure Adams berated himself for his lax study habits. Far from a poor student, Adams was setting very high intellectual expectations for himself. His goal was to be a learned man, even if he was still unsure precisely what he wanted to be learned about. By the time he was admitted to the Massachusetts bar in 1758 Adams had convinced himself that developing an understanding of law and government was the most useful of human endeavors. Among Adams's notes written in that same year we find this plan for estimating human worth: "We are not, therefore, to measure . . . Admiration of a man by the Number alone, but by the Utility and Number jointly of the Propositions that he knows, and his dexterity in applying them to Practice."[8] Adams idealized political theory which could be usefully applied to practice. He had found his mission, to which he turned his substantial ambition.

This fragment from 1758 contains a short essay on the nature of genius. Adams's definition of a genius was someone who is capable of the "invention of new Systems or Combinations of old Ideas." There were many different kinds of genius within this general rubric: one could be a genius in the physical world by inventing a new machine; or one could be a genius at writing, inventing a variety of characters and placing them together in a finely crafted play or story; or one could discern laws about natural phenomena or find in human nature laws of morality. Finally, one could be a political genius. "He who has a Faculty of combining . . . these [laws of human nature] into Rules, for the Government of Society, to procure Peace, Plenty, Liberty, has a great political Genius."[9] Adams did his utmost to develop this last talent and always hoped that he possessed this kind of genius.

While learning the law in a two-year apprenticeship with James Putnam in Worcester, Massachusetts, Adams read the great legal theorists of his time. After being admitted to the bar, he did not stop his course of study, seeking out reading lists from some of the state's most learned men and setting himself to work on their suggestions.[10] He joined the Sodality, an exclusive Boston-area book club, which discussed a variety of works of political philosophy. He used much of his spare income to buy books, and quickly compiled one of the finest libraries in New England. This library came in handy when Adams wrote about colonial rights in the Novanglus letters. He was proud that his argument for American independence from parliamentary laws rested partly on information obtained from a book that was neither possessed nor read by any other person in the colony.[11] In collecting books, Adams specialized in government and law.[12] When a friend asked him to read a book on the anatomy of caterpillars, Adams flatly refused, saying, "I doubt not the Book is worth studying. All Nature is so.—But I have too much to do, to Study Men . . ."[13]

Adams's aspiration to be a genius in applying theoretical knowledge about government to practice was no passing fancy. To a surprising extent he lived out his own ideal. Like other politicians of his time he was committed to a version of personal freedom, but Adams often complained that the pursuit of freedom backfired among the unlearned. They did not realize that personal liberty had to be accompanied by a stable, well-constructed government if it was to last. An abstract commitment to freedom was useless. A crusade for it was counterproductive if authority was not also firmly and properly established.

Lessons about how to properly establish government while maintaining popular rule and personal liberty were catalogued in the writings of key political philosophers, like Machiavelli and Montesquieu. Adams felt that his reading of them was highly instructive. They helped him learn how to apply useful ideas in practice to benefit humankind.

As president he retained the view that reading in political theory was useful. In 1798 the undergraduates of the College of New Jersey (now Princeton University) wrote to Adams to complain about offenses that the United States was suffering on the seas at the hands of the British and to protest Adams's raising a large army to oppose the French. Adams responded to their letter diplomatically but forcefully. The students were right to be offended by the British depredations at sea. But indignation would not produce a positive result. Many of the world's most noble characters had boiled with indignation and had fought tyranny ardently, but to no avail, because they did not do so smartly. They were "inexperienced in freedom, *and had very little reading in the science of government.*"[14] This phrasing suggests that if these leaders had consulted political philosophy expertly, they might have succeeded. Their lack of book knowledge made them unworthy to their cause, and their ignorance yielded results worse than what would have happened had they never lived.

In Adams's response to the College of New Jersey undergraduates, the presumption that those with book knowledge are naive is turned on its head. Those who *lack* book learning fail to temper their ardor with the gathered wisdom of the ages about what works in politics. Only those who *do* read are capable of overcoming a kind of impetuous naiveté. In Adams's frequent example of the ardent reformers with good intentions who made the world worse, the reformers were the philosophes, the intellectual leaders of the French Revolution. Adams knew many of them personally. They failed, in large part, because they did not heed the wisdom of the ages contained in Western political philosophy. They may have been smart, but they did not have the intellectual background to be "political geniuses." Others criticized the French revolutionists for being too enamored of political theory. For Adams, it was their ignorance of theory that was the problem. While he could do little about the course of the French Revolution, he could urge the College of New Jersey's undergraduates to become better informed than those who had created messes because they were "inexperienced . . . in the science of government."

Central to Adams's confidence that he understood politics better than others was his devotion to a version of the scientific method. Adams sometimes used the word "philosopher" pejoratively. When he did so, he was not referring to all theorists, just the ones who did not base their understanding of something on lived historical experience. Adams's manufactured synonym for this pejorative sense of the word "philosopher" was "ideologian," which better expresses his meaning. An ideologian is driven by a priori ideas, which he or she might bring to politics without the benefit of consulting experience. Valid understandings of politics, by contrast, could only be discerned from the recurrent patterns of lived experience. Only by consulting what really was could one come to know the immutable laws of politics.

Writers who based their analyses on systematic observation of past events, like James Harrington, Cicero, Machiavelli, Montesquieu, and Aristotle, set themselves apart from writers like Jean-Jacques Rousseau, Thomas Paine, Mary Wollstonecraft, the Marquis de Condorcet, and Plato, who Adams felt simply formulated what they wished to see, regardless of whether or not it was achievable in practice.[15] Philosophy, properly understood, was a science, deriving useful laws from lived experience. When they resumed their correspondence in their twilight years, Adams wrote to Jefferson, "Phylosophy is not only the love of Wisdom, but the Science of the Universe and its Cause."[16] Political philosophy was the specialized science of discerning the laws of human interaction. In his effort to understand how politics works, Adams read histories voraciously, and admired the authors who derived patterns from among those histories. They provided a guide to the politically possible.[17]

A variety of authors influenced Adams to adopt this "empirical" political science. Machiavelli in particular had dismissed prior writings on politics as unrealistic and touted his own ideas as a great improvement because they were based on actual experience. "Many have imagined republics and principalities that have never been seen or known to exist in truth," the Florentine theorist wrote in chapter 15 of *The Prince*. By contrast, it was his "intent . . . to write something useful." He did so by "enter[ing] upon a new way, as yet untrodden by anyone else," which would correct a "lack of proper appreciation to history, owing to people failing to realize the significance of what they read."[18] Among the American founders, it was unusual to admit that one had even read this "teacher of evil." Adams went beyond that admission, forthrightly acknowledging that he was "somewhat a student of Machiavel," even though Machiavelli was "disagreeable to me because I could never know whether he was in jest or in earnest."[19] It was Machiavelli's political method that was appealing to the straightlaced New Englander, not his wry irony.

Henry St. John, known as Viscount Bolingbroke, was a British admirer of Machiavelli who greatly expanded on Machiavelli's bare-bones explanation of why historical observation was so vital to the development of a true understanding of politics. After a remarkable early career in politics—he was made secretary of war at age twenty-seven—Bolingbroke wrote several political treatises, including one called *Letters on the Study and Use of History* (1738). *Letters* was animated by the pithy observation that "history is philosophy teaching by examples."[20] Though he rejected much of Bolingbroke, Adams accepted this understanding of what historical experience taught wholesale.

Unfortunately for Adams, he was never able to convince contemporaries of this understanding of how to develop political knowledge. His assessment of those who differed from him was not charitable. Adams wrote copious commentary in the margins of the books he owned, and because he was writing only for himself he often comes off as testy and exasperated. Among his comments is this: "I am stark mad, or every one of these [Benjamin Franklin, the Marquis de Condorcet, Anne-Robert-Jacques Turgot, Wollstonecraft, and Francois Le Rochefoucauld] was an idiot in the science of government."[21] He called those who admired Plato's political ideals "all a little cracked."[22] They were deficient because "the Science of Government, like all other Sciences, is best pursued by Observation and Experiment—Remark the Phenomena of Nature, and from these deduce the Principles and the Ends of Government."[23]

The science of politics was every bit as discernible as natural science, Adams believed. However, it was not making as much progress. The reasons for this were several. History was easily forgotten. Lazy politicians did not read. Key texts were deliberately destroyed by political and ecclesiastical authorities aiming "to conceal their frauds."[24] "Fools" like Franklin and the philosophes stepped into the void with their untested and unlikely dreams.

Citizens of the United States were lucky to have enough right-thinking people at the Constitutional Convention that the system created was not wholly inadequate. The French were not so lucky. The views of "ideologians" like Turgot, Condorcet, Voltaire, and Rousseau enabled the horrors of the French Revolution. Their lack of understanding about the need for checks on popular government helped facilitate the Reign of Terror's bloodbath and led inevitably to the unfortunate dictatorship of Napoleon. Even before his presidency, Adams had sadly concluded that "the feelings of mankind are so much against any rational theory [of politics], that I find my labor has all been in vain."[25]

Adams was confident that in his *Defence* and *Discourses on Davila* he had worked out the rational theory of politics from the various historically proven building blocks he found in political philosophy. This confidence yielded a remarkable stability in Adams's political thought. Quite simply, he felt that he had discovered the truth about politics. Nothing that occurred in the last forty years of his life shook this confidence. On the contrary, his experiences confirmed to him the accuracy of his understanding. To one correspondent late in his life he wrote, "You will live to see that I am precisely right."[26] Though the percentage of fools and schemers in the political world would not diminish, he had confidence that his views would be applied in many nations across the globe, because what he had to offer worked. Experience was, as always, the true test of value.

Adams was unconvincing to others in part because he was a poor writer. John Patrick Diggins, who admires Adams greatly, calls his *Defence* "dense, meandering, sprawling, [and] disconnected. . . . [It is] a jarring blur of free association about Western political philosophy." James Grant points out that "the work . . . reveals a lay scholar of astonishing breadth in reading and knowledge but also of a remarkably short attention span."[27] As anyone who grades papers knows, deficiencies in writing often indicate deficiencies in thinking. This is as true for a president as it is for a high school student. Adams's writings were typically prepared in haste, while he was busy with government service. If he did have the aspiration to be a renowned author— and there is every reason to believe that he did—he should have taken more care in the preparation of manuscripts. He would have benefited from a severe editor and much critical feedback. What he was attempting to do in these works was quite sophisticated. He was presenting a unique synthesis of a traditional view of how government institutions should be set up with a liberal empiricism emphasizing liberty and the wisdom of lived experience, combined with a strand of thought which comprehensively interpreted human nature. If this is not political theory, what is? The very ambitiousness of this project helps to explain some of Adams's awkwardness as a writer. Yet Adams was so sure of himself that he did not seek or accept feedback. He did serious research. He laid out his findings like a lawyer aiming to write an exhaustive brief, expecting to win his "case" convincingly. When he did not, he blamed "the jury" for their ignorance. And yet the salient fact remains that John Adams was absolutely devoted to political theory. He did his utmost to construct a useful and applicable political theory from political philosophy's true ideas, and then worked to apply these ideas to practice as president.

No Simple Form of Government Can Secure Man

Adams's political thought covers an array of subjects, and it is a challenge to do justice to his views in a short space. Nevertheless, because he consistently emphasized certain matters his views are readily outlined and his self-professed debts to various thinkers emerge. His primary political concerns were institutional dynamics and how institutions represent societal interests. He was a fierce advocate of the "mixed constitution," in which one house of the legislature represents "the people," a second house of the legislature represents the aristocracy, and a powerful executive independently pursues the course he thinks best. All three of these institutions would have to compromise to make law. This institutional design had proved its worth in practice because it squares with the realities of human nature—most importantly a self-regarding "passion for distinction" which animates human action. Alongside these ideas about institutional dynamics, Adams was committed to the most familiar enthusiasms of his day: liberty, individual rights, the rule of law, and consent of the governed. Because of his understanding of political theory, his manner of pursuing these commitments was more conservative, but it was no less ardent, than that of most of his contemporaries.

Adams stressed that just three major political discoveries had occurred since Lycurgus formulated Sparta's ancient constitution. Each of these three was a necessary part of any successful regime: representation; the separation of executive, legislative, and judicial powers; and the participation of multiple representative institutions in the lawmaking process—the familiar arrangement of the mixed constitution.[28] This last concept already had a history two millennia long. In any society, most of the populace had very different interests from the few in it who were wealthy and powerful. Severe conflict between the "people" and the "aristocracy" was the likely result, unless that strife could be contained by a political structure. The Greeks and Romans were the first to formulate the idea of a "triple equipoise" of institutions, as Adams called it, where the many and the few were each represented in separate legislative bodies, as was a monarch or executive who would possess a sufficient interest in stability and harmony to mediate disputes between the two groups.[29]

The separation of powers was familiar Enlightenment fare. John Locke and other British Whigs had stressed the importance of keeping the legislature and the executive in distinct hands. The mixed constitution provided, however, a distinctive kind of separation of powers that Locke had not expressly advocated, to Adams's chagrin.[30] The darling of early Enlightenment thought, Montesquieu, had. Montesquieu also went beyond

Locke to stress that the judiciary, too, should be powerful and independent of the other branches, an idea which Adams endorsed. Montesquieu was, however, only one among many writers who had defended the mixed constitution. Adams understood his own *Defence* to be the latest in a long line of written works championing the idea. Aristotle had touted its benefits. Adams admired Aristotle's devotion to moderation, which was embodied in his plan for the mixed constitution. The concept traveled to Rome, where it was praised in the works of Polybius and Cicero—and not coincidentally seemed to be replicated in the Roman republic. The great admirer of Rome, Machiavelli, revived the ideal during the Renaissance. It subsequently came to England, where it took shape in the workings of the British government, with its House of Commons, House of Lords, and monarch. There it was argued for by Harrington, Jonathan Swift, Bolingbroke, and many others. Finally, it reemerged on the European Continent in the writings of Montesquieu and Jean Louis DeLolme.

Adams highly prized DeLolme's *Constitution of England,* which was published in 1776 and first read by Adams in the 1780s. In it he found a cogent explanation of why the British government was the most stable in Europe and why it produced a regime which valued liberty more than others: it best approximated the mixed constitution. The House of Commons and the House of Lords, representing different classes, were forced to compromise with each other. They did so under the watchful eye of a monarch who possessed an absolute veto to check them both. DeLolme's argument was not new. He simply expressed as well as anyone what Adams had believed and read since the 1750s: historical experience proved that the mixed constitution was the best institutional arrangement for government and that the British government had approximated it better than any other nation ever had.

Adams's friend Mercy Otis Warren accused him of becoming enamored of the British and their form of government during his years as a diplomat in England. Not so, Adams complained, protesting that he had been wronged by her characterization of him in her *History of the Rise, Progress, and Termination of the American Revolution* (1805). The former president asserted, "My opinion of the British Constitution was formed long before I had any thing to do in public life, more than twenty years before I ever saw the British Island." A staggering array of authors had been involved, which he proceeded to catalogue: "Fortescue, Smith, Montesquieu, Vattel, Achersley, Bacon, Bolingbroke, Sullivan, and Blackstone, and De Lolme, and even Marchamont Needham, Algernon Sydney, James Harrington, and every other writer on government, and from all the examples I had ever read in history."[31] As a young man he had scribbled in a notebook the understanding that "no simple form of Government [a monarchy, or an aristocracy, or a simple democracy—any government with one lawmaking institution], can possibly secure Men against the Violences of Power." Upon rereading his own comment fifty years later Adams wrote beside it that this "has been the creed of my whole life."[32]

To work properly, the mixed constitution had to be "balanced," which was one of Adams's favorite words. In practice this meant that each of the three institutions involved in lawmaking had to be able to stop the other two from doing what they would do without the others' presence. If any institution could not cancel legislation, there would be an imbalance, as that institution would be weaker than the others. The British monarch could veto legislation, which gave him or her the power that an executive required, and Adams made no secret of his admiration for the power of the British monarchy. Because of the Americans' experience with King George III, most Americans, at least in the 1770s, favored weak executives. That Adams continued to praise the British monarchy and its powers throughout his life was scandalous to many. They believed—and others were willing to mislead them in thinking—that Adams was being traitorous instead of merely advocating the idea that executive power could provide a beneficial counterweight against the inclinations to excess of representatives of the people or of the well-to-do.

Though almost all of the newly independent American states adopted a three-institution system of lawmaking, Adams found that the executive in each of them was too weak. No American governor had been given an unqualified veto. This meant that the American governments were unbalanced—too much power resided in the legislative branches. Though several states moved to strengthen governors in the 1780s and the president of the United States was made relatively powerful for an American executive, the president still did not wield an unqualified negative. The Constitutional Convention could have done far worse in framing the Constitution, Adams believed, yet executive weakness was a significant flaw in the American system.

In order to work, the mixed constitution needed to segregate out representatives of the aristocracy and house them in an upper legislative chamber, while reserving the lower chamber for representatives of the common people. The British did this effectively in their House of Lords and House of Commons. In a famed passage from the *Defence*, Adams wrote,

> The rich, the well-born, and the able, acquire an influence among the people that will soon be too much for simple honesty and plain sense, in a house of representatives. The most illustrious of them must,

therefore, be separated from the mass, and placed by themselves in a senate; that is, to all honest and useful intents, an ostracism.[33]

The idea that aristocratic and democratic elements needed to be separated was as old as the mixed constitution, but the formulation that the separation was to be strict and absolute, an "ostracism" of sorts, had been articulated by DeLolme. Unfortunately, the Americans did this rather haphazardly, with many falsely insisting that there was no aristocracy in America to segregate in the Senate.

Adams was excoriated during his political career for having aristocratic pretensions. No other charge so irked the sensitive New Englander. Adams was not rich, nor was he profligate in his lifestyle. There was great irony in his being accused of favoring the wealthy while his friend and rival Jefferson, who enjoyed a much more opulent existence, became renowned as a champion of the common man. To Adams this was all a big misunderstanding. Aristocracies were inevitable—in any society some people would have more wealth, more education, or more talent than others. These were empirical facts. The interests of these wealthy, educated, and talented people would differ from the interests of most others, and their power would be formidable. The mixed constitution would help to preserve popular rights and the liberty of all by keeping the aristocracy's influence confined to a single chamber. If the aristocracy were not so confined, they would likely come to dominate the entire government.

Those who rejected the mixed constitution because it was undemocratic were naive. They did not recognize the inevitability of the aristocracy's establishing itself and asserting power. Adams had little patience for fantasies about unicameral governments which would supposedly be more democratic than their bicameral cousins. Single-chambered legislatures would come to be dominated by aristocrats. In the margins of Mary Wollstonecraft's *Historical and Moral View of the Origin and Progress of the French Revolution* Adams peevishly wrote, "Does this foolish woman expect to get rid of an aristocracy? God Almighty has decreed in the creation of human nature an eternal aristocracy among men. . . . All that policy and legislation can do is to check its force by force."[34] Like Wollstonecraft, many French philosophes preferred a unicameral legislature. Adams's *Defence* was specifically designed to discredit this dangerous but increasingly popular view.

However, even if these writers were correct and democratic views could prevail in a single legislative body, there would be trouble. Unchecked democracy was even worse than unchecked aristocracy. Envious of the wealthy, democratic forces might be tempted to redistribute wealth or issue paper money, devaluing the currency. The passions of the common people were no less dangerous than those of the aristocracy, and as a group they were typically less cautious. Democracy was, in fact, the most unstable and thus the worst of the simple regimes. Monarchs would aim to promote civil peace to retain their power, and aristocrats would want stability to protect their property. Democratic agitation would likely provoke a reaction from a disenfranchised aristocracy. History demonstrated that simple regimes cycled from one to the next. This concept of political development had been offered up in Plato's *Republic,* in Aristotle's *Politics,* and in Machiavelli's *Discourses.* Adams endorsed Plato's understanding of this progression as the most accurate. He quoted Plato on the subject in the *Defence*—the longest of these quotations covers well over ten pages in the version edited by Charles Francis Adams.[35] Adams, like Plato, thought the likely successor to a short-lived democratic regime was a dictatorship. Napoleon's accession to power in France demonstrated to Adams this axiom's truth. To avoid this cycling, the more complicated institutional machinery of the mixed constitution was a necessity.[36]

To the prophet of democracy living out his retirement at Monticello, Adams wrote, "Checks and balances, Jefferson. However you and your Party may have ridiculed them[, they] are our only Security, for the Progress of the mind, as well as the Security of the Body. . . . Know thyself, human Nature!"[37] As indicated by this quote, Adams felt that the necessity of the mixed constitution was grounded in the facts of human psychology. Adams incorporated psychology into politics in the typical Adams way, by importing the views of political philosophers. Machiavelli had improved on previous authors by basing his prescriptions on how human beings really were rather than how they ought to be. Yet Adams found Machiavelli's views of human nature unrealistically austere. But he was at least closer to the mark than those who insisted that to work, government had to rely on altruistic behavior.[38]

A more realistic view of human behavior was offered by the thinkers of the Scottish Enlightenment. The Scots suggested that everyone has a kind self-regarding motive in the actions they take. People want to be seen and approved of.[39] As much as Adams wished that humans were inherently good, he knew that this was not the case. The philosophers who based their political prescriptions on this more measured view had "the phenomena all in their favor."[40] Humans could do good or they could do evil. Which they did depended a great deal on what would be most noticed and esteemed. If people were lauded for contributing to the public good, they would do good. If there were no rewards for contributing to the public good, people would not engage in public service. Whether good or ill is being done, Adams felt that "self-love operates in all stages of sociability."[41] So a goal in constructing a constitution was to build in rewards for working through constitutional channels and engaging in public service. Fame, or awards, or honors, or even money could entice people to do good. There was no reason government should not use them to channel behavior. In fact, doing exactly that was a vital part of constructing a good society.

This was why Adams favored honorific titles like "his majesty" for the president and vice president in 1789—a suggestion traceable to the Swiss thinker Emmerich de Vattel.[42] However, as with the conception of the mixed constitution, numerous authors with similar ideas contributed to Adams's thinking on human psychology. Once again Bolingbroke was an important influence.[43] Bolingbroke also influenced members of the Scottish Enlightenment, foremost among them David Hume and Adam Smith, who wrote exhaustively on the idea that self-regard is at work even when humans are cooperating. Twelve essays in the *Discourses on Davila* are dedicated to the subject of human psychology. As Alfred Iacuzzi relates, the writing "follows closely that of Adam Smith," whose book *The Theory of Moral Sentiments* was better known in Adams's time than Smith's *The Wealth of Nations*.[44]

Representation, the separation of powers, and the mixed constitution alone did not fully define the good regime for Adams. Other components of the good regime were, however, logically affiliated with these three political inventions, including individual rights, liberty, self-government, the rule of law, and consent of the governed. Conservative by nature, Adams could help lead a revolution partly because Locke's thinking about what made governments legitimate was so universally accepted. If the British would not allow the citizens of Massachusetts to govern themselves, something Locke wrote that all people had a right to do, then Adams felt he had reason to protest. If the situation was not rectified, then he felt the colonists had every right to withdraw their consent from the tyrannical British regime and declare their independence. This was all good Lockean theory translated to practice.[45] While these Enlightenment ideals had been most innovatively and forcefully articulated in his *Second Treatise*, Locke's thinking did not materialize out of thin air. He had intellectual precursors, and thinkers who came later expanded on his ideas. Adams read them and agreed with their support for self-government, rights, and the rule of law. Among these thinkers, now usually considered peripheral to Locke, Sir Philip Sidney was particularly admired by Adams.

Vattel also provided an Enlightenment gloss on views of international relations originally offered by Samuel Pufendorf and Hugo Grotius. These theorists stressed the benefits of establishing reciprocal rules of behavior to contain the damages of war and promote free commerce. While Adams praised these international legal theorists, he harbored doubts about how fully their ideas could be implemented. As fully sovereign entities, all governments could incorporate the international norms suggested by Vattel, Grotius, and Pufendorf into their own statutes, or conclude treaties with other nations to uphold them. They could not force other nations to abide by these rules. Reciprocity was a norm of international relations, and it logically recommended implementing the humane suggestions of these theorists. However, one could not count on reciprocity, particularly when there were severe imbalances of power between nations. Adams understood that the United States was weak compared to Britain and France, particularly in naval power, and that until the United States built its navy it was unlikely to be treated as an equal.

Finally, Adams's thought reflected a deeply conservative strain. Though the differences between him and Edmund Burke are both numerous and deep, they converged on one idea: to be sustained, political change must be gradual.[46] Whether Burke influenced Adams, or Adams influenced Burke, or both came to similar conclusions independently is a matter for conjecture. The speech Burke delivered in Parliament which was the precursor of *Reflections on the Revolution in France* was widely circulated. Adams, in England at the time serving as the U.S. ambassador, almost surely read the speech. His own views and writings may have been read by Burke. Most likely Burke articulated views Adams already believed because of his devotion to Aristotelian moderation. The two came to similar, exasperated judgments about a spate of political reformers, and likely viewed the writings of the other as evidence of his own correctness. Reformers often meant well, but they tended to bring their a priori ideas to politics with too little attention to what would work. As a result they failed to do good, and succeeded only in bringing harm.

Even before he took office, a President Adams could be expected to guard executive independence. If he were true to his ideals he would use the office to moderate the extreme views offered on the one hand by the nation's aristocrats, who he saw had organized themselves as the Federalist Party, and representatives of "the people" on the other, who had organized as the Republican Party. His devotion to the rule of law would keep him from exerting as much power as he hoped an executive would have, but he would not hesitate to use the veto to cancel legislation that he perceived violated the common good. In short, as president, Adams would place himself in the lonely position of guarding the mixed constitution.

"Independence Forever!"

Adams had already been applying theory to practice for decades by the time he became president. His proudest accomplishment in this regard was the Massachusetts Constitution, which he suggested "is Locke, Sidney, and Rousseau, and de Mably reduced to practice."[47] Since Adams thought that the most important determinant of whether a regime could succeed was its institutional structure, he naturally believed that the most crucial time to apply theory to practice was during a regime's founding or the writing of a new constitution. Once a framework for government was adopted, those who acted under its auspices were constrained to act within it, unless it was so defective that the people withdrew their consent. Thus as president, Adams could not pursue his ideals to their utmost, because as president he did not have the latitude of a constitution builder. However, his respect for the constitutional structure was itself a reflection of his political thought, demonstrating his deep commitment to the rule of law.[48]

As president, Adams seemed indecisive and unsteady to many, but this judgment was made by those who misunderstood Adams's theoretical views. In reality he hewed closely to his long-held beliefs. A "right" knowledge of political theory did not provide Adams with inevitable answers to the questions of the day, but it was a good foundation from which to make the judgments required of a president. Adams did chart a fiercely independent course. It was this very independence which led to many perceived failures, like his estrangement from the cabinet and from Federalists in Congress. These are considered failures mainly because today we expect the president to coordinate activity in the executive branch and among his congressional partisans. Adams's own political thought dictated a different standard of presidential success. He was less interested in coordination than he was in exercising independent judgment. The cabinet was regularly consulted for advice and Adams would find ways to cooperate with Congress, but if he alienated others in his pursuit of what was best for the nation, it demonstrated that he had not sacrificed his judgment for popularity or for appearances.

Given his understanding of politics, it is not difficult to imagine how Adams viewed the events of the 1790s: after the American Revolution the United States had followed the pattern of every other nation in world history, dividing into two opposing factions, one aristocratic in nature and the other more democratic in its enthusiasms. The aristocratic Federalists favored Britain, a nation they were more comfortable with because the House of Lords served to protect wealth and promote stability. The democratic Republicans favored France, a nation which purported to be a pure democracy and which acted rashly as a result. Neither the aristocratic party's comfort with Great Britain nor the democratic party's ill-founded enthusiasm for revolutionary France would make for good foreign policy. A strong, independent executive would need to curb the excesses of each. Unfortunately the aristocratic party and the democratic party disagreed with each other so strongly that civil war was a distinct possibility. The remedy to this animosity rested in the moderating hand of a dispassionate, independent executive.

The clearest example of Adams's independence was his decision to reopen peace negotiations with France in 1799. Relations with France—a single issue—dominated the Adams administration in a way that is characteristic of no other presidency.[49] French naval vessels and privateers had been boarding American ships and confiscating their cargo for several years. France and Britain were at war and the French wished to stop the extensive trade flowing between the United States and Great Britain. In 1798 Adams sent three envoys to meet with the French government to end this practice and to seek reparations. Unfortunately, agents acting on behalf of the French leader Charles-Maurice de Talleyrand-Perigord asked the American ambassadors to pay a bribe. The Americans refused, and Talleyrand spurned them. When this "XYZ Affair" became public, it caused a sensation in the United States.[50] Not only was the nation injured by the French, now it was insulted as well.

Relations with the French had been the subject of a bitter, decade-long dispute between the Republicans and the Federalists. Republicans had defended the French revolutionaries, thinking of them as freedom fighters who were to be supported in that they brought down a tyrannical regime and established a popular government. In the view of most Federalists, Adams included, these same individuals were dangerous zealots. They were not surprised that the French Revolution had turned horribly violent. The most ardent of the French wished to spread their democratic revolution across the globe. For years, the Federalists had worked to cement a close alliance with the more sober British and distance the nation from the reckless French. The new French offenses gave Federalists an opportunity to fully realize their foreign policy.

One of Adams's first official acts as president was to call Congress into special session, where he asked its members to pass laws raising the nation's military preparedness. Most Federalists took this as a positive sign—if France did not immediately desist from disrespecting the United States there would be war, which would serve to end the French insults, draw the United States closer to Great Britain, and vault the Federalist Party into a long-lasting majority. Adams was expected to follow this path because of his well-known admiration of Britain and his antipathy toward the French.

But the Federalists were mistaken in thinking that Adams would readily lead the nation into war. His understanding of history led him to be wary of taking such a course, particularly against a relatively large and wealthy nation. Further, what he admired about the British was their constitutional form—not the nation itself, of which he was wary. True, the British had translated the theory of the mixed constitution into practice, but his skepticism about human nature, fueled by his reading and his experience, led him to be wary of an alliance with the British against the French. This was the same skepticism which had kept him from endorsing the French Revolution. And political gain was no reason to go to war. While he would seriously contemplate asking Congress to declare war, Adams concluded that a diplomatic solution was preferable. His call for military preparedness was prompted by his understanding of international relations. To be respected as a nation in the way that Vattel, Grotius, and Pufendorf suggested nations should be, the United States had to be armed. Building up the nation's military would make the world's superpowers think twice about picking on the United States. Adams was an international-relations realist in an age when others seemed to let their feelings about democracy, whether positive or negative, dictate whether or not to go to war.

Adams's early messages to Congress made clear that French actions were unacceptable and had to stop. After the XYZ Affair, he left open the possibility that if France would receive American envoys in good faith, he would send a new delegation. Not desiring an active war, Talleyrand made conciliatory gestures. In 1799 Adams responded to these gestures by appointing a new envoy. Many Federalists considered this action tantamount to treason. With an army of 50,000 in the field led by party architect Alexander Hamilton, they believed that by dealing with Talleyrand, Adams was throwing away a chance to restore national dignity, extend national borders, and keep the Federalist Party in the majority.

In short, Federalists mistook Adams's preference for the British institutional structure for an enthusiasm about allying with Great Britain. Adams's judgment about the national interest differed from theirs; he thought the wisest course was to maintain American neutrality, if possible. His commitment to executive independence dictated that he would oppose those who had elected him president to pursue this diplomatic course, even though doing so would severely disappoint them. Preparing for war and then negotiating peace satisfied few, because it offended the extreme options proffered by both the aristocratic Federalists (war) and the democratic Republicans (eviscerate the military).

Adams acted moderately and independently through the quasi-war crisis, tempering each party's potentially dangerous enthusiasms. He made clear that the United States had been wronged by France and that he expected them to change their ways. He bided time to build the nation's military capability, resisted committing to war, left avenues for compromise open, and insisted on American neutrality. At a critical juncture Adams asked his cabinet whether he should send another minister to France or request that Congress declare war. The cabinet's Hamiltonians favored war. When Adams chose the route of conciliation by appointing William Vans Murray as envoy to France, members of the cabinet were "thunderstruck." Adams could have saved himself some trouble by more clearly signaling that he was going to reject their advice or in more forcefully arguing that neutrality remained the preferable course. However, he frequently took action independent of cabinet officers who showed signs of being infected with the disease of Federalist extremism. In his understanding, the nation deserved the president's best independent judgment. This included independence from cabinet members if they advocated partisan measures. Adams did not feel that his decisions needed to pass scrutiny in the cabinet or with the public. If Adams had asked for war, his popularity and that of the Federalists would have surged. He would almost surely have won a second term. But these benefits might have come at a very high price for the fledgling nation.

As Stanley Elkins and Eric McKitrick relate, Adams's presidency was defined by his seeking balance: balance between the Federalists and the Republicans, balance between France and England, and balance between preparing for war and keeping peace.[51] Understanding Adams as he saw himself in the chief executive's chair requires acknowledging that this balancing act was part of his theory-informed approach to the job. Adams's independence from party politics leads John Patrick Diggins to draw a sharp distinction between Adams's presidency and all subsequent presidencies. Diggins asserts that Adams was the last honest president. He made decisions primarily on the merits of the case rather on the basis of what would benefit his party or his political legacy. Diggins suggests that this cannot be said of any subsequent president. What made Adams different was not just his character, though it too may have been different. What set him apart was a solid commitment to the ideals he had discerned from political theory. Diggins asserts that "henceforth [after Adams's presidency], there would be little relationship between theory and practice in electoral politics."[52]

Adams's wariness of democratic excess was also on display in the way he treated the diplomatic correspondence of the American ministers involved in the XYZ Affair. When Congress requested that this correspondence be made public, Adams intentionally released the documents gradually. Dribbling documents out over several months bought time, allowing cooler heads to prevail in the United States and giving the French time to rectify their provocations. When conciliatory dispatches did arrive from Talleyrand, the president released them quickly to justify his action and to cool the nation's war fever.[53]

During Adams's term Congress passed several important pieces of legislation concerning immigrants, as well as the Sedition Act and the Judiciary Act of 1801, which expanded the federal judiciary. This legislation was acceptable to Adams and he signed each of these bills into law. What is usually called the Alien Act was actually several bills. One of them made individuals who immigrated to the United States wait fourteen years before they were eligible for citizenship.[54] This requirement was aimed squarely at French immigrants. The upheaval caused by the French Revolution meant that many refugees had recently come to the United States from France. The fourteen-year waiting period would prevent them from quickly becoming citizens and disrupting American politics with their radically democratic ideas.

Another bill allowed the president to deport any non-citizens who he believed endangered public safety. This was also directed primarily at the French. In 1793 a French diplomatic officer, Edmond Genet, had come to the New World with instructions to spread the principles of the French Revolution in the Americas. It was his hope to rouse the people of Canada, Florida, and Louisiana to rise up against their colonizers. In pursuing this mission, Genet expected to recruit Americans as sailors to man armed ships which would prey on British vessels. This was a stunning breach of diplomatic etiquette.[55] If Genet had been successful, his mission would likely have prompted the British to declare war against the United States. Genet responded scornfully to remonstrances against his behavior, and he threatened to take his case to the American people. An angry President Washington requested that the French relieve Genet from his service.

In 1796, the French interfered in American electoral politics. Their ambassador to the United States, Pierre Adet, wrote letters and broadsides favoring the election of the Francophile Jefferson over Adams.[56] By long-standing tradition, a government could request that a foreign nation's diplomats be replaced, but if resident aliens tried to influence American electoral politics as Genet or Adet did, they could now be expelled too. To Adams, these were reasonable measures to take against democracy's zealots, who were so intent on spreading their creed that they disregarded national borders. The deportation bill would help preserve American sovereignty against the possible assault of those foreigners so fervently at odds with the mixed constitution. These acts were logical steps to take when viewed as an alternative to war and foreign infiltration.

Today Adams is most severely criticized for signing the Sedition Act into law, because it is supposed that by doing so he was an enemy of free speech. Adams did value free speech, but like other values it was not absolute.[57] It was proper to set bounds on speech because speech could be used to falsely undermine the people's trust in government. And this is precisely what the Sedition Act, as it was written, aimed to do. The act allowed the federal government to prosecute "false, scandalous, and malicious" accusations against the government or its officials. Prosecutors enforcing the act would need to prove that a writer or speaker intended to defame an official or bring him into disrepute through false words. Truth was a valid defense against prosecution.[58]

In signing the Sedition Act into law, Adams believed that the nation was striking a well-crafted balance. Tyrannical and aristocratic governments would err on the side of limiting too much speech. Experience showed that they tended to ban any criticism of the existing regime. Democratic regimes would err too, in allowing anything to be spoken or written regardless of its truth or its consequences. Allowing false and malicious speech to be prosecuted struck the right balance between freedom and order. Certain prosecutions under the law were overzealous and suspect, but Adams's approval of the law was prompted by his commitment to moderating unhealthy extremes. He was still the conservative revolutionary, devoted to liberty, but was also concerned with promoting order and stability.

Adams's role in the Judiciary Act of 1801 is usually thought of negatively as well. The Judiciary Act intentionally created new federal offices which were to be filled by Adams with Federalist partisans immediately, before the Republicans gained control of the nation's governing institutions. Because of the term "midnight judges" we have an image of Adams filling out Federalist commissions in a fit of partisan pique by candlelight shortly before he ungraciously fled Washington by coach to avoid Jefferson's inauguration. It is true that partisanship was involved in the appointments Adams made, but his thinking was not that of a party hack. He was less interested in rewarding Federalists than he was in preventing the incoming Jefferson administration from seizing control of the judiciary and canceling the checks which were so central to Adams's political philosophy. In the federal elections of 1800, the Republicans had not only captured the House by a wide margin (69 to 36), they had also gained a majority in the Senate (18 to 13), and their party leader Thomas Jefferson was likely to become president.[59] Federalists realized that their only remaining hold on power was in the federal judiciary. They expanded the federal judiciary with the Judiciary Act of 1801, passed during Congress's lame-duck session. Adams signed the bill into law and started appointing Federalists to the newly created positions because he viewed it as an opportunity to counterbalance the Republicans' new power.

Despite all his fine attributes, which Adams "always loved," Jefferson was an unabashed democrat.[60] He would not provide balance or exercise judgment independent of his party in the president's chair precisely because he was the acknowledged and unapologetic leader of his party. Nor would the Senate be able to counterbalance the House, as both were held by the popular party. To Adams, the election of 1800 exposed deep flaws in the selection processes for both the president and the Senate, but what he could do about them as president was tightly circumscribed by the Constitution.[61] He could not single-handedly change electoral outcomes or engineer a more aristocrat-favoring selection process for the Senate. Within the constitutional structure he could only appoint Federalist judges as an ad hoc counterweight to the democrats' designs. As Adams saw it, these appointments were not personal payback. Rather, his interest was in preserving some semblance of balance between aristocratic and democratic factions by stacking the federal judiciary with the more aristocratic Federalists.[62]

With the Federalists and Republicans bitterly opposed in the late 1790s, Adams feared the nation might be headed for civil war. In this setting arose a domestic disturbance. In 1799 a tax revolt occurred in eastern Pennsylvania called the Fries Rebellion. John Fries gathered 150 men angry about the new taxes designed to support the enlarged army. The group marched on Bethlehem, where they forced a U.S. marshal to free several prisoners who were being held for having taken federal revenue officers captive. With the Federalists in no mood to put up with lawlessness, Fries and two others were charged with treason and sentenced to death for their actions. Adams had been disturbed about the possibility of lawlessness and he supported the prosecution of Fries. However, he felt that the charge and the sentence were excessive. Adams, the great believer in the rule of law, expected Fries to be punished. But the legal norm of making punishments proportional to the seriousness of the crime was also a key Enlightenment ideal which Adams endorsed.[63] After consulting legal precedents, Adams pardoned Fries and his cohorts, alienating "law and order" Federalists in the process and further diminishing his opportunity to get reelected.[64] In this, as in his other actions as president, Adams based his actions on his theoretical understanding of what an executive was to do. Though uttered in an entirely different context, Adams's last statement to the American public captures his theoretically informed view of how a good president would act in relation to politicians and organized groups: "Independence Forever!"[65]

Conclusion

Throughout his political career, Adams followed the dictates of his theoretically informed view. In doing so he lived out his own ideal of an individual who would translate what he knew from theory into practice for the benefit of humankind. He "acted as though dedicated intelligence might make a difference."[66] As a legal theorist and constitution builder the breadth of his political thinking was impressive. Richard Alan Ryerson suggests that "alone of the Founding Fathers, he provided an explicit link to nearly every writer who became a major source for America's political and legal traditions, from Plato and Justinian, to Blackstone, Rousseau, and Beccaria."[67] It does not go too far to suggest that Adams's relationship to political philosophy defined who he was.

Particularly in regard to France, Adams proceeded temperately and well when he could easily have pandered to Federalists by initiating a war (against a nation with a much greater population and a vast advantage in wealth). He would have been less likely to exert his independence from those who made him president without the intellectual tools political theory gave him to resist partisan pressures and political opportunism. A good deal of Federalist commentary attributed Adams's decision making to his obstinate personality rather than his political thought. These Federalists were right, to a point. Adams *was* obstinate. That personality trait was reinforced, *but it was also directed* by a theoretically informed understanding of how he should act. If he had been merely stubborn, Adams might have been the most staunch Federalist partisan American politics ever knew. But to the benefit of the nation his stubbornness served his principles. Theory provided a critical direction which led him to resist the clamorings of both parties, avoiding both war and "entangling alliances."

It was easy to misinterpret Adams's theory-based admiration for the British government and distaste for France as a preference for an alliance. Adams may never have been able to bridge the rift between himself and the Hamiltonians, but he could have prevented them from being surprised. He could have made independent decisions while being less aloof. Always the student of himself, Adams understood his own deficiencies. Writing to Jefferson in 1813, Adams told his friend, "I have been so unfortunate as never to be able to make myself understood."[68] Though the former president was speaking specifically of his ideas on aristocracy, this sentiment could be applied to Adams's political thought in general. Theoretical commitments are not easy to articulate, nor are they quickly understood. Adams wrote volumes of dense prose to get his point across. Perhaps he should have written much less to be more understood.

However, to the discerning eye his actions were predictable. Adams himself recognized that he would be able to satisfy neither party. Just before the election of 1796 Adams wrote, "I am not enough of an Englishman nor little enough of a French Man for some People. These would be very willing that Pinckney should come in, Chief. But they will be disappointed."[69] Benjamin Rush opined that "it was [Adams's] misfortune to administer the Government of his country at a time when it was alternately attracted and repelled by two of the most powerful nations of Europe, contending by a furious and extensive war for the supremacy of the globe. In the vibrations of parties, he retained a fixed point, by which means he offended both."[70] Doing this destroyed Adams's chances for a second term.

The heart of Adams's political thought centered around institutional dynamics. In other areas treated by political theory he was less well versed. For example, Adams was a believer in the theory, stressed since the days of ancient Rome, that there could be no "imperium in imperio" or "power in power." In any one place, a single government was sovereign. If a constitution attempted to split sovereignty among different levels of government, one entity would come to dominate. Adams believed that the national government was fully sovereign, meaning that he never fully came to grips with the innovative relationship that the Constitution defined between the national and state governments. While Jefferson and Madison offered ideas about federalism that are still discussed, Adams did not. If Adams was greatly informed by two millennia of political theory, he was also, in a way, trapped within its familiar constructs.[71] What has been in politics is not a foolproof indicator of what can be, and Adams's approach to political theory denied the possibility of finding something new under the sun.

There was also an unrecognized circularity to his commitment to the mixed constitution. Many English thinkers praised the mixed constitution and resuscitated classical authors who touted its benefits because in doing so they confirmed to themselves that their own government was ideal. Though skeptical of many, Adams may not have been sufficiently skeptical of the tendency of the British to idealize the British-style mixed constitution. Subsequent history demonstrates that democracies can be stable. This includes the British government, which moved substantially away from the mixed constitutional form during the nineteenth and early twentieth centuries, draining the House of Lords and the monarchy of their political power. Many democracies function passably well without three lawmaking branches arranged in "triple equipoise"—something which Adams would never have predicted.

Few members of the public read what Adams wrote or bothered to think about the points of difference between his understanding of why the United States had three institutions making law versus James Madison's understanding of this same matter. In the politics of his day—probably always in politics—Adams's opponents had great incentives to misunderstand, mischaracterize, and distort his views. Political theory was a two-edged sword to John Adams. Though his keen interest in political theory set him down the path that led to the presidency, and provided important guidance throughout his tenure in office, his specific commitments caused him to be disliked. For solace, Adams turned to—who else—a political philosopher. In Plato, Adams found vindication for his independence. *The Republic* teaches that what should be esteemed (e.g., genius, character, virtue) is not, and what is esteemed (e.g., beauty, wealth, fame) should not be. Adams felt the truth of this teaching in a way that was personally painful. He felt that he suffered for his adherence to the truth—to the science of politics which was to be found in political philosophy.

It is exceedingly rare for a politician both to have served as the highest officer in a nation and be renowned for contributions to political theory. Adams scholars insist that he should be recognized as an important political thinker.[72] A half century ago Clinton Rossiter suggested that "the richest portion of Adams' legacy to our America is his political theory."[73] Adams's synthesis was unique, and if he had been a better writer, his political thought would be better known and he would be recognized as a powerful modern conservative with a notable perspective on the American institutional design, including the role of the president.

Chapter 3

Thomas Jefferson: Notes from a Prophet of Progress

You wrote for Europe, while . . . I think for America.
—Thomas Jefferson, letter to Jean Baptiste Say

They [Native Americans] too have their antiphilosophists who find an interest in keeping things in their present state, who dread reformation, and exert all their faculties to maintain the ascendancy of habit over the duty of improving our reason and obeying its mandates.
—Thomas Jefferson, second inaugural address,
March 4, 1805

Thomas Jefferson provides a stark contrast to John Adams. Adams found the time to both read and write dense tomes of political thought. Jefferson had little taste for such endeavors. Adams believed he had found the one form of government which worked well from his study of history and political theory. Jefferson thought Adams's discovery and most of the books that he had studied to find it were rubbish. Where Adams carefully sifted and winnowed what was useful from the chaff in the historical tradition of political theory, Jefferson could whisk it all away in a rhetorical flourish, as merely a chronicle of past follies. To Jefferson, history was not philosophy teaching by examples. Quite the contrary—in one of his characteristically pithy statements he wrote that "history in general only informs us what bad government is."[1] Jefferson dismissed what Adams accepted: that within the long tradition of political theory was an accumulation of the wisdom of the ages.

Yet Jefferson did not dismiss political philosophy out of hand. He keenly felt himself to be part of an intellectual movement which would re-form the world. He, more than any other major American-born figure involved

46

in the founding, agreed with Thomas Paine's ambitious and revolutionary sentiment that "we have it in our power to make the world over again." And the ways in which he wished to see the world made over were greatly informed by contemporary political theorists and by those from the recent past who had blazed a trail for these later thinkers.

Thus Jefferson was deeply ambivalent about political theory. He was suspicious of how it had affected politics historically. At the same time he was deeply invested in the new "scientific" political philosophy. Jefferson also felt himself unbound by the ideas of any particular theorist. As he himself recognized, "I never submitted the whole system of my opinions to the creed of any party of men whatever in religion, in philosophy, in politics, or in anything else where I was capable of thinking for myself."[2] Adams claimed not to be original. He had built the edifice of his political theory from bricks fashioned by others. The quirky, eclectic theory that Jefferson built contained some materials directly from political theorists, others which were inspired by their work but intentionally altered, and a good deal of material of his own devising.

Jefferson always professed a love of reading, and he assembled what was perhaps the most impressive private library in the Americas before he sold it to Congress to replace the one the British burned in Washington during the War of 1812. Yet his reading habits were very different from Adams's. In a letter of January 11, 1817, the retired Jefferson marveled at the amount which Adams had read in the past year: "Forty three volumes read in one year, and 12. of them quartos [large books]! Half a dozen octavos [small books] in that space of time are as much as I am allowed."[3] If Jefferson's estimate of his own book reading is accurate, Adams read roughly ten times the amount that Jefferson did in 1816.

Even if the disparity in the amount they read was significantly less when they were young, Jefferson's reading was more eclectic, limiting the amount of time he spent on any one thing. While Adams refused to read about caterpillars so that he could concentrate on political theory, Jefferson's inclinations were precisely the opposite. He was fascinated by nature and the sciences in all their facets. He was quite willing to lay aside the dusty tomes of politics' yesteryear in favor of the burgeoning amount of scientific work inspired by the Enlightenment.[4]

One reason that Jefferson told the French economist Jean Baptiste Say "you *wrote* for Europe, while . . . I *think* for America" is that he was not a professional author and did not have the time to write down his thoughts on political economy. But for this prolific letter writer, not setting down his thoughts about politics in a comprehensive or theoretical manner was a deliberate choice—as deliberate as was Adams's choice to do so. What we know of Jefferson's political thought comes from ideas set down in letters or in documents like the Declaration of Independence or his inaugural addresses. For Jefferson, it could hardly be otherwise. By personality and intellectual habit he was not one to draw fine distinctions or to make extended arguments. What he found correct was "self-evident" to him, bolstered by the facts of empirical science and not in need of great explication or elaborate argumentation. Either others saw it too, or they were hopelessly lost.

While others might enjoy prattling on about traditional political philosophy, Jefferson was engaged in the far more important business of making the world anew according to the dictates of science. To him, taking a scientific approach to life meant devoting oneself to the pursuit of human happiness, which required being free of familiar dogmas or patterns of living. He would not be one of those "antiphilosophists" who would "find an interest in keeping things in their present state . . . dread reformation, and exert" themselves to preserve old habits and customs. He, like other Enlightenment thinkers, would be ruthlessly committed to what would make life tangibly better for humankind. He had an incredible opportunity to do this in America—which was as blank a political canvas as existed anywhere in the world. When he "thought for America," he believed he was thinking as a hard-headed empiricist, unbound by the past, which was dominated by various dogmas.

For scholars, finding the "real" Jefferson has been like a quest for the Holy Grail. In Carl Becker's formulation he was a devoted Lockean; to Adrienne Koch he was a devotee of the French philosophes; Lance Banning argues that Jefferson transported the British "Country party" or Whig opposition ideology of the 1720s and 1730s to America; Joyce Appleby rejects Banning's view, forwarding the claim that Jefferson was an economic progressive whose thinking harmonized with the now-obscure Antoine DeStutt de Tracy; Garry Wills emphasizes Jefferson's debt to the Scottish moral-sense philosophers, such as Francis Hutcheson.[5] Such arguments would almost surely strike Jefferson as needless. To find the "real Jefferson" in one thinker or another is to make the kind of fine distinctions about the Enlightenment-era writers that Jefferson himself would not make. It also posits a kind of devotion to people rather than ideas, which made Jefferson uncomfortable. Without pausing a beat, Jefferson claimed to have gained inspiration from a great variety of thinkers. He did not worry that their ideas did not cohere or that he might have to choose among them. Despite his admiration for them, he felt perfectly free to alter what they had said, because scientific reasoning was his guide, not men.

Jefferson read political philosophy, but both his predecessor and his successor in the office of the presidency read much more. Nor was his understanding of political philosophy anywhere near as deep or as meticulous as theirs was. This is not a criticism so much as it is a description of Jefferson's own deliberate choice. Despite his relative aloofness to political philosophy, Jefferson gained much from his acquaintance with it. He felt a kinship with the one true philosophy, as indicated by the quote from his second inaugural address at the opening of this chapter. Those who opposed his administration and the good that it would bring by applying Enlightenment republicanism were "antiphilosophers," disingenuously protecting their privileged status or unimaginatively stuck in familiar ruts of thought. Privilege had justified itself for more than two millennia through the use of various "antiphilosophies." Jefferson's "Revolution of 1800" attempted to relegate privilege to the past forever, for the benefit of humankind.

"All Theory Must Yield to Experience"

Jefferson's approach to political theory bolstered his push for radical political change. Anyone devoted to the status quo was suspect in his mind. An important example of this can be found in Jefferson's second inaugural address, delivered at the height of the third president's popularity and influence. The speech has a triumphalist tone. It was the work of a self-assured intellectual at his most confident. Jefferson believed wholeheartedly that his revolution in government was working and he wanted the American people to know it. There are only a few passages which acknowledge that not everything was going according to plan. One of these passages contains the excerpt about Native Americans quoted in the second epigraph to this chapter.

Jefferson had very specific ideas about "Indian policy." His primary goal was to encourage Indians' "domestication" by "teach[ing] them agriculture and the domestic arts." In his own mind he was motivated by a humane consideration: after being pushed off of their traditional lands, native tribes could not effectively subsist by hunting and gathering. But his administration's "endeavors to enlighten them" were foundering by March 1805. Jefferson's understanding of why this was occurring is telling. He felt that "crafty individuals among them who feel themselves something in the present order of things and fear to become nothing in any other" were to blame. "These persons," he continued,

> inculcate a sanctimonious reverence for the customs of their ancestors; that whatsoever they did must be done through all time; that reason is a false guide, and to advance under its counsel in their physical,

moral, or political condition is perilous innovation; that their duty is
to remain as their Creator made them, ignorance being safety and
knowledge full of danger; in short, my friends, among them also is
seen the action and counteraction of good sense and bigotry; they too
have their antiphilosophists who find an interest in keeping things in
their present state, who dread reformation, and exert all their faculties
to maintain the ascendancy of habit over the duty of improving our
reason and obeying its mandates.[6]

This extraordinary paragraph tells us much about Jefferson's attitudes.
"Reason" told Jefferson that traditional ways were to be given no credence
simply because they had the stamp of longevity. The Indians' way of life
was simply not very productive, and the sooner that their nomadic ways
were abandoned in favor of farming, the better. "Reason" did not stand for
some elaborate argument, or a theorem with a proof, but the Enlightenment's simple test of utility, guided by science.[7] All Jefferson felt he had to
consider was whether the nomadic Indians or farmers were faring better.
The only thing required to answer this question was data on the amount
of food produced by the average person engaged in these two different
ways of life. In that calculus, farming was the clear winner. Encouraging
Indians to farm was, to Jefferson, simple common sense dictated by empirical reality. To him, choosing agriculture over hunting and gathering
was so obviously beneficial that those who opposed the policy were either
motivated by selfishness (tribal leaders who wanted to maintain their positions) or bereft of reason (rank-and-file tribal members without education who were duped by their leaders). By extension, those who argued
for any human arrangement, political or otherwise, that was disutile were
enemies to the one true philosophy.
    Jefferson's racial insensitivity need not detain us long here, other than
to acknowledge that it informs these observations.[8] And yet, Jefferson
thought precisely the same antiphilosophic dynamic was at work within
"white" society. For centuries European societies had been dominated
by kings, aristocrats, churches, and other guardians of tradition. Those
who had power in these societies effectively kept themselves in power by
touting the benefits of their favored institutions. They duped citizens into
thinking that only absolute monarchy or the mixed constitution promised
stability, or that the institutions they administered were ordained by God.
To Jefferson that was all patently false. These institutions provided narrow benefits to the very people who argued that they were universally
beneficial and indispensable. They harmed the vast majority.

Some of the beneficiaries of unreason were so articulately crafty, so smartly devious, that their arguments had great sticking power. When couched in political terms, this *was* traditional political philosophy. Repeated over and over, these arguments could become the conventional wisdom, fooling even a highly intelligent man of goodwill like John Adams. Instead of treating traditional political philosophy as a compendium of wisdom, Jefferson felt it should be approached warily if at all. It threatened to lead one astray, from a dedication to universal human happiness toward hierarchy and tyranny. Additionally, theories were self-reinforcing: "the moment a person forms a theory, his imagination sees in every object only the tracts which favor that theory." The antiphilosophies of political theory's past were closed systems, from which its adherents could interpret any phenomenon. Science was the solution to combat these prejudices, and in making that point Jefferson counseled that "all theory must yield to experience."[9]

Traditional political theory had to withstand the withering scrutiny of the scientific method. Locke's *Essay concerning Human Understanding* had warned against the false association of ideas. Humans were often fooled into thinking that two occurrences which took place in succession were due to some relation between the two, a cause and effect. Locke urged caution in making such attributions. Much of the effort of the Enlightenment centered around dispelling false associations and establishing true causal relationships. The eighteenth century's best minds broke the world down into its constituent parts and conducted research on which phenomena really caused other phenomena. Jefferson was unabashedly devoted to this scientific method. Science was of such importance to Jefferson that he considered the world's foremost scientists to be the "greatest men that have ever lived, without any exception." The three greatest were Locke, Bacon, and Newton.[10]

While Adams chose to focus his attention on the "big picture" theme of the performance of institutional structures, Jefferson, true to the Enlightenment, chose to break down and compartmentalize. This is what he did in his only book, *Notes on the State of Virginia*. He approached components of his native state, including its soil and climate and individual laws. Each was to be taken on its own terms and determined to be of value or not. There was no "big picture" for Jefferson except what was created by the summation of these constituent parts. Thus it was that Enlightenment political thought separated itself out from all previous thought because it took more care in analysis and kept its goal of human happiness constantly in mind. Jefferson valued Enlightenment thought because it had found the effective way by which to increase human happiness. The movement promised to use science in all of its manifestations to make life better for people regardless of their status. Only the political writings which took this scientific approach did Jefferson hold in high regard.

The Enlightenment was already increasing human happiness through the dissemination of knowledge, the invention of superior tools, and the discovery of more effective medicines. None of these had been brought about by government. They had been accomplished by the genius of private individuals engaged in scientific research. In its political phase, the Enlightenment championed restrictions on government as a means whereby individuals could effectively structure their own lives in the way that they saw fit. Freedom would yield happiness. By contrast, almost all pre-Enlightenment thought was built around some abstract value (e.g., what does God want?) rife with false associations and unscientific thinking. It used government—and often a very heavy-handed government—to stifle freedom and to perpetuate itself. This ethic would be crushed by the new science.

This dismissive attitude toward traditional political theory did not impress John Adams. In the summer of 1800, when it seemed like Jefferson would become the next president, Secretary of State Timothy Pickering asked President Adams about his friend's education. Pickering's report of the conversation indicated that Adams said, "Why yes, he has a certain kind of learning in philosophy, &c., but very little of that which is necessary for a statesman."[11] This is not the public ranting of a political foe who knew his opponent only in caricature. Adams knew Jefferson well, and he was privately lamenting the fact that he did not take political theory more seriously.

Jefferson's argument in his second inaugural address was a deliberate allusion to what was happening in Western society: *they too* have their antiphilosophists in native communities, Jefferson said, meaning that this phenomenon was even more apparent among Americans of European descent. Before 1800, Jefferson believed the antiphilosophist Federalists had done their best to corrupt the American government, duping the people with their theories. The tyrannical forces of aristocracy had had the upper hand in Europe for centuries. In 1800 they harbored affection for a dying way of life, destined to be extinguished because of its counterproductive and unreasonable ethic of privilege.

The new philosophy of government was based on lived experience. Elaborate, difficult written arguments did not have to be constructed to support it, as was the case with the old philosophy. One could simply observe its benefits and see the truth. When Adams ran across a book he found hopelessly false, he wrote snide notes in its margins all the way to its conclusion, sometimes totaling thousands of words. Jefferson simply stopped reading, declared the book useless, cast it aside, and moved on.[12] Thus he confessed to Adams after he was seventy years old that he had "scarcely ever had patience to go through a whole dialogue of Plato."[13]

When asked about Aristotle's *Politics*, Jefferson wrote, "So different was the style of society then, and with those people, from what it is now with us, that I think little edification can be obtained from their writings on the subject of government." The ancients had not even discovered representation, and thus they had not conceived of democracy within a nation-state, the only form which promised citizens liberty and self-government. Considered a patron saint of education by many for his advocacy of public schooling, Jefferson radically devalued the books that had been a standard part of an advanced curriculum in politics for two centuries. The relative primitiveness of the Greeks and Romans "relieves our regret if the political writings of Aristotle, or of any other ancient, have been lost, or are unfaithfully rendered or explained to us."[14] The loss of ancient wisdom about politics did not much matter to Jefferson, because it was hardly worth preserving in the first place.

A good deal of modern political theory was no better. Initially enthusiastic about Baron de Montesquieu, Jefferson came to understand in middle age that his book *The Spirit of the Laws* was in many ways erroneous, though it seemed to be based on scientific observation. He came to believe that the book would be better if much of it could be significantly altered, critiqued, or updated to reflect empirical reality. Montesquieu had been cited as the great authority who proved, through a demonstration of historical examples, that popular governments were not possible in nations with large territories. The United States offered proof, Jefferson believed, that this hypothesis was utterly false. In his retirement he spent months translating Antoine DeStutt de Tracy's *Commentary and Review of Montesquieu's "Spirit of the Laws,"* which argued against Montesquieu's position that republics had to remain small and also countered his endorsement of the mixed constitution.[15]

Jefferson's books and his early writings were almost all destroyed in a fire that burned his boyhood home, Shadwell, to the ground in 1770, when he was in his late twenties. One of his few extant possessions which predated the Shadwell fire is his commonplace book, in which he copied passages from key authors whom he wished to remember and reference. His early entries consist almost entirely of legal definitions, summaries of case law, and excerpts from legal commentaries. For a young lawyer, this is not surprising. But in 1774, when Jefferson was over thirty and a representative in the Virginia legislature, he turned to copying passages of political philosophy. What he copied were whole sections of *The Spirit of the Laws* and Cesare Beccaria's *On Crimes and Punishments*. These were two of the most widely read political writings of the time. Jefferson thus seems to have become a serious student of political theory only years after his formal education ended. Had he been a serious student of political theory before then, he would have copied out those passages years earlier. The editor of a modern edition of Jefferson's commonplace book, Gilbert Chinard, finds that "it is remarkable that in a book of this character, political philosophers occupy so little space."[16]

Jefferson's relative inattention to political philosophy is underscored by his 1771 compilation of titles to be included in a "gentleman's library." Just a year after the Shadwell fire, he had already compiled a library larger than the one that had burned. It was in this context that a friend, Robert Skipwith, asked him to send a list of important books to buy. Jefferson's response was a curious one for someone with the reputation of being a devotee of philosophy: he offered an elaborate defense of reading fiction. Its "entertainments" are "useful as well as pleasant." Fiction helps to "fix in the principles and practices of virtue" because we abhor bad behavior when we read of it in these works, and think highly of charity, gratitude, and beauty. While reading, "we never reflect whether the story we read be truth or fiction," so that fiction's lessons are equally powerful as those culled from real life. But fiction has an edge on reality because examples can be more readily or starkly drawn for a purpose. By contrast, actual history provides "too infrequent" lessons. For example, "filial duty is more effectually impressed on the mind of a son or daughter by reading King Lear, than by all the dry volumes of ethics, and divinity that ever were written." Jefferson listed nearly 200 titles for Skipwith to buy, under nine headings. By far the largest group of books was under the heading "Fine Arts," in which novels, plays, and poetry were housed. "Politicks, Trade" warranted just eight titles.[17]

Political philosophy's ideas were in the air during the founding, however, and Jefferson clearly internalized enough of them to be profoundly influenced. Yet the image of Jefferson the philosopher is highly exaggerated if what we mean by "philosopher" is one with a deep and thorough understanding of a certain body of writings. If, however, we use the term to denote someone who is starkly original, then Jefferson has a much more solid claim. His thinking was clearly influenced by others. Jefferson agreed with scores of influential authors who stressed the importance of human happiness, making dubious the claim that any particular book was Jefferson's inspiration. Jefferson himself did not care where the idea was from as long as it expressed the truth.

Even the way Jefferson explained the intellectual provenance of the Declaration of Independence indicates a certain carelessness about political theory. At the end of his life the third president recollected that in authoring the Declaration he was "neither aiming at originality of principle or sentiment, nor [was it] yet copied from any particular and previous writing." The ideas he put to paper were common ones at the time, and "all American Whigs thought alike on these subjects." "Its authority," he said, rested "on harmonizing sentiments of the day, whether expressed in conversation, in letters, in printed essays, or in the elementary books of public right, as Aristotle, Cicero, Locke, Sidney, etc."[18]

The Declaration's debt to Locke and Sidney is obvious: both argued that revolution is a valid response when one is governed by a tyrannical regime. But crediting Aristotle and Cicero demonstrates the lack of fine distinctions Jefferson made when he approached political philosophy. What they have to do with the document is not at all clear. These ancients were guardians of the "res publica," or a government which serves the public interest instead of private interests. Apparently that vague connection is what Jefferson is referring to. Given his explicit dismissal of ancient authorities elsewhere, this "influence" is very tenuous indeed.

Daniel Boorstin makes a study of Jefferson's "philosophical vagueness" in *The Lost World of Thomas Jefferson*. He describes Jefferson's intellectual life as a kind of paradox: he was a nonphilosophical philosopher. He possessed a philosophy, but did not think he had one. "What he asked of his political theory," Boorstin contends, "was no blueprint for society, but a way of discovering the plan implicit in nature."[19] To Jefferson, science, common sense, usefulness, and philosophy, properly understood, all coincided, merging seamlessly in his political thought. And this was all rather simple, self-evident, and natural.

Jefferson's relationship with political theory, then, was a deeply ambivalent one. He was dismissive of the vast majority of historical theory and put surprisingly little effort into understanding the massive body of work that he was rejecting. Simultaneously he embraced the modern scientific metatheory of the Enlightenment in all its phases, including its "political science." Like others steeped in Enlightenment thought he tended to break subjects into constituent parts for analysis, focusing on cause and effect. He believed that the thinkers who did that were worthy of consideration. Of even greater value were the individuals who had discovered and publicized the scientific method. He borrowed from Enlightenment thinkers, but he also prided himself in his independence from their ideas. He was ruthlessly devoted to human happiness, rather than being beholden to any particular thinker. As such he was not meticulous about political theory. He was not in the least ashamed that John Adams outread him in it. Adams had been misled by all that reading. He, Jefferson, had gained the proper attitude about and approach toward political philosophy from much less reading. He had found the obvious truths which did not require elaborate arguments—they just required champions in government who would do the people's work—and who would, more importantly, let the people do their own work for themselves.

"A Government Rigorously Frugal & Simple"

As the nation anticipated the presidential contest of 1800, Jefferson, like Adams, did not engage in electioneering. However, from private letters we have a clear understanding of his political principles heading into this epic contest. To Elbridge Gerry, Jefferson wrote that he was against the national government's accruing power that belonged to the states; he was against the executive's eclipsing the power of the people's representatives in the legislature; he was for "a government rigorously frugal & simple" and for eliminating the national debt as soon as feasible; he supported a minimal defense establishment, with the nation relying almost exclusively on militias; he favored a minimal diplomatic corps and political alliances with no nation, but open trade with all.[20]

Jefferson's letter to Gerry indicates that his primary hope was to pare an already small national government down to almost nothing. A variety of influences from political theory informed him and bolstered his position. Like Adams, Jefferson grounded his ideas about politics on an understanding of human psychology. Their preferred sources on this matter were similar. In Adam Smith and others, Adams found the idea that humans desire to be seen and esteemed. To Jefferson, the Scottish Enlightenment emphasized a more sunny and cooperative view. Francis Hutcheson, Adam Smith, Lord Kames, and Thomas Reid argued that human beings possess a natural moral sense or feeling for others. This leads people to cooperate most of the time, a phenomenon much more readily apparent in real life than Thomas Hobbes's "war of all against all," or even Adams's desire to be seen and esteemed. Human beings are naturally sociable.[21] Relations between people are much more often mutually beneficial than they are "zero-sum." One person's well-being does not prevent another's, and it makes little sense to conceive of humans as atomistic, or existing in a hypothetical "state of nature."

In an 1814 letter to Thomas Law, Jefferson wrote, "I sincerely, then, believe with you in the general existence of a moral instinct. I think it is the brightest gem with which the human character is studded, and the want of it is more degrading than the most hideous of the bodily deformities."[22] In addition to his fealty to moral-sense philosophy, this quote makes clear that his was not a naive view. Jefferson recognized that there are individuals who do not care for others and who engage in antisocial behaviors. They are the exceptions to the rule. Largely because of these exceptions, government is a necessity. But also because they are exceptions, very little government is, in fact, needed.

Because humans possess an innate moral sense, the presentation of elaborate arguments about it is unnecessary. Writing from France in 1787 to his nephew Peter Carr, Jefferson opined that

> I think it is lost time to attend lectures on moral philosophy. He who made us would have been a pitiful bungler, if He had made the rules of our moral conduct a matter of science. . . . [Man] was endowed with a sense of right and wrong. . . . [that] is as much a part of his nature, as the sense of hearing, seeing, feeling; it is the true foundation of morality. . . . State a moral case to a plowman and a professor. The former will often decide it as well and often better than the latter because he has not been led astray by artificial rules.[23]

Jefferson had great praise for Kames's *Historical Law Tracts,* which accepted the moral-sense theory as a given. He never expressed similar praise for Smith's epic and influential *Theory of Moral Sentiments,* which argued the same point much more thoroughly. In fact, he called Smith's writing "prolix and tedious."[24] Carr, like most of his fellow human beings, already treated others well and was in no need of lectures on moral philosophy. Thus Jefferson took the curious position described by Daniel Boorstin: he was possessed of a philosophy that he thought was no philosophy at all, because it was self-evident.

Jefferson called himself an Epicurean, a philosophy based on the ideas of Epicurus, a Greek philosopher from the third century B.C. who believed that the enlightened pursuit of happiness was the end of life. This was a typical enthusiasm of Enlightenment thinkers, from the Utilitarians, to the Scots, to Beccaria, to the French thinkers Claude-Adrien Helvetius and the Baron D'Holbach. Jefferson viewed himself as part of this movement, the goal of which was to increase the overall happiness of humankind by ensuring that liberty would flourish. Freedom could increase happiness greatly. Different people liked different things, and within reason each could choose to live the life he preferred in a free regime—a point made by Locke and repeated innumerable times by many others in the eighteenth century. Liberty did have to be worked for and constantly guarded, though, because it was always threatened. In fact, the vast majority of human institutions worked to curtail liberty. While Jefferson thought with Locke that the earliest governments were founded on consent, it was not an exaggeration to think of their subsequent histories as chronicles of corruption.

Typically Britons offered the view that their liberties expanded through time. In this understanding of history, English citizens first got a taste of freedom with the signing of the Magna Charta in 1215. Various legislative acts through the centuries expanded the prerogatives of individuals, and the rights of citizens became confirmed by the English bill of rights of 1689. To Jefferson, this thesis of progressive freedom had things backward. The original Anglo-Saxon government had been noncoercive. It had been corrupted by increasingly centralized and heavy-handed institutions which restricted popular freedom and served the few at the expense of the many. The history of England was the story of the progressive *loss* of freedom and self-government, not its discovery. In his commonplace book he wrote that "English liberties are not infringements merely of the king's prerogative, extorted from our princes by taking advantage of their weakness; but a restoration of that antient constitution, of which our ancestors had been defrauded by the art and finesse of the Norman Lawyers."[25]

England's history was not unusual. Jefferson gathered evidence that all of the northern kingdoms of Europe originally had popular councils, most of which could depose their king.[26] Thus he made the point that kings were not originally all-powerful and unchecked. They had become so only after political power had been consolidated and cunning "antiphilosophies" had formed to justify an unquestioned status. Kings originally had to serve the public to continue in their positions, and the early "parliaments" ensured that the people's will was done, often deposing kings who did not satisfy them. Only through time did kings claim to rule by divine decree. When that argument was accepted, they became untouchable. While this version of European history is as questionable as the belief that freedom has made constant progress, Jefferson did believe in it, in part because of the distinguished authors he read who advanced this "Saxon myth." The British legal scholars Lord Kames, Sir Edward Coke, Sir John Dalrymple, and Obadiah Hulme all offered versions of this idea in their writings, as did Algernon Sidney in his *Discourse on Government*.[27]

The idea that governments have benign foundings but that citizens lose their liberties through time because of the growth of governmental institutions had powerful advocates in England decades before the American Revolution. As Sir Robert Walpole consolidated power under what is now recognized as the first prime ministership, his opponents offered this same critique in apocalyptic terms. These opponents decried the concentration of power in an administrative arm of the government at the expense of the people's legislature. They also complained about the burgeoning use of debt and taxation to saddle citizens with unnecessary burdens and the birth of a standing army which might be used to enforce heavy-handed laws in peacetime. Among these writers were John Trenchard and Thomas Gordon (who wrote editorials together as "Cato") and Viscount Bolingbroke.[28] Whether their polemics "count" as political theory or not is debatable. However, they popularized the theory about government that the concentration of power and increasing corruption are natural trajectories, and that the only way to check them is for citizens to be aware and vigilant in countering these tendencies.

Jefferson's own experience seemed to fit this Whig narrative. The British had become increasingly aggressive in their pursuit of revenue from their colonies in the 1760s and 1770s. They had threatened self-government in the process. Virtuous colonists revolted, forming their own popular governments through a consensual process. In the late 1780s and through the 1790s, the elite Federalists attempted to consolidate these states into a centralized regime and create a powerful national government. Alexander Hamilton seemed to be an American version of Walpole: he advocated a powerful executive, a national banking system, and a standing army in peacetime, which would create the need for extensive taxation and long-term debt. The familiar patterns of history were repeating themselves on the American stage. Power was concentrating—a movement engineered by the few who would benefit from this occurrence. If Jefferson could be elected president and the Republicans could control Congress, then much of the damage Federalists had done to liberty could be reversed by paring the national government back to its bare essentials.

Not surprisingly, given this mind-set, Jefferson stressed the need for checks on government power. He repeatedly proposed a four-tiered government:

> Let the national government be entrusted with the defence of the nation, and its foreign and federal relations; the State governments with civil rights, laws, police, and administration of what concerns the State generally; the counties with the local concerns of the counties, and each ward direct the interests within itself. It is by dividing and subdividing these republics from the great national one down through all its subordinations, until it ends in the administration of every man's farm by himself . . . that all will be done for the best.[29]

The "ward" was Jefferson's own brainchild, but it reflected the Enlightenment's suspicion of concentrated power, its belief in the capabilities of average people (or average men, at least), and its commitment to popular government.[30]

Jefferson's *Notes on the State of Virginia* indicates his other commitments. He criticized the state's property requirement for voters.[31] He did not believe that freed African Americans and whites could live together harmoniously. He disliked Virginia's malapportionment. He praised bicameralism, but suggested that the state's Senate and its House of Delegates were too homogeneous because they were selected at the same time, by the same people, from among the same pool of candidates. Jefferson felt that Virginia's legislature was too powerful because it not only possessed legislative power, but also wielded some executive and judicial functions. The three entities should be strictly separated. The legislature should also not be able to change the Constitution at will, nor determine the number of legislators that had to be present to conduct official business.[32]

Jefferson's penchant for checks and balances was familiar Enlightenment fare. One of Locke's English contemporaries, James Harrington, had proposed an elective upper chamber in his *Commonwealth of Oceana* (1656), and Jefferson's belief that an upper chamber should be a kind of "natural aristocracy" of talented individuals resembles Harrington's vision. His devotion to strictly separate executive, legislative, and judicial arms of government was in line with Montesquieu's revision of Locke.

In 1788, while serving as American ambassador to France, Jefferson received a copy of *The Federalist* from James Madison. In Jefferson's characteristically gracious way he praised the book's contents to Madison, writing that he had learned from it.[33] From Jefferson's subsequent writings, it appears that the one key idea that he adopted from *The Federalist* was that republics were suited for large territories but not for small territories, the most important correction Jefferson thought needed to be made to Montesquieu.

Through the rest of his life, Jefferson would proudly point out this discovery to correspondents. He did so without crediting Madison's Federalist No. 10, where the argument first appeared publicly. His own summaries of the argument are unmistakably Madisonian, delivered with a tip of the cap to empirical experience:

> I suspect that the doctrine, that small states alone are fitted to be republics, will be exploded by experience, with some other brilliant fallacies accredited by Montesquieu and other political writers. Perhaps it will be found, that to obtain a just republic . . . it must be so

extensive as that local egoisms may never reach its greater part; that on every particular question, a majority may be found in its council free from particular interests, and giving, therefore, an uniform prevalence to the principles of justice. The smaller the societies, the more violent and convulsive their schisms.[34]

One of Jefferson's more interesting enthusiasms was the idea that "the earth belongs in usufruct to the living."[35] Jefferson felt that the decisions of prior generations should not bind the present generation and that decisions made in the present should not bind future generations. Since the problem with government is that its institutions gradually consolidate power and snuff out liberty, requiring the political slate to be wiped clean is a perfect solution. Each generation should make its own rules. Laws and constitutions should not be allowed to be in force more than seventeen years, Jefferson thought, his estimate of the length of a generation.

While this idea of generational justice is unusual, it is not original to Jefferson. The French mathematician and civil servant Marquis de Condorcet offered a vision of generational justice which limited the power of laws to the length of a generation. Condorcet's plan was "strikingly similar to Jefferson's." Joseph Ellis maintains that the congruence was almost surely not a coincidence because the two shared a physician in France. Jefferson also seems to have come to this idea quite suddenly in the latter half of 1789, suggesting that he came upon Condorcet's proposal and endorsed it enthusiastically (without crediting him directly) because it fit with his enthusiasm for self-government, his distaste for tradition, and his tendency to think that governments degrade through time.[36]

Jefferson much preferred peace to war. Yet he so disliked tradition and was so enthused by the idea of wiping the political slate clean that he sometimes endorsed violence. In response to the debtors' uprising in western Massachusetts called Shays's Rebellion, Jefferson commented that he "liked a little rebellion now and then. It is like a storm in the Atmosphere" because it clears the air.[37] Shays's Rebellion had been nearly bloodless, but this view also seemed correct even if bloodshed was significant, as it was in the American Revolution. He persisted in making such comments even after the French Revolution, in which millions perished. In an 1823 letter to John Adams he confided that to attain free government "rivers of blood must yet flow, and years of desolation pass over. Yet the object is worth rivers of blood, and years of desolation."[38] Adams must have been appalled. What might legitimate the use of force against government is a frequent object of inquiry in political theory. Sidney and Locke had argued for it where governments do not have the consent of the governed. The French philosophes and Thomas Paine were committed international democratic revolutionaries. Jefferson possessed their sureness about reform as much as he did any specific idea they presented about the use of force.

One thing that Jefferson did not want to change over time was the predominantly rural nature of the United States. An agrarian political economy produces political benefits. Farmers are self-sufficient. An individual farmer needs almost no government. He has to make his own decisions in running his farm—good preparation for the active citizenry required in a democratic state. By contrast, manufacturing relies on hired laborers. Hired laborers are dependent on their employers. They are also not accustomed to making their own decisions and are therefore ill prepared to be democratic citizens. The French physiocrats Francois Quesnay and the Marquis de Mirabeau had emphasized that land was the creator of value in an economy. Jefferson may have been impressed by them. His assertion of the political advantages stemming from a predominantly agrarian economy had long roots in the Whig country party. For nearly a century before Jefferson became president, many British thinkers had noted the relative degeneracy of people in cities compared to those in the countryside. Two of Jefferson's favorite writers, Lord Kames and Adam Ferguson, had praised the virtues of farming and of a predominantly agrarian society. Jefferson brought renewed zeal to this strain of thinking rooted in his observation of an increasingly populous, urbanized, and corrupt Europe and a rural, still virtuous America.

A number of writers on international law had applied "moral sense & reason" to questions of international relations, according to Jefferson. He thought they had done the world a valuable service. As secretary of state, he wrote that where Hugo Grotius, Samuel Pufendorf, Christian Wolf, and Emmerich de Vattel "agree, their authority is strong." When they did not agree, "we must appeal to our own feelings and reason to decide between them."[39] Perhaps there was not "natural law" to regulate international relations, but there was a common-sense foreign policy that was humane and promised to benefit the citizens of all nations.

Jefferson believed that republican governments would generally avoid war. Their interests would center around peaceful trade rather than projecting their power on the global stage. This understanding was in the spirit of the humane international lawyers. Jefferson's own gloss on their thinking was that republics would have no need for an extensive military, particularly in peacetime. Professional militaries had served to prop up and enrich those in power. Republics would not have this need. Their military posture would be exclusively defensive. When the globe would become covered by republics, peace would prevail. Unfortunately, until that time, the American ship of state would be tossed on the stormy seas created by the globe's most powerful tyrannies. The best courses of action for the United States were to set a good republican example by not arming except for defensive purposes and to continue trading goods openly with all nations. The phrase "beware entangling alliances," often credited to George Washington, was in reality coined by Jefferson.[40] This was the way for the world's only "empire of liberty" to act in a world full of tyrannical governments.

Jefferson's political thought is a unique amalgamation. Some of his ideas were borrowed directly from political theorists. Others have recognizable roots in political theory but were breezily modified to suit his own whim. Still others came from Jefferson's experiences or imagination. Whatever else can be said about the election of this quirky theoretical mix of ideas to the presidency in the person of Thomas Jefferson, it surely promised a new direction in American politics. Jefferson could be expected to be an activist in favor of a minimalist national government, favoring a rollback of Federalist innovations. He would expect a democratic people to take care of almost everything for itself, either individually or in its subordinate divisions of government. He would favor legislative supremacy, the separation of powers, checks and balances, and the separation of church and state. But since his standard of success was human happiness, he might be willing to compromise any of these forms when the promise of favorable results dictated a departure. He believed in the extended republic as much as his collaborator Madison did, and he was motivated in this regard by the superior value he perceived in an agrarian way of life. He would prefer peace to war. He would minimize the United States' military establishment. He would avoid entangling alliances. But he would also be willing to strike radically (and even violently) at threats to self-government and he would be very willing to extend the United States' borders.

Utility to Man Is the Standard

Jefferson had applied the ideas of political theorists to practice prior to becoming president. Carl Becker suggested that "Jefferson copied Locke" in the Declaration of Independence.[41] Besides the two thinkers' commitment to natural rights, Locke's *Second Treatise* argued that a revolution was warranted only after a "long train of abuses" that a government refused to remedy, and the bulk of the Declaration consists of a listing of abuses that the colonists felt were perpetrated by King George III. Others note additional influences on this renowned writing. Garry Wills points out that Jefferson's use of the concept of the pursuit of happiness was cribbed from Beccaria, Helvetius, and Hutcheson. Morton White stresses that the Swiss legal scholar Jean-Jacques Burlamaqui influenced Jefferson to pronounce these rights "sacred" and inspired the phrase "Nature and Nature's God."[42]

During the 1770s Jefferson had worked on a comprehensive review of Virginia's laws as a state legislator. This massive effort resulted in the presentation of 126 bills, approximately half of which were written by Jefferson. These bills reflect the great breadth of Enlightenment aspirations. Jefferson proposed to eliminate the benefit of primogeniture; he suggested that the salaries of elected officials be made public; rotation in office would be required; the poor would be supported through public charity; more humane treatment was prescribed for runaway slaves; local schools would be established, and so on. The two most famous of these bills have clear Enlightenment roots. The "Statute for Religious Freedom" was inspired by Locke's "Letter concerning Toleration."[43] Jefferson's "Bill for Proportioning Crimes and Punishments" applied Beccaria's ideas from *On Crimes and Punishments* to the Virginia penal code.[44] Both the official recognition of religious freedom and the reform of Virginia's criminal code were low-hanging fruit for a devotee of the Enlightenment. The reforms themselves did not come easily, but they were readily identifiable ways to turn the new philosophy to public benefit. Thus Jefferson did not come to the presidency without a reputation for applying theory to practice. And as chief executive he continued to do so.

The major contours of Jefferson's presidency are understandable as logical moves given his theoretical commitments. He worked to radically cut the nation's professional military, moved to retire the nation's debt as quickly as feasible, and reduced internal taxes to zero—all things that a committed Whig theorist could imagine to make the minimalist state a reality. With Jefferson at the helm, power would not concentrate and a republican example would be set that others could follow. Freedom and self-government would be preserved. A general extension of happiness would result. Church and state would remain separated, a concept of Locke's that Jefferson made his own. Locke also inspired the Native Americans' benevolent "father" in Washington to oversee a policy which would facilitate the adoption of farming, with the promise of great benefits for them. Having adopted Madison's defense of the extended republic, Jefferson jumped at the opportunity to extend the nation's size with the Louisiana Purchase. He also convinced Congress to fund one of the greatest Enlightenment projects ever undertaken—the Lewis and Clark Expedition—which proved to be of both scientific and political value.

His understanding of international law theory led to an insistence on the rights of neutral nations. When other nations would not conform to the new norms of international law, he formulated an embargo as a humane tool of international coercion. And Jefferson changed the presidency forever, using the Enlightenment's democratic spirit to forge a more popular and democratic institution than what was envisioned by most founders.

Jefferson's theoretically informed view that governmental power was prone to corruption and that it should therefore be minimized was put into practice by slashing the professional military establishment to almost nothing. The nation relied almost exclusively on militias and gunboats in its harbors for defense. This allowed him to propose, and the Congress to enact, a reduction of internal taxes to zero. The federal government would gain its revenue exclusively from taxes on imports. By his second inauguration Jefferson would brag, "What farmer, what mechanic, what laborer ever sees a taxgatherer of the United States?"[45] Scores of other civil-service posts were eliminated. And Jefferson offered Congress a plan to retire the nation's debt in less than two decades, which it accepted. His was a radical plan to virtually eliminate any internal footprint made by the federal government. Lance Banning observes that in these years the Jeffersonians came as close as any group ever has to managing a nation "in accordance with an ideology that taught that power was a monster and governing was wrong."[46] This course of action was, of course, consistent with the Saxon myth's claim that government destroyed freedom through time. It was also a vision of government deeply informed by what a Whig could do with the reins of government.

Jefferson's second term was consumed with foreign affairs. The temptation to take advantage of a largely disarmed nation was just too great for Britain and France, who were again engaged in a struggle for global supremacy. The British had begun to stop American ships at sea, looking for goods traveling to her enemies and sailors who had been (or still were) British subjects. When British captains found these goods and men they took them. These were not isolated incidents, but official British policy.[47] Jefferson's defensive military posture could do nothing to stop the British, who boldly stationed their ships just outside of the busiest American ports.

The president responded by assigning homework to the secretary of state, James Madison. During the summer of 1805 Madison was "surrounded by books," and he "piled up evidence from international law theorists, treaties, and admiralty court decisions" to prove that the British policy "had no legal foundation whatever." Madison biographer Ralph Ketcham relates that the resulting 204-page pamphlet "quoted the standard theorists, Grotius, Pufendorf, Bynkershoek, Martens, and especially

Vattel" to demonstrate that the British policy was illegal.[48] Jefferson had hoped the document could be released as an official government publication. However, he came to the realization that the British would not listen to Madison's reason or the authority of the aforementioned international law theorists. In the end the secretary of state's pamphlet was circulated anonymously. Season after season, the Americans continued to protest British actions, insisting on the rights of neutrals as outlined by international law theorists, and hoped that British policy would change.

British actions did not change—at least not for the better. The British government proceeded to require all American ships bound for any European port to register, be inspected, and obtain a license from it. Meanwhile, Napoleon declared that American trade with Britain was prohibited. With both Britain and France effectively prohibiting neutral trade, by the end of his presidency Jefferson's hope for a republican foreign policy was in tatters. On June 22, 1807, things got even worse. After refusing to be boarded, the USS *Chesapeake* was fired upon by the HMS *Leopard*. Three of the *Chesapeake*'s crew were killed, eighteen were wounded, and four were taken prisoner by the British. This was an act of war, and Jefferson would finally have to respond more strongly than to have his secretary of state write a treatise on international law.

At Jefferson's urging, Congress declared an embargo in reverse. American ships would not ply the high seas and American goods would not be sold abroad. This had the advantage of preventing additional incidents from occurring, but its main purpose was to hurt Britain economically. It was thought that to regain access to American raw materials and food, Britain would pledge to treat American ships with respect. This policy originated in the fertile imaginations of Madison and Jefferson, who remembered the effect that embargoes had on relations with Britain preceding the Revolutionary War. Nevertheless, in the embargo was a kinship with the ideas of Grotius, Pufendorf, Vattel, and others who offered visions of how to limit the occurrences and destructiveness of international disputes. Unfortunately, the embargo harmed the American economy far more than the British economy, and it did not achieve its purpose.

Like his predecessors, Jefferson disliked the presence of European powers in the Americas. If territory in the Americas could be wrested away from colonial powers and added to the United States, more of the earth would be republican and the United States would have a better chance of succeeding because of the benefits found in an extended republic. Thus, Jefferson favored almost anything which would secure the United States' foothold in the New World. Jefferson hoped that a relatively weak colonial power, Spain, would be receptive to selling New Orleans and Florida to the United States for cash. However, in a secret deal Spain transferred the vast tract of land known as "Louisiana" to France shortly after Jefferson became president. To have Louisiana, a territory as large as the United States had settled, controlled by France was a nightmare for Jefferson. The war between Britain and France would likely come to the Americas, and the United States would be caught between the world's two superpowers. But Napoleon surprised Jefferson by offering him Louisiana in exchange for cash. Napoleon was willing to part with France's presence on the North American mainland for the funds which would fuel his war machine.

Jefferson jumped at the opportunity to buy Louisiana, even though the action offended his minimalist government scruples. Not sure whether the nation possessed the legal authority to purchase new lands, the president considered presenting Congress with a constitutional amendment which would explicitly sanction such an act. But Napoleon wanted the deal done quickly, and Jefferson obliged him, dropping his plans for the amendment. The decision to purchase Louisiana and to borrow the money to do so was made unilaterally, with Congress presented with a virtual fait accompli. Jefferson saw a chance to extend the "empire of liberty" even though it meant temporarily subordinating his governmental minimalism and strict attention to the separation of powers. This was a paradoxical act: the president moved forcefully to enhance the long-term prospects of minimalist government. But *results* were his barometer of success. In exchange for one action which possibly exceeded his (and the government's) constitutional authority, the nation could look forward to many more generations of decentralized, agrarian self-government. His actions were justified by the only calculus which mattered: utility.

New states carved out of the Louisiana Territory could be trusted to self-government because of the validity of moral-sense philosophy. These distant blank canvases would help prevent the concentration of power, which all good Whigs feared. The natural rights and religious tolerance of Locke would hold sway there because of the Constitution. The agricultural potential of this purchase would enthuse the physiocrats. And enabling such a decision was Jefferson's Federalist No. 10–inspired understanding that the minimalist superstructure for this republic was more likely to work if it encompassed a large territory.

To gain useful information about this land and what lay west of it, Jefferson conceived of an expedition into its interior. This "Corps of Discovery" would map the region, collect samples of its flora and fauna, and make contact with its native tribes, hoping to establish friendly relations. The Lewis and Clark Expedition was a quintessential Enlightenment project, gathering useful information. The most important objective for this group would be to find a way to the Pacific Ocean. If that could be done, the United States could claim the land, build a nation as big as the continent, and open up new trade routes with Asia. The utility of this enterprise was not merely scientific, but eminently practical. And if *"utility* to man [is] the standard of virtue," as Jefferson believed, then this enterprise was worthy.[49] In funding the Lewis and Clark Expedition, Jefferson's frugality gave way to his ambition for American citizens.

Like they have with all presidents, citizens presented Jefferson with petitions and requests. One sent by the Baptists of Danbury, Connecticut, urged the president to proclaim a day of thanksgiving. Jefferson appreciated the group's kind words for him, but he would not oblige their request. In his reply, he wrote a line which is still quoted more than two centuries later, that the Constitution's First Amendment had built "a wall of separation between church and State."[50] It was, therefore, not in his power to suggest how American citizens should praise God and worship. This response reflected Jefferson's own convictions, but they were convictions which had intellectual roots in Locke's "Letter concerning Toleration" and various theorists' devotion to liberty and minimalist government.

Jefferson's conception of the presidency was far different from that of his predecessors. Both George Washington and John Adams felt that the president should act independently, unswayed by "political" considerations. They felt the president should make decisions based solely on his judgments about what was good for the country rather than what might be popular. Jefferson possessed much greater faith in the choices and decisions of average people than did Washington and Adams. He conceived of the presidency as a position which would serve the people by reflecting their values. In his response to the Baptists of Danbury, Jefferson wrote, "My duties dictate a faithful and zealous pursuit of the interests of my constituents."[51] This is a statement which neither Adams nor Washington would ever have made. This new ethic of service to popular wishes is why both John Patrick Diggins and Joyce Appleby (the respective authors of the Adams and Jefferson biographies in the recent Times Books series) stress the pivotal nature of Jefferson's presidency. For Diggins, Adams was the last honest president, who exercised his independent judgment rather than calculating what would increase his public support. He stresses that Jefferson initiated a long line of pandering presidents. Appleby offers a less jaded view, but the change she thinks Jefferson's presidency brought is no less profound. To her, Jefferson's claim to have presided over a "second revolution" in American politics rings true. He alone among the founders championed popular democracy, and he brought meaning to this commitment as president.[52]

The invention of a more "popular" presidency was Jefferson's own, something that he has been blamed for and credited with throughout the last two centuries. Yet Jefferson could not have conceived of the president's job as the defender of his constituents' interests without intellectual support from the Enlightenment. Nor would this view have gained much traction without the commitment to popular politics forwarded by Enlightenment thinkers. Happily for Jefferson, Congress was filled with Republicans throughout his tenure—Republicans who saw eye to eye with the president on almost every issue. Thus Jefferson was not confronted with the difficult choice of what to do when the people's representatives in Congress did not agree with the people's representative in the Executive Mansion. Would Jefferson have remained true to his commitment to legislative supremacy? We will never know.

Jefferson's Indian policy has already been referenced, but not the specific philosophical backing for his position. Empirical data about the productiveness of farming versus hunting and gathering convinced him that he was being benevolent, but it also must have been important to Jefferson that his intellectual idol, John Locke, offered up a version of the idea. In chapter 5 of the *Second Treatise,* Locke argued that "an acre of land that bears here [in England] twenty bushels of wheat, and another in America, which, with the same husbandry, would do the like, are, without doubt, of the same natural, intrinsic value. But yet the benefit mankind receives from one in a year is worth five pounds, and the other not worth a penny."[53] In Locke's understanding it was the labor of farming that made land productive. Locke used this argument to explain how private property was carved out of what had been common land during prehistory. In the "state of nature," farmers were entitled to the land they improved because they had imparted the vast majority of value to it. Jefferson applied the principle in a new way, because it occurred in a constituted government. Though many Americans and Locke himself believed that Native Americans were in "a state of nature," that is, that they possessed no government, Jefferson did not consider them to be so. To him, they had primitive governments, based on consent and reliant on informal but very real institutions. The United States offered farmland to Native Americans in exchange for their hunting lands. To Jefferson, Locke's point was still useful. It could help to make the lives of the Native Americans much more comfortable.

Political theory inspired President Jefferson to map out and preside over a radical departure from Federalist policies. He would not have had the intellectual wherewithal or the confidence to do this without the intellectual backing of Enlightenment political theory. Thinkers of the Enlightenment were sure that they could create a better world through a radical departure from the past. The Jefferson administration took its tone from those thinkers. His borrowings were not straightforward, however. Jefferson needed to do the significant work of interpreting theory and fleshing out what abstract ideas would mean in practice. He borrowed as he thought ideas were useful, feeling free to reinterpret, reshape, and riff on them as he saw fit. The way he did these things qualifies Jefferson as an important figure in the history of political thought.

Conclusion

If stark originality, the desire to effect fundamental change, and the claim of universal applicability define what "counts" as political philosophy, then Jefferson may be the president who is closest to being a political philosopher. His ambition was to create the world's first sustained republican government, and accomplishing this in 1801 required a radical turn in the American government. Under his leadership, the United States' positive example would, he hoped, change the world. In service of that end Jefferson attempted to translate ideas to practice which no political leader had ever applied before, many of which had recognizable origins in the Enlightenment. If John Adams's political thought has a uniqueness because it borrowed key ideas from an array of different thinkers, Jefferson's is unique because he adapted and stubbornly turned the work of various writers into his own vision.

As president, Jefferson found himself in a role that constrained but did not end his ability to apply philosophy to politics. Dumas Malone argues that if Jefferson's "greatness lies in the fact that he applied to the shifting problems of his age an enlightened and humane philosophy, there was no other period when his purposes shone forth with the same purity, or the fundamentals of his philosophy seemed so clear" as during the Revolution. Afterward "his services to his fellow men never again squared quite so well with his fundamental principles."[54] A president probably never has the same degree of freedom to voice his views and advance them as the revolutionary has. Even so, while he was president Jefferson did preside over several radical turns in policy suited to his own thinking that were inspired by various strands of Enlightenment thinking.

One of the ways in which Jefferson found himself constrained was that at times his principles clashed with each other. Ideally, all of a politician's principles will cohere neatly. However, practical considerations can throw principles up against each other, making politicians prioritize from among their commitments.[55] Jefferson starkly stated his ambitious principles in abstract terms before he was entrusted to be the nation's chief executive. Few literate observers were unaware in 1801 of what kind of government he preferred. While he was president he had to choose whether to expedite the purchase of Louisiana to make sure that the purchase occurred, or to slow that process down to heed proper procedural and constitutional forms. Jefferson chose to expedite the process. To him it was more important to gain territory than it was to make absolutely sure that the government was heeding the letter of its procedural rules. Moving forward quickly had the advantage of guaranteeing vast new tracts of land would be opened to farmers, preserving America's agrarian political economy as far into the future as anyone could imagine. The purchase promised to bring many new states into the Union which were blank slates, uncorrupted by the residue of colonialism and slavery or the taint of the Federalist Party. The resulting enlarged republic would also be more stable, because it would not be "convulsed" by factionalism, the argument that Jefferson lifted from Madison's Federalist No. 10.

Any president with a well-formed set of ideals heading into the presidency should be prepared to deal with the possibility of his ideals clashing at some point. There is no evidence that Jefferson lost any sleep over what he did regarding Louisiana. He had a standard by which to judge clashes of principle: do what would best serve public utility. He made a calculated decision in 1803. He would loosely construe the Constitution on the point of extending national territory and risk taking action before Congress did—action which would have to be approved after the fact—in order to present millions of Americans with open farmland for generations. This was an easy utilitarian choice in Jefferson's mind. With the success of the Lewis and Clark Expedition, republicans could envision a nation of popular governments, emphasizing local control, stretching across the entire continent. Fifteen million dollars and a possible constitutional indiscretion was a small price to pay, he believed.

Jefferson's actions were not without their problems. He was stubborn because he was so sure of himself. What was supposed to set science apart from religion was that the former was based on empirical reality, while the latter was based on belief. In Jefferson's hands, science became something of a religion. Farming *is* invariably more productive than hunting and gathering on an acre-by-acre basis. Yet expecting native populations to embrace a new lifestyle at odds with their traditional ways of life exposed the Enlightenment's tin ear for culture. Jefferson dismissed the idea that culture might place real limits on the quest to make the world over again. To the extent that habitual ways of life impinged on rational progress, they were always to be cast aside. For someone who professed to take others' choices seriously, this is a significant contradiction. Jefferson's insistence on a minimal military also exposed the United States to depredations by world powers. Britain and France were quite willing to take advantage of American weakness—a fact that would harm James Madison's presidency even more than Jefferson's. By creating a populist presidency Jefferson was also setting in motion a dynamic that would lead the president to accrue a great deal of power, often at the expense of Congress. Jefferson himself helped to create an institution with which he would be very uncomfortable.

For all of the connections that Thomas Jefferson made between political theory and political practice, undoubtedly the greatest is the credo penned into the beginning of the Declaration of Independence. The words that "all men are created equal" and that they have "inalienable" God-given rights breathed life into the United States and have continued to provide a beacon of hope in a murky world. One cannot imagine the Union's relentless pursuit of victory during the Civil War, the Fourteenth Amendment's admonition to the states to provide equal protection of the laws and due process, the fight for women's suffrage, or the Civil Rights Movement without reference to the promise contained in the Declaration. Those words have power, even if Jefferson himself failed to live up to the ideals that he expressed. Jefferson's emphasis on freedom limited the reach and scope of government, an enduring American tradition. None of the developments over which Jefferson presided are without attendant problems, but the problems associated with many alternatives are worse.

When Adams and Jefferson resumed their correspondence in 1812, it was Adams who was the more eager correspondent by far. Adams articulated and embraced the idea that "you and I ought not to die, before we have explained ourselves to each other."[56] Though he made an effort to politely answer this call, Jefferson did not wish to fully explain himself to Adams or to anyone else. As he so often did in public, he preferred to round off, to minimize, and to otherwise soften the differences he had with others. He was happy to discuss health, the brain, language, death, spiritualism, and current events with Adams, and he did so in touching and eloquent prose, but he was not drawn into an extended discussion of political theory.[57] The man who many people credit with the famous dictum that there are self-evident truths probably believed that Adams lacked the gift to see the self-evident truths of politics.[58] His old friend's devotion to traditional political philosophy got in the way. Getting into a quarrel over this matter at their advanced age was useless.

Both John Adams and Thomas Jefferson thought of themselves as hardheaded empiricists, but they came to radically different conclusions about the truths elucidated by empirical experience. They could have engaged in a very illuminating dialogue with each other about this, but they did not explore the matter deeply, mainly because Jefferson did not want to. As close as he got was to chide Adams: "You possess, yourself, too much science, not to see how much is still ahead of you, unexplained and unexplored."[59] Thus he pleaded with Adams not to consider the past as prologue. Adams looked to the past for answers; to Jefferson it had none. Republican governments in large nation-states were something new under the sun and Jefferson's hopes for them would not be bound by past theories.

Jefferson was at once the most open-minded and one of the most closed-minded of presidents. He was open to the spectacular leap of faith that Enlightenment principles could make the world over in an unprecedented, positive way. He was absolutely certain that in the future life would be better than it ever had been for the vast majority of people at any time in human history. However, Jefferson's dismissal of most political theory out of hand indicates a closed-mindedness that is an enduring character trait. Jefferson was prejudiced about African Americans. He was prejudiced about women. This did not make him an unusual politician of his time. But it should be noted that this pattern of behavior was also applied to political theory. He was prejudiced about it. He might have made an exercise of articulating why Plato, Aristotle, Machiavelli, Adams, and others were wrong. He might have done so in a robust correspondence with Adams that would have been particularly illuminating. Sadly, he did not feel it was necessary to do this beyond the barest of observations because their wrongheadedness was so self-evident to him.

It may be that politicians should not be blamed for lacking a knowledge of political theory. However, if a president shows significant interest in it, then it is fair to judge whether he has dealt with it in an intellectually responsible and fair-minded manner. Jefferson's superficial approach to much of political philosophy fails this test. His own sense of sureness led him to his most problematic policies. This sureness might have been tempered if he had given more thought to thinkers and theories outside of the Enlightenment. But then one must pause to wonder whether this would have muted his inspiring push for universal rights and the happiness of all humankind.

Chapter 4

JAMES MADISON: POLITICAL THEORY MUST BE MADE TO
COUNTERACT POLITICAL THEORY

Theoretic politicians, who have patronized this species of government [democracies], have erroneously supposed that by reducing
mankind to a perfect equality in their political rights, they would,
at the same time, be perfectly equalized and assimilated in their
possessions, their opinions, and their passions.

—James Madison, Federalist No. 10, November 1787

A government deriving its energy from the will of the society, and
operating by the reason of its measures, on the understanding and
interest of the society . . . is the government for which philosophy has been searching, and humanity has been fighting, from the
most remote ages. Such are republican governments which it is the
glory of America to have invented, and her unrivalled happiness
to possess.

—James Madison ("Helvidius"), letter to the *National
Gazette*, February 20, 1792

James Madison is one of the few politicians who are routinely recognized as political theorists. Madison's reputation as a profound, original political thinker is based primarily on his efforts in formulating and
explaining the nature of the United States Constitution. He did so most
famously in *The Federalist*, the newspaper editorial series he coauthored
with Alexander Hamilton and John Jay which argued for the Constitution's ratification in 1787 and 1788. In the preceding months he had written the Virginia Plan, the template for discussion at the Constitutional
Convention. In succeeding years he served in the House of Representatives, where he wrote the proposed amendments which became the Bill

of Rights and organized the opposition party which objected to the Federalists' stewardship of the new national government. In each of these endeavors, Madison consulted political philosophy and thought in characteristically theoretical ways.

The pair of quotes above go a long way in explaining how Madison approached political theory. He was not shy about concluding that "theoretic politicians" were wrong. In fact, he frequently found that political theory and those who consulted it fell prey to erroneous generalizations. For example, many who were devoted to popular government made unwarranted assumptions that utopian results could be achieved merely by "reducing mankind to a perfect equality in their political rights." These thinkers were misinformed. It took the Americans to "invent" and implement workable republican governments. Madison was too modest to say it, but he himself had played a critical role in developing the workable republican theory which they had implemented. In doing so he had drawn on and built up alternatives to the conventional wisdom which had been offered by other political theorists. Madison's relationship to political theory was that of a believing skeptic.

Madison placed a great deal of emphasis on discerning the proper theory of politics. His reading in the discipline may not have been quite as varied or as consistent as John Adams's was, but what he lacked in constant attention, he made up for in depth of insight. Adams divided political theory into two broad categories: the good—the writings of historically grounded devotees of the mixed constitution—and the bad—the "ideologians" who tried to impose their own preconceived and untested notions on politics. There was not great subtlety in this approach. In a strangely similar manner, Thomas Jefferson had a polarized perspective as well: ancient theories had to be cast aside in favor of the new and true science of politics outlined by Enlightenment thinkers.

Madison was much less prone to make such stark categorizations. He delved into political theory more deeply than Jefferson and considered it more critically than Adams. As a result his political thought was more nuanced than either of his predecessors in the presidency. To Adams, the major discoveries in political thought were very few and these discoveries were to be jealously defended. Adams did not even dare to hope to make a new discovery in the theory of politics himself; it was difficult enough to convince people of the few truths which had been discerned across the millennia. To Jefferson, the Enlightenment was the philosophy of common sense. Its embrace did not take great intellectual effort. Government was properly a bare-bones framework which would allow free individuals to invent the lives and the things which would help remake the world.

Unlike Jefferson, Madison *did* expend massive intellectual effort on political theory, and unlike Adams, in doing so he *intended* to make new discoveries in the theory of politics.

When Thomas Jefferson received a complimentary copy of Adams's *Defence of the Constitutions of Government of the United States of America,* he broadly praised it to Adams, remarking that he disliked just one thing: the Confederation Congress was really a legislative assembly, not a diplomatic assembly, as Adams had described it. It fell to the more meticulous Madison to point out to his fellow Virginian that "many of the remarks in it . . . are unfriendly to republicanism" and that the book might unfortunately "revive the predilections of this Country for the British Constitution."[1]

When Madison read political theory he tried to discover the intricacies of a variety of subjects. He also took care to discern the subtleties of the positions taken by other thinkers, and he mined a broad array of writings for useful ideas. This was hard intellectual work, but the potential payoff made it worthwhile. Through concerted effort, Madison felt he helped formulate something that philosophers had "been searching [for] . . . from the most remote ages," a new theory of republican government. This new theory signaled the dawn of a new age in politics, in which popular governments would not be unstable. Though he approached political theory much differently from Jefferson, it was no wonder that he and Jefferson were allies. Both felt humankind was poised at the brink of a hopeful new age which would alleviate suffering and increase happiness.

And thus it is that Madison is remembered as a political theorist, even though for more than a century this understanding of him was essentially lost.[2] Madison is particularly well remembered for Federalist No. 10, which Robert Dahl points out is the most "compactly logical, almost mathematical, piece of theory" written by an American.[3] In it Madison reversed the commonly held idea that popular governments had to remain small. Only in an "extended republic" could factionalism be contained by the governing process. No one faction in a large, heterogeneous republic would be a majority and use that status to dominate others. Madison was immensely proud of and excited about this discovery. He featured the idea in his first contribution to *The Federalist,* wrote it into the "Vices" memo he prepared in anticipation of the Constitutional Convention, delivered it in one of his first major speeches at the convention, and described it in a letter to Jefferson, and he wedged an abbreviated version of it into Federalist No. 51. Madison obviously realized the significance of this breakthrough in thought.

Why had this discovery not been made previously? The short answer is that it had, but the idea had not been accepted, or even much remarked. As Douglass Adair discovered, Federalist No. 10 seems to have been inspired by David Hume's short essay "Idea of a Perfect Commonwealth."[4] Hume suggested that political theorists had been misled into thinking that republics had to remain small only because it was difficult to set up a republic in a large nation. Hume noted that if a republic were successfully established in a large nation, then it would be difficult to get rid of, because any change in government would be difficult to coordinate. He insisted that a republic could work just as effectively in a large, more diverse nation as it could in a nation with little territory; the trick was merely in starting it up in the first place. However, Aristotle's and Montesquieu's ideas to the contrary continued to dominate people's thinking through the latter half of the eighteenth century. In another essay, "Of Parties in General," Hume wrote that factionalism in politics is inevitable and that it produces a taxonomy of groups. Madison synthesized these two ideas and supplemented them to form his theory of the extended republic: republics would inevitably develop factions, and if a faction was a majority it would trample on others. Popular governments would therefore be unstable *unless* they encompassed a vast territory, because only with an extensive territory would there be no majority.

The "theoretic politicians" who were most excited about political equality (he was likely referring to Plato and Jean-Jacques Rousseau) believed that political equality would produce an equality of views, an equality of enthusiasms, and even an equality of possessions. This could never be. As Madison put it, factionalism is "sown in the nature of man." The trick to popular government was to render factionalism relatively harmless, not to hope that it could be eliminated. With the proper republican structure governing a large nation, the worst tendencies of popular rule could be contained, so that private rights would be secure.

In taking Hume's idea, fleshing it out, and fitting it with his other commitments, Madison was writing political theory. It was political theory designed to dissolve preexisting ideas which created mental barriers, ironically erected with the help of political theory itself. It was the good fortune of Americans to have been sufficiently open minded to have conceived of and applied the new theory of republican politics. Madison's revised understandings of how to achieve popular rule in practice were to stay with him through subsequent years, when he turned from constitution building to governing. Like his two immediate predecessors in the presidency, Madison's ideas about political theory would accompany him into the Executive Mansion and be employed by him there.

"A Decent Regard to the Opinions of Former Times"

Works of political theory were John Adams's constant companions. James Madison's reading in political theory seemed to be done more in spurts. Particularly when confronted with a challenging problem, Madison turned to books. He carefully reexamined the view that most informed people held, often finding that it was not validated by history or that it contained faulty inferences. Where Adams and Jefferson were prone to endorse or reject individual thinkers, Madison more often dealt with a smaller unit of analysis: the idea. He was willing to adopt a useful idea from anyone, even those thinkers, like Hume, with whom he generally disagreed. Well before he became president, Madison had a near-comprehensive knowledge of political theory as it then existed. He had also been so successful in solving problems with the help of political theory that he had great confidence in his ability to figure out political patterns and tendencies, even when few others discerned them. This joint meticulousness and confidence produced both benefits and drawbacks for President Madison. However, well before he assumed that office had come his own triumph of political theory: his contribution to *The Federalist,* which I will focus on in this section as an illustration of Madison's relationship with political theory.

William Lee Miller observes that "James Madison was called a 'scholar,' either in praise or derision, all his life."[5] There was good reason for both his allies and his opponents to focus on this aspect of the fourth president's life. To quote Stanley Elkins and Eric McKitrick, Madison engaged in "massive prior preparation" to understand political issues.[6] An indispensable part of this effort was a thorough digest of relevant sources of political philosophy. In the course of his readings, he came to well-formed views about the proper conduct of national foundings, the nature of constitutionalism, the preferred structure of domestic institutions, political economy, and international relations. In forming these views, he did not hesitate to reject what most others thought and to develop new understandings more consonant with empirical experience and his preferred normative values.

Madison's studiousness had been well established at Princeton.[7] In Madison's final two years his primary teacher was the college's president, Reverend John Witherspoon. Under Witherspoon's tutelage a generation of students read Adam Smith, David Hume, Francis Hutcheson, and the English Whig opposition writers. Witherspoon's enthusiasm for political theory helped to make him and many of his students forceful advocates of American independence. Perhaps more importantly, Witherspoon's students were taught to think for themselves. Madison and his fellow students did not engage in the rote memory exercises featured at other schools. Instead, Madison learned to investigate for himself.

As the former colonies' independence was being won, Witherspoon and his former pupil served together in the Confederation Congress. Among their work was a bill written in committee proposing a library for the new Congress. At the time, it was common practice for the person who first spoke in favor of a proposal to chair the select committee which designed a bill. Madison was the committee's chair and therefore he was probably the first and most vocal proponent of assembling a "library of Congress." Typical of Madison, he did the lion's share of the committee's work. The final list of books Madison compiled, with recommendations from Witherspoon and Jefferson, totaled 300 titles contained in roughly 1,400 volumes, including many histories and works of political theory.[8] Congress failed to execute the committee's plan. Madison's advocacy and effort indicates that he felt much more than did the other members of Congress that the wisdom contained in books could help representatives govern.

Always an avid reader, during times of political crisis Madison assigned himself homework projects in which political theory took center stage. In these assignments Madison hoped to find remedies to his nation's political ills. During these episodes he read and took extensive notes on the philosophers and historians who treated the subject in question. He weighed what they had to say against what actually happened, then compiled a memorandum which reflected his newly informed view. When the United States faced a severe financial downturn in 1778 and 1779, the young delegate "sat down before the fireplace at Montpelier, his books around him, to compose his thoughts and write an essay he entitled 'Money.'"[9] The essay laid out a position on fiscal policy which he advocated during subsequent sessions.

A year prior to the Constitutional Convention, Madison turned to his library again. In preparation he had requested that Jefferson, then the American ambassador to France, send him a "literary cargo"—all the books that could be found on the subject of confederations. Madison read them with a purpose in mind: he wanted to learn all that he could about this arrangement, and particularly why various confederations had failed in the past. Armed with that knowledge he diagnosed what afflicted the American confederation. The result, elucidated in "Of Ancient and Modern Confederacies," was that confederations failed because the central authority in them was too weak. Later the same year he wrote a companion essay titled "Vices of the Constitution," which proceeded to describe the failings of the American confederation. Douglass Adair called this work, because it gave direction to Madison's efforts at Philadelphia, "the most fruitful piece of scholarly research ever carried out by an American."[10] Finally, while he was secretary of state Madison wrote a 204-page pamphlet protesting British actions at sea. The result was a more public document than his previous homework projects, but it too was steeped in political theory—this time in the theory of international law and the history of international relations.

Madison's contributions to *The Federalist* serve as an illustration of the ultimate fruit of one of these projects. His contributions are quoted frequently and have been analyzed in numerous books, but rarely are they seen as contemporary readers were supposed to see them—through a basic working knowledge of political theory. Madison's early essays are all aimed at rectifying some flaw in the Antifederalist understanding of political philosophy. Unwarranted orthodoxies were being repeated by the Constitution's critics. Authors were described as supporting one position when they actually supported another. Antifederalists were confused about terms and this confusion enabled them to mislead their readers. Rectifying these erroneous views was necessary to vindicate the Constitution.

In Federalist No. 10, Madison refuted the idea that a republic had to be small in size to function well. In so doing he contradicted what many citizens had learned from thinkers from Aristotle to Montesquieu, and from the Antifederalist writers who were citing them.[11] In an age when political theory was taken seriously, the authority of political philosophers carried weight and threatened to give the Antifederalist argument an intellectual heft that it did not deserve to enjoy. Madison's elaboration and adjustment of Hume's skeletal ideas allowed him to counteract the Antifederalists' faulty assumptions about the proper size of republics.

His next contribution, Federalist No. 14, continued to draw a distinction between what was meant by a "democracy" versus a "republic," something he had discussed briefly in Federalist No. 10. In a democracy, he explained, all citizens could participate in lawmaking. In a republic, representatives are chosen to make laws. Representation allowed republics to be much more extensive than democracies, because only the representatives would need to assemble in a capital city. A democracy had to remain small enough that all its citizens could gather in one place, in a city like Athens in the fifth century B.C. Distinguishing between representative governments and direct democracies showed that democracies were particularly prone to upheaval. Their relative homogeneousness did not solve the problems of factionalism. One group tended to dominate in them, ruling in a way that was problematic for anyone not in that group. Most analysts did not distinguish between democracies and republics, so they mistakenly thought that all popular governments were prone to upheaval. Thus "some celebrated authors, whose writings have had a great share in forming the modern standard of political opinions," argued strenuously for monarchy or the mixed constitution, to the exclusion of popular republics, which were dismissed as unworkable.[12] The conventional wisdom had to be set straight by the careful delineation of terms. Democracies were prone to upheaval; well-constructed republics were not.

Madison's remaining contribution to the first part of *The Federalist* was in Nos. 18 through 20. In these essays he argued that confederacies failed because there was too little central authority over constituent states. This argument also turned the Antifederalist view on its head. The critics of the Constitution were arguing the familiar position that power in confederacies inevitably concentrates, culminating in a tyranny. Madison refuted them using historical evidence about the Achaean League, the Amphictyonic Council, the German confederacy, and the united Netherlands. Each of these real confederacies demonstrated that confederations with meager centralized powers were ineffectual or short lived.

The Antifederalist argument to the contrary relied heavily on the authority of the English Whigs, the same authors who had often been cited to justify the Revolution. Madison felt that the Antifederalists were taking the Whig suspicion of power to an unwarranted extreme. The Antifederalists' deeply held theoretical enthusiasms were clouding their practical judgment. The actual history of confederacies proved them wrong. "Experience is the oracle of truth," he wrote. Experience showed that it was the weakness of the central government which was debilitating. Like a political scientist trying to figure out the validity of a theory, Madison sought out patterns to test popular assumptions. When he found that common assumptions were erroneous he searched for other theoretical views which were validated by the facts. In the case of confederations Madison cited an author rarely referenced, in stark contrast to Montesquieu. In his examination of the Achaean League, the Abbe de Mably had pointed out that a confederacy can work, but only if there is sufficient "general authority."[13] Madison's study of confederations validated de Mably's view, and refuted the one preferred by the Constitution's detractors.

Alexander Hamilton wrote the next sixteen essays. When Madison returned as Publius, he continued to champion unorthodox solutions to familiar problems. In Federalist No. 37 he pointed out a misunderstanding that he would feature in Federalist No. 47: legislative, executive, and judicial functions cannot be cleanly separated. The Antifederalists were complaining vociferously that the sharing of powers in the Constitution violated the strict separation argued for by Montesquieu. Madison pointed out that the Antifederalists were mischaracterizing Montesquieu. The safety of the separation of powers derived from preventing any one person or group from wielding power over something, which the Constitution accomplished. It was not necessary, and probably impossible, as Montesquieu had admitted, to avoid the sharing of powers between branches. In fact, as Madison would make clear in Federalist No. 51, the sharing of powers between branches was actually an advantage of the Constitution's design, an innovative way of preventing tyrannical overreaching.

In that celebrated essay, Madison clarified why a complicated structure of government, as opposed to a unicameral form, remained necessary in a republic. The new federal government seemed to retain the form of a mixed constitution, with a more numerous lower branch of the legislature, a more exclusive upper chamber, and a single executive. Federalists like John Adams believed that the new government was an attempt to set up the mixed constitution in the United States. Many Antifederalists felt so too, and they were upset by this, believing that popular governments had to depart radically from the old familiar forms in which elites possessed more influence than their numbers alone would merit.

Federalist No. 51 attempted to educate them, demonstrating that a republican regime required multiple governing institutions so that each would continue to do the people's work. With multiple institutions involved in lawmaking, each representing the people, ambition would "be made to counteract ambition."[14] The new government's institutions would look something like a mixed constitution, but it would be quite different *because it would be fully republican.* Each institution would represent the people. Properly understood, the Constitution had not simply adopted an old form. Rather, it used an arrangement similar to the old form to construct a new, stable republican form.

Madison's political thought—in *The Federalist* and elsewhere—reflected what he said about the American people in Federalist No. 14. They "paid a decent regard to the opinions of former times and other nations," but they did not "suffer [from] a blind veneration for antiquity, for custom, or for names, to overrule the suggestions of their good sense, the knowledge of their own situation, and the lessons of their own experience."[15] Madison drew on a variety of sources, both traditional and obscure, and added his own imagination to form a new republican political theory. He altered forms familiar to anyone with a passing acquaintance with political theory, to serve the people by setting up a government that was both popular and stable.[16]

Madison may have been a more productive thinker during the ratification era than he was at any other time, but his approach to political theory during these years was characteristic of him. He observed that the ideas of frequently read and much-loved thinkers were mischaracterized. Close attention was required to understand what they really meant. He knew that the most cited political theories were frequently incorrect. They had to be tested against experience. He found that terms were often misused or imprecise, leading to confusion. A more precise formulation of them was often in order. The regime in which political theory was an authority was prone to error because of these mistakes. Yet political theory itself could be used to correct these mistakes. If one was careful, if one was accurate, and if one championed ideas in line with lived experience, then political theory *could* be authoritative, and Madison took great pains to construct just such an authoritative political theory.

James Madison and other Americans did not invent a stable republican government by rejecting everything the past had to offer or by ignoring political philosophy. Nor did they succeed by slavishly following old forms. As he told readers in a later essay, written for the *National Gazette,* Americans had "a government deriving its energy from the will of the society, and operating by the reason of its measures, on the understanding and interest of the society." This was "the government for which philosophy has been searching, and humanity has been fighting, from the most remote ages"—not a shabby accomplishment, if he did say so himself.[17] Madison had used political philosophy, lived experience, and his own imagination to help craft a new political theory for a new age. Not surprisingly, once he figured out this theory he was its fiercest advocate. As Ralph Ketcham notes in his biography,

> Until a question had received careful study and had been turned around and around in his mind, and until the proper priorities had been settled, Madison was indecisive, and doubtless until then, he did evade and obfuscate. However, after study and reflection, Madison was able to take such strong, well-founded positions that he held them tenaciously, argued them persuasively, and usually prevailed in councils.[18]

During his political career, Madison felt he had worked out a science of politics covering the entire range of the political. In subsequent years this science would rarely be adjusted by its author.

Madison's own confidence in the republican political theory that he helped to construct is a significant part of the story of his relationship with theory. By the time he was president, Madison literally felt that he had formulated a more precise understanding of what politics should be like in all of its major phases: international relations, political economy, domestic institutional arrangements, and constitutional law. Much of the United States' distinctive contribution to politics was formulated by James Madison. However, as events unfolded which did not vindicate all the ideas that Madison championed, his confidence prevented quick readjustment. Madison was still open to adjustments, but they had to be done with the same great care he had used to construct his original theory. It took him years to make these changes in his views, years during which the nation suffered some serious setbacks.

Reconstructing Republicanism

To Madison, keeping citizen rights secure was the essence of what a popular government did. The arrangements which best secured rights informed his thinking across political dimensions, from institutional arrangements to the extent of government power, and from international relations to political economy. Doing justice to Madison's intellectual debts requires touching on each of these subjects. Marvin Myers, a leading rediscoverer of Madison's thinking, points out that "the uninitiated reader of Madison who sets his sights for a general philosophy of man, society, and government will find the blurred tracks of many predecessors in a well-worn trail."[19] The tracks of Madison's philosophical predecessors are blurred largely because the creation of a republican political science required him to adjust and refit the ideas he found in political theory. He did not adopt a familiar concept and leave it essentially unchanged, as John Adams had. As a result, Madison's intellectual influences are eclectic and challenging to definitively identify.

Concerning institutional arrangements, Madison learned from those who advocated the mixed constitution, but he turned the form to something decidedly more popular. Like Adams, Madison knew well the critique that Plato, Aristotle, and Machiavelli had built up against the six "simple" regime types distinguished by how many people ruled—one, the aristocratic few, or the democratic many—and whether those who ruled governed for themselves or for the community as a whole. Madison accepted their view that the problem with each of the simple regimes is that they are unstable. This argument undergirded Madison's emphasis on the definitional distinction between simple direct democracies and more complex republics in Federalist No. 10 and No. 14. It also informed his idea that democracies are prone to upheaval and are not long lived. Most importantly, it contributed to his vision for a viable republic. A simple regime which attempts to be popular will fail; a multi-institutional republic, where each institution redundantly represents the people, might succeed. Madison had borrowed the form of the mixed constitution from the various thinkers who had influenced Adams, and he had changed it by insisting that the executive and the upper legislative body represent the people along with the more numerous lower legislative chamber.

Unlike the advocates of the mixed constitution, Madison did not believe in segregating aristocratic interests from democratic ones. Yet in his conception of how the new republican form would work, he borrowed an understanding of how politics might successfully contain conflict. The advocates of the mixed constitution felt that the structure of government could provide the benefit of institutionalizing interests within the law-making process. This would temper the wishes of each major group in society; each would have to compromise to make law. Multiple institutions would check and balance each other, preventing tyranny and producing laws that approximated a common good. Madison adopted the theme of checks and balances, again with the new stipulation that all institutions would have to represent the people, either directly or indirectly. Madison's assertion that "the most common and durable source of factions, has been the various and unequal distribution of property" was familiar to readers of political theory because the idea had its roots in the theory of the mixed constitution.[20] Adams, Harrington, Bolingbroke, and before them Machiavelli each advocated an aristocratic institution and a democratic institution because of the predictable rift between those with property and those without it. Madison rejected their remedy, but acknowledged that these writers had discovered something profound. They discerned that differences in the distribution of property produced the most enduring political disputes, that these disputes had to be authoritatively reconciled by a government, and that the only way to do this effectively was to represent both those with property and those without it in the institutions of government.

The idea that there should be distinct legislative, executive, and judicial branches had been formulated by Montesquieu. Acceptance of this division was commonplace during the founding era and Madison concurred with the idea. But Michael Zuckert points out that Madison's debt to Montesquieu on this subject was much deeper than an embrace of three distinct branches. Montesquieu's purpose in separating three governmental functions from each other was to guarantee that the rule of law would prevail. The legislature would be subject to the same laws as everyone else because an independent executive would enforce written laws that applied to everyone. This had been Locke's argument. Montesquieu added a new wrinkle: the executive could only use his coercive power to enforce the law "out of doors," that is, in society. Once someone was apprehended and charged with a crime, it was the judicial branch which took over. Only judges and juries could convict and punish someone. This design served to avoid arbitrary rule by *both* the legislative branch and the executive branch. Because of the limits on its power, each branch of government would have to heed the rule of law, which would promote justice and stability.

Madison's hope for checks and balances between the branches was similar. It was a significant alternative to what Zuckert calls "short-leash republicanism," the prominent American view which we have seen espoused by Jefferson. Short-leash republicanism emphasized that good government had to be minimalist.[21] By contrast, Madison explicitly endorsed "energy" in government (Federalist No. 37). Government needed to be up to the task of formulating laws, applying them to all citizens, and effectively enforcing them. A weak executive or judiciary could not accomplish this. In short, Madison and Montesquieu favored a robust version of the separation of powers, focused on making government power safe to use rather than minimizing it. Without this vigor, government could not succeed.

There was no question that the legislative branch would still be the most powerful branch in any truly republican government. The legislature would have the power to tell the executive and the judiciary what the law was. This was an additional reason to separate the legislative branch into two entities so one institution would not predominate—an idea advocated by Montesquieu.[22] Madison acknowledged this in Federalist No. 51, contending that "it is not possible to give to each department an equal power of self-defence. In republican government, the legislative authority necessarily predominates."[23] And this was as it should be. This branch was more proximate to the people because its members would be made up of the people's representatives, selected by frequent elections (directly in the House and through the people's state representatives in the Senate). The Constitution codified this legislative supremacy as the law of the land, giving numerous specific legislative powers to the Congress.

That the Constitution dictated legislative supremacy was meaningful to Madison because of his understanding of the social contract. Madison was well acquainted with the contractarian tradition in political philosophy. Gary Rosen's *American Compact* argues that the idea of the social compact is "the fundamental idea of Madison's political thought." His ruminations on the social contract "suggest a long acquaintance with the thought of Hobbes, Locke, and their followers." At the same time, Madison "was no mere acolyte," and he offered his own unique view of how a social compact should be constructed, what it should protect, and how it could be legitimately altered.[24] The most important innovation in the social contract that Madison embraced was that like the American colonial charters, a written constitution would serve as the definitive social contract. This contract was to be unalterable on a whim by anybody, so long as it had received an explicit sanction from "the people." Madison advocated the idea that popular conventions should be used to ratify the Constitution. In this he followed the thinking of Emmerich de Vattel, who stressed that legislatures should not be able to adopt or alter constitutions.[25] Legislatures themselves were to be a subordinate party beholden to the social contract, not its architects.

The other key aspect of the social contract that Madison emphasized was the Lockean premise, already emphasized for decades by Americans, that a social contract determined what was beyond the power of government. Madison acknowledged this aspect of the social contract most explicitly in the Bill of Rights, where he began one of the proposals, which would become the First Amendment, "Congress shall make no law . . ." In 1787 Madison had believed that a federal bill of rights was unnecessary. His spurning that option was prompted by his understanding that the Constitution as it was written was already a document of limited, enumerated powers. A federal bill of rights was unnecessary because Article I, Section 8 of the document spelled out the various items on which Congress could legislate. If the subject in question was not on that list, then Congress could "make no law."[26]

Madison's scruples in regard to constitutional limits were clearly on display when Hamilton proposed and Congress debated chartering a national bank. He agreed with the object of a national bank, to spur credit, and he had supported a similar structure during his time in the Confederation Congress. However, chartering a national bank was not something Congress was empowered to do in Article I, Section 8, so he argued against the proposal on constitutional grounds. In 1791 the National Bank was chartered over his objections. Yet he never gave up on the idea that the federal government was limited in its powers, generally confined to the list set down in Article I, Section 8, with all other functions resting with the states and their people.

As a metaphor about human nature, neither Locke's relatively benign view nor Hobbes's "solitary, poor, nasty, brutish, and short" version of "man's natural state" was satisfying to Madison. His experience put human nature somewhere in between their visions. Humans *needed* governance in a way not fully acknowledged by Locke. And unlike Hobbes, Madison did not fear that open disputes would typically turn violent. Madison's more measured view is rooted in the Christian tradition and the thinkers who reflected it.[27] The potential for human depravity prefigures a need for governance, which reflects but also is capable of containing conflict. A whole range of thinkers, from Aristotle to Harrington, stressed that cooperative and other-regarding potential exists alongside selfishness in humans. A good constitution would work to promote accommodation among individuals of free will and to blunt the sharp edges of selfishness.[28]

Madison agreed with Locke and others that rights are pre-political. Government does not grant people rights; government's purpose is to secure rights people already possess. As with Locke, a government is to be a contract designed to protect the rights which each human possesses. Madison spoke of these rights as the property of each individual, just as Locke had, broadly suggesting that a person's liberty, safety, and ideas are their rightful possessions, to be safeguarded by government.[29] Like Locke and Hume, Madison stressed that the primary part of justice was the securing of property rights.[30] Madison also championed the rights of conscience. Madison's toleration went significantly further than Locke's, however. He believed that the right of conscience was complete and absolute. The reasoning he used to reach that conclusion was thoroughly Lockean.[31] Jefferson may have written the Virginia Statute for Religious Freedom, but it was Madison who worked tirelessly to get the Virginia legislature to adopt it, finally succeeding nearly ten years after it was first proposed.

Madison's views on constitutional politics are fairly familiar, but few realize that he also possessed well-developed views of international relations and political economy. In his view a republican nation needed a republican foreign policy and a republican political economy. Madison had formulated both. International affairs had been a sorry litany of needless and destructive wars entered into by those who generally did not suffer from their consequences. While Madison was under no illusion that republics would always be peaceful, he was confident that they would be more reluctant to go to war than dictatorships or other tyrannical regimes. A globe full of republics adhering to a functional international law would not be anywhere near as belligerent as the world was in the eighteenth century.

The great advocates of international law like Hugo Grotius, Samuel Pufendorf, and Emmerich de Vattel helped Madison to come to this view. They self-consciously understood their writings as a humanitarian project. Each attempted to explicate "natural law" as they saw it, a code of conduct between states that would replace a more savage Hobbesian or Machiavellian free-for-all in which each state conducted its affairs with only its own immediate interest in mind and might made right. At stake was whether an international-relations regime which respected rights could be placed alongside the constitutional structure which would safeguard them in the domestic sphere. Madison aimed to craft this new humane foreign policy while he was in Congress and then as Jefferson's secretary of state.

Grotius had argued that prisoners of war should not be killed or enslaved, that property ought not to be destroyed except for military necessity, and that the vanquished retained some autonomy, like religious liberty. He also emphasized that neutrality was a legitimate and safeguarded position for nations in a time of war.[32] These views fit well with Madison's philosophy of limited government and universal human rights, but they were only a first step on the way to fully humane international relations. Later thinkers refined Grotius's views in ways amenable to Madison's thinking. Pufendorf elaborated a concept of sovereignty wherein all states are considered equals. This view was of critical importance to Madison. As a nation which lived in the shadow of European powers, coequal sovereign status was a means of ensuring that the citizens of the United States would not be trampled on. Citizens in every country had as much right to be respected as the citizens of the globe's superpowers. Acknowledging sovereign equality was a significant step toward ensuring that Americans would not be treated as the pawns of Great Britain or France.

Of equal importance was a workable concept of neutrality. If the United States could declare itself aloof from the controversies that embroiled the European powers in war, it would only be a matter of time before it could become a great "empire of liberty," too strong to be threatened by any nation. The Dutch jurist Cornelius van Bynkershoek helped develop neutrality by defining its conditions: a neutral nation could not offer advice, arms, passage, or soldiers to combatants. In exchange, neutral trade had to be respected by belligerents just as it would be if the belligerents were not at war. Nations at war could board neutral ships to search for contraband, but the prohibited items were clearly defined and directly related to the conduct of war. If this concept were adopted as an international convention, then a nation determined not to go to war could ensure that its citizens and its property would remain unharmed.[33]

Vattel elaborated on "prize law," or what belligerents could rightly confiscate when they searched neutral vessels on the high seas. He proposed arbitration to resolve international disputes so that relatively minor offenses would not rupture into full-blown war. Vattel's contributions to international law were especially well regarded by Americans, and Madison praised the "liberal spirit" he added to previous thinkers' views. In *The Ideological Origins of the American Revolution*, Bernard Bailyn notes that "in pamphlet after pamphlet the American writers cited . . . Grotius, Pufendorf, Burlamaqui, and Vattel on the laws of nature and of nations."[34]

Where Madison did not agree with their particular views, he agreed with their spirit, which was to define international law such that relations between states would be made more peaceful and predictable. Nations would come to respect the individual rights of the citizens of all nations. When disputes arose between nations they could be resolved peacefully with reference to this international law, or if this law were not definitive on a particular issue the dispute could be settled by arbitration.

Madison was particularly sensitive about how the nation's economy would affect its foreign relations. His reading of history led him to the conclusion that nations often go to war because of money. Those leading the charge were typically those who could benefit from war—a nation's royals and aristocrats. The foreign policy of a republican government would reflect its inhabitants—it would be more frugal and simple than nations with aristocratic classes, and less belligerent. Visions of capturing riches would not induce the citizens of republics to go to war like they did the ostentatious monarchies of Europe. The push to go to war would be reduced even further if the present generation would have to pay for it, rather than borrowing to put off the financial cost, a suggestion Madison offered in a *National Gazette* essay titled "Universal Peace." Madison credited this idea to Rousseau, but apparently it was actually borrowed from the Abbé de Saint-Pierre.[35]

Drew McCoy points out that it was commonplace for early political economists to view economic development as a four-stage process, moving from hunting and gathering, to "pasturage," to agriculture, and then to commerce. This staged view of economic development made sense to Madison and he employed it in his construction of an ideal moral economy. Madison's preferred political economy was predominantly agrarian, but not exclusively so. Like Jefferson, he praised agriculture's productiveness over hunting and gathering or pasturage. He also believed that farming encouraged beneficial traits in individuals and in political communities. On an individual level, farming encouraged industriousness and a respect for property rights. It also promoted decision-making skills and a sense of equality. Developing an economy primarily devoted to manufacturing and trade would be politically disastrous. During the early part of the eighteenth century, English "Country party" thinkers had warned of this development. Additionally, the Scots Lord Kames and Adam Ferguson had similarly praised farming.[36] In the aggregate, a predominantly agricultural economy could help a nation be self-sufficient when it needed to be. Following Adam Smith, Madison hoped that a robust international trade would increase standards of living, but he understood that in a world that was still almost exclusively non-republican, a dependence on foreign trade could be disastrous to an existing republic. Self-sufficiency built on agrarianism would allow the nation to steer clear of international disputes when it needed to.

In *The Wealth of Nations,* Smith warned of the debasement and dehumanization of the laboring classes in an advanced commercial society. Smith theorized that the law of supply and demand would push wages ever lower in areas where the supply of labor was high, in cities. The result would be ever-greater disparities in wealth among citizens. Madison hoped to create a political economy which would keep the nation agrarian, poised at the cusp of a commercial society, rather than advancing into the commercial stage of economic development, with its attendant personal and political difficulties.

The government's role in fostering an agrarian political economy was, mainly, to not interfere. Ideally, the United States would produce a surplus of agricultural goods, which would be exported. These would be sold for cash, producing a favorable trade balance. Seeing the nation's prosperity, many would emigrate to America, hacking ever-more farms out of the wilderness and increasing the size of this "empire of liberty." European powers had colonized most of the earth to bring revenue into their treasuries. Madison's vision for the United States was different. Barring an emergency, the nation would carry no debt and be involved in no wars, it would be a full signatory to humane international law, and it would practice a political economy which promised prosperity without the ills of luxury or vast disparities of wealth.

Given the logic of Federalist No. 10, a bigger republic was better. While most of his fellow countrymen were still thinking small, Madison had formulated the vision of the extended republic. Hume's contribution to this theory has been described above, but others must be credited as well. As a young state legislator, Madison worked to protect Baptist preachers from prosecution by the Anglican establishment. Meanwhile, in Pennsylvania, he knew that numerous sects coexisted without rancor. This led Madison to find truth in Voltaire's aphorism "If one religion only were allowed in England, the Government would possibly become arbitrary; if there were two, they would be at each other's throats; but as there are such a multitude, they all live happy and in peace."[37] The extended republic was the wisdom of Voltaire's aphorism applied to public policy generally. Finally, the definition of "faction" contained in Federalist No. 10 would have been familiar to those versed in political theory. Bolingbroke had stressed that "parties, even before they degenerate into absolute factions, are still numbers of men associated together for certain purposes and certain interests, which are not . . . those of the community."[38] To both Madison and Bolingbroke this put a premium on figuring out a way to contain their worst impulses.

"The Rightful Authority to Which Governments Are Limited"

As Madison prepared to assume the presidency he could have been expected to be a fierce protector of popular rights. Doing so, he believed, required him to follow the letter of the Constitution carefully, with its relatively clear divisions of power. This meant that he would defer to the legislature on almost all things, except when he would find it acting in a way that was unconstitutional. He would also defer to the states in matters where the Constitution did not empower the federal government. A President Madison would be happy to add territory to the nation, as his illustrious predecessor had, keeping the United States predominantly agrarian as far forward into the future as anyone could see. He would do his best to keep the country free from foreign entanglements, asserting the right of neutrals, as formulated by key international legal theorists, something he had already been doing as secretary of state. The transition to the Madison presidency would generally be marked by continuity. At the same time, any differences could be expected to correspond to the difference in theoretical emphases between Jefferson and himself. Jefferson was more immediately utilitarian, more willing than Madison to sacrifice proper legal and institutional form for what he considered to be beneficial. Madison believed that the most beneficial course in the long run was almost always to regard proper constitutional form and the rule of law.

Relations with Britain continued to be the most pressing issue faced by the federal government during Madison's presidency. As related in the previous chapter, the bitter Napoleonic wars prompted both France and Britain, but Britain in particular, to offend the United States on the high seas. Madison and Jefferson crafted a response designed to be distinctly humane and republican. They protested through Madison's pamphlet titled *An Examination of the British Doctrine,* which pointed out that the British were violating precepts laid out by the leading authorities of international law and common practice. And they formulated a coercive policy which aimed to rectify the situation through an embargo rather than through war. By prohibiting American ships from leaving port they expected Britain—a commercial nation which relied on trade—to feel the sting of the boycott. To resume trading with the United States, the British would have to promise to respect American shipping rights.

However, in the last two years of Jefferson's presidency the British withstood the boycott. Britain's diverse economy and vast empire did not rely on American goods as much as Madison presumed it did. The cash-poor United States, meanwhile, relied more on British purchases than Madison could admit, and the implementation of the Nonintercourse Act coincided with a severe economic downturn in the United States. The small national government also had little ability to enforce its edict other than to rely on voluntary compliance. Many New Englanders who had traded with Britain before the embargo engaged in smuggling. Instead of abandoning the embargo, Madison remained true to his theoretical understanding of the workings of political economy, maintaining that if enforcement were better, an embargo would still work to coerce the British. In this he seemed to be a prisoner of his own assumptions. Madison might have rethought his position if he had known more about how the embargo was working in practice. But the paltry information available to him about the embargo's effect both in Britain and in the United States did not help him use experience to adjust his thinking.

Madison still hoped that he could negotiate a solution to the diplomatic crisis. Events in the first month of his presidency led him to conclude that such a breakthrough was at hand. In March 1809 Madison negotiated an agreement with British envoy David Erskine, who pledged that the British government would pay damages for the *Chesapeake* incident (see Chapter 3) and that it would respect American shipping rights, even to the European continent. This agreement reinforced Madison's predisposition to think that the embargo had worked. Unfortunately, in negotiating the agreement Erskine exceeded his instructions and the accord was rejected by the British government. Erskine was recalled and President Madison was back to square one, as the original embargo had expired when Jefferson left the presidency. Madison was left to insist that the British should respect American shipping because of the principles of international law and to hope that Congress would enact a new embargo.

Through a bill introduced by Nathaniel Macon, a representative from North Carolina, Madison attempted to get Congress to readopt the embargo in a new form. Instead of prohibiting American ships from plying the high seas, Macon's bill proposed to close American ports to both French and British ships while letting American ships go where they wished. This would expose American ships to being boarded, but it would allow native merchants and shippers to sell goods and make money. This was a significant concession on Madison's part. The original embargo had been designed to starve the British and French of raw materials. Now those raw materials would be allowed to cross the Atlantic Ocean. The coercive effect of this revised embargo would come about as a result of losses incurred by British shipping interests. Since more goods flowed to

Britain from the United States than in the opposite direction, this restriction might prove less effective even though it was both more enforceable and more politically palatable than the original embargo.

Not favoring this new proposal, a coalition of New Englanders and opposition figures within the Republican Party amended the bill in Congress in an effort to restart bilateral trade. They decided that if *either* Britain *or* France lifted its restrictions on American shipping, then President Madison could impose an embargo on the other nation *if* that nation persisted in refusing to lift its own restrictions. Proponents of this amendment felt that either Britain or France would promise to respect American shipping rights (they did not agree about which would). If one of the major world powers did this, then the other might follow suit, solving the diplomatic crisis. If the other nation did not come in line, then the coercive pressure of the embargo would fall entirely on the recalcitrant power. Macon's Bill #2, as the revised version was called, received a majority of votes in both the House and the Senate, and it was presented to President Madison to sign.

Among the problems with the revised Macon Bill was that it threatened American neutrality. If one of the belligerents took the offer and the other did not, the United States would seem to be taking sides between the two warring superpowers.[39] Madison could have vetoed the bill on these programmatic grounds and insisted on his own preferred policy. He chose not to because of his understanding of the limited role of the executive in the legislative process.

Because Britain could effectively stop most shipping to the Continent, France had little to lose by pledging to respect American shipping. Napoleon took advantage of the incentive provided to him by the new policy, forcing Britain either to pledge not to interfere with American ships or to have a unilateral embargo placed on its ships going to the United States. After receiving assurances from the French and waiting for a favorable response from Britain, Madison declared a unilateral embargo on British ships coming to the United States. Napoleon undoubtedly hoped to drive the wedge between Britain and the United States deeper in adopting this course of action, and he succeeded.

Of this episode Jack N. Rakove explains that "to some extent, Madison was a prisoner of his constitutional convictions." Deferring to Congress "was a noble judgment in principle, but one that presented Madison with political and diplomatic problems. For his failure to persuade a fractious Congress to support his foreign policies not only exposed him to political embarrassment at home, it also undermined his complicated diplomatic strategies abroad."[40] His accepting Congress's alterations to Macon's bill indicates the seriousness of Madison's commitment to legislative supremacy. Had Madison agreed with Adams's fierce commitment to executive independence and strength, the result would likely have been a veto. Had he continued Jefferson's practice of holding dinner parties at which the president subtly lobbied members of Congress, he might have won a majority over to his position. And had he not had any acquaintance with political theory, he would likely have used his prerogative to veto the revised Macon Bill. Madison's own work in political theory had given him a different perspective—one which required the president to defer to Congress's legislative wishes in all cases except those of unconstitutionality.

In legislative matters the president was merely allowed "from time to time give to the Congress Information of the State of the Union, and recommend to their consideration such Measures as he shall judge necessary and expedient." Madison informed Congress and he recommended that they consider his favored policies, but he stopped well short of publicly advocating them.[41] A key example of this arose coincidentally with the reimposed embargo. Instead of facilitating a substantial increase in military spending, Madison left the matter entirely to Congress after simply suggesting in his annual message of 1811 that its members "consider" such increases. Congress voted to reinforce the army but not the navy. With American ships headed back into hostile waters this lack of naval preparedness proved troublesome. When war came, the navy acquitted itself very well, but its victorious vessels had been built during the Washington and Adams administrations.[42] Madison also yielded to congressional sentiment when it came to the cabinet. This led to several appointees' being unfit for the job they held or not working well with Madison. The "amiable but inept Robert Smith," Madison's first secretary of state, was unsuited to be the nation's top diplomat and he did not get along well with the president.[43]

Madison's institutional scrupulousness was accompanied by advantages, but these advantages were less tangible than the disadvantages. Other presidents have used war or the threat of military action to augment their power. Madison refused to use the dispute with Great Britain to increase his chances of getting his way, which in his mind would have had the side effect of warping the Constitution to favor greater presidential power at the expense of Congress. Madison allowed Congress to make its own mistakes. Proceeding this way satisfied Madison's understanding of the separation of powers which was set up by mutual agreement in the Constitution. Many politicians of the founding era supported legislative supremacy and constitutional limits, both as abstract concepts and as useful tools in their specific battles with political opponents. Madison's commitments to legislative supremacy and to constitutional rule persisted even when he believed that the specific outcome chosen by Congress was highly problematic. Reinforcing the sanctity of the Constitution was a very important positive example, even if the benefits of doing this were less immediately apparent than some of the drawbacks which accompanied his scrupulousness. Yet this clearly demonstrates Madison's fealty to an emerging view of constitutional law and the Enlightenment's emphasis on elevating the "rule of law" above the "rule of men."

Madison also kept republican principles in mind when it came to law enforcement. Many northerners understandably resented the embargo, as it threatened their livelihoods. New England's partisan press savaged the administration. Many New Englanders flouted the law by smuggling goods across the Canadian border or on illegally loaded ships. They were doing business with a regime that was increasingly hostile toward the United States. When war came, these merchants were unsure when, if ever, their access to the British markets might be restored. By 1815 delegates to the Hartford Convention were openly discussing the possibility of secession. None of these trying events induced Madison to curtail civil liberties. While smuggling would be treated as the crime it was, Madison did not push Republicans to prosecute those who criticized him or the government's policies, a temptation which others have not been able to resist. None of the members of the Hartford Convention faced federal charges, and Madison did not even suggest making the advocacy of secession illegal. These men were entitled to their views, and they were even entitled to publicize their views. As long as they pursued their goals peacefully, the United States government had no ability or need to prosecute them. These were commitments that were unthinkable without the Enlightenment commitment to free expression.

In interpersonal relations Madison tended to be affable but somewhat timid. Thus it may come as a surprise how aggressive he was in promoting the idea that the United States would control the entire North American continent. As president he worked to expand the boundaries of the United States along two specific fronts: south into Florida and north into Canada. These efforts arose out of the political events of the time, but they were simultaneously a reflection of Madison's hope for an extensive "empire of liberty." The theoretical vision of the extended republic, inspired by Hume, underlay his policies, as did the hope that the United States would remain poised on the cusp of an agrarian-commercial economy. Madison hoped that republican governments would cover the globe. He was under no illusion that this process would be swift or inevitable. The failure of the French republic meant that throughout his presidency the United States was the only republican nation that conformed to the model he had worked out in the late 1780s. The extension of U.S. territory was a kind of advance, a liberation of inhabitants and territory.

This outlook dictated an aggressive policy toward Spanish Florida in his first term and prefigured his initial ideas about strategy in the War of 1812. In the Louisiana Purchase of 1803, Madison and Jefferson thought that they had bought what is now the panhandle of Florida, then called West Florida. However, boundaries were ill defined and documents relating to the purchase were vague and contradictory on the subject. The Spanish claimed West Florida and refused to surrender any territory to the United States. Spain was a relatively weak power, though, and Madison viewed this weakness as an opportunity.

For almost its whole length, the border between the United States and Spanish Florida was simply an imaginary line drawn from east to west across a map. With no natural boundary to restrain them, American homesteaders had crossed into West Florida during the years of the territorial dispute. By the time Madison became president, these settlers were sufficiently numerous that the administration wished to press the issue. "Late in 1810, Madison authorized a confidential agent, William Wykoff, to stir up demands within West Florida for America to take possession of the area."[44] Madison thought the Spanish would recognize that they did not have a sufficient presence in this territory to put such demands to rest. When word came that the territory was effectively occupied by Americans who wished to be citizens of the United States, the Spanish might peacefully renounce possession or submit the claim to arbitration.

The American settlers of West Florida did not quite get the message. They went well beyond what Madison hoped they would do. They marched on Baton Rouge, captured the Spanish governor, and declared West Florida to be an independent state. To end the confusion and to impose federal rule, Madison sent federal troops to occupy West Florida. In his zeal to add to the extended republic, Madison had unintentionally encouraged a coup against the territorial government of a nation with whom the United States was at peace. This was a troubling international incident, backing him into the very kind of military adventure that he believed republican governments would shun, even though the number of troops involved was small and it did not eventuate in bloodshed.

Madison's expansionist views also informed strategy during the War of 1812. His hope was to invade Canada and to take much of its sparsely populated territory from the British. Southern Canada was well suited to farming. Taking it would preserve the United States' agrarian character, just as the Louisiana Purchase had. This aspiration ran at cross-purposes with the Republicans' long-standing distaste of national military power.

The federal government had dismantled much of its military when Jefferson took office. The United States was slow to mobilize in 1812. Timid, untested generals and poorly trained American troops failed to act effectively in the initial stages of the war. A numerically inferior British detachment captured the American fort at Detroit, effectively ending the American hope to appropriate what is now southern Ontario.

Madison did his best to avoid war with Britain from 1809 to 1812. Accepting war did not require Madison to change his thinking. It is, in fact, a testament to how much faith he put in the standards of international law that their violation could prompt a military response. He had never believed that republican nations would never go to war. None of the international-law theorists he consulted were utopians who believed they could end war forever. They had attempted to make war less likely and less dangerous when it did occur. United States citizens had been mightily and consistently provoked for many years by the British. By seizing American goods, preventing free trade, and impressing American seamen into service on British ships, they had trampled on American rights. The Americans had made many attempts to solve the dispute with Great Britain peacefully, but by 1812 it seemed certain that Great Britain would not respect American rights unless there was a war. On June 1, 1812, Madison recommended the state of British-American affairs to the attention of Congress. To Madison, declaring war was "a solemn question which the Constitution wisely confides to the legislative department of the Government."[45] By the standards of international law which Madison so frequently cited, war was justified. If a nation consistently disregarded the standards of international law set down in the writings of Grotius and his successors and refused to heed protests which asked them to mend their ways, then these norms would have to be enforced through the force of arms. In retirement in Braintree, John Adams wrote that "a more necessary War was never undertaken. It is necessary against England; necessary to convince France that we are something: and above all necessary to convince ourselves, that we are not, Nothing."[46]

Like Jefferson, Madison was committed to a rigorously frugal republican regime. Above all this meant that the nation's primary defense would be "an armed and trained militia[, which] is the firmest bulwark of republics."[47] Largely because of this policy, Britain felt it had nothing to fear and much to gain from disregarding international conventions at sea. But the United States could not successfully insist that Great Britain abide by standards of international conduct without having a professional military.[48] By the end of the War of 1812, Madison realized that frugality in government could not be maximized without endangering public safety. In one of the few times he acknowledged changing his mind, he told American citizens in his Annual Message of 1816 that "experience has taught us . . . that a certain degree of preparation for war is not only indispensable to avert disasters in the onset, but affords also the best security for the continuance of peace."[49] A primary pillar of Madison's "Quaker" foreign policy had given way, adjusted by what experience had taught him. In the wake of the War of 1812 Madison did his part to ensure that the nation would never again "speak loudly while carrying no stick at all."[50]

Another area in which Madison adjusted his thinking was in regards to the National Bank. During his presidency the original twenty-year charter of the bank expired. If this entity were to continue its existence, it would have to be reapproved by the same person who had led the charge against it in the House of Representatives on the grounds of its unconstitutional nature. Madison did accept reauthorization, suggesting that the bank's long acceptance by the American people had rendered it constitutional. In doing so, he was continuing to develop republican constitutional theory on the fly, suggesting that practices which were long accepted as legitimate by a people passed constitutional muster. This concession was not accompanied by a general relaxation in his views about setting new precedents of dubious constitutionality. In the final days of Madison's presidency, Congress sent him a public works bill. The bill was the fruit of Henry Clay's "American Plan," which touted the universal benefits of building roads and canals. Madison vetoed the bill, reminding Congress that "internal improvements" were a state responsibility according to the Constitution, not a national one. Because Congress was not authorized to make laws concerning transportation within the states, the bill was an unconstitutional extension of federal power.

As president, Madison continued to champion the rights of conscience. In 1811 he vetoed a bill which would have incorporated the Episcopal Church in Alexandria, then a part of the District of Columbia. In his veto message to Congress, Madison adopted good Lockean form, noting that "the bill exceeds the rightful authority to which governments are limited by the essential distinction between civil and religious functions."[51]

Attention to the "rightful authority" of governments and the proper authority of each of its constituent parts was Madison's lifelong work. Discerning proper boundaries was his theoretical forte. He had drawn on experience and the theories which seemed to fit experience to develop well-considered ideas about the rightful boundaries between the power of government and the liberty of the people, between the legislative branch and the executive branch, between the federal government and the state governments, and between the prerogatives of the British government and rights of United States citizens. When given the opportunity to practice politics as the executive, he put into practice the "science of politics" that he had discerned with the aid of his deep knowledge of political theory. He insisted on the rights of neutral nations. He deferred to the legislative will and to constitutional boundaries, even when doing so came at a tangible cost, because he felt that damaging the rule of law would produce even greater problems. His policies were consistent with one who is a champion of popular rights, even for those who disagreed with his policies. He continued to support the idea of the extended republic by actively seeking to extend American sovereignty into Florida and Canada. Madison also demonstrated that he was sufficiently open minded to adjust his thinking when his own commitments proved problematic. By the end of his presidency he acknowledged that the United States needed a professional military. With better information, he might have adjusted his thinking about the embargo as well. His science of politics was a work in progress, an ongoing attempt to find a workable republicanism. For someone who had already figured out so much and who had been so instrumental in making the United States what it was, it is remarkable that he was still open to these changes. President Madison was more interested in creating a working republic than in protecting his own theoretical views or in receiving credit for having figured out how to do it.

Conclusion

Of all the American presidents, James Madison has the most valid claim to being a political theorist because of the combination of his serious engagement with theoretical concepts and his skepticism toward theory which prompted him to formulate new views. If the hallmarks of political philosophy are creativity, innovation, consistency, and breadth of aspiration, then Madison is a political philosopher—and the only president worthy of the title. This means that it is often not the case that he derived a specific policy directly from an individual thinker. Rather, like most political philosophers, he displays an array of intellectual influences which he used and adjusted to forge a new theory. Though some of his commitments caused him troubles, to his credit Madison was both willing to put up with some troubles to preserve worthy principles and capable of adjusting his views. This suggests that his presidency should be considered more favorably than it has been. Recent commentators, employing a paradigm of power maximization inspired by the modern presidency and the writings of Richard Neustadt, judge Madison to be a failure. Underrated in presidential rankings are a president's commitment to the rule of law and to the preservation of citizen rights, particularly in times of national danger. Along these two metrics, Madison was an excellent president.

Madison attempted to live out his theoretical ideals every bit as scrupulously as John Adams had. The primary casualty in Adams's case was his own political career. With Madison, events were such that the nation came perilously close to paying for his theoretical ideals with its life. His preference for a frugal military establishment, his unwillingness to aggressively lead Congress toward a greater level of preparedness in 1811, and his insistence that all nations follow the niceties of international law were a toxic mix. These commitments could not be pursued simultaneously without putting the United States in serious jeopardy. They prompted a war which the United States was ill prepared to fight. The burning of the capitol building and ransacking of the White House need not have occurred even with this poor preparation, but it is an appropriate symbol for Madison's presidency that it did. All of Madison's commitments were well thought out. What was not particularly well thought out was whether they fit together. Despite the narrow escape, there was a fortuitous conclusion. As Adams acknowledged about Madison, "Notwithstand[ing] a thousand Faults and blunders, his Administration has acquired more glory, and established more Union, than all his three Predecessors, Washington, Adams and Jefferson, put together."[52]

Two matters in particular deserve to be emphasized: the meticulous work which went into forming Madison's understandings and the tenacity with which he held these views. These two observations are related. It was *because* Madison put such effort into forming a true republican theory of politics that he was so confident that he was correct. Madison was not merely a politician acquainted with political theory, he was a political theorist deeply invested in his own innovative discoveries. They were discoveries that Madison had confidence in because he worked to see that they squared with a scientific study of lived experience. Ralph Ketcham characterizes Madison brilliantly:

> By scholarly and intellectual habit, he weighed matters carefully, sought subtle and sophisticated insights, and suspended judgments as long as possible; this tendency caused many to see him as a "closet politician," too little in touch with the practical world and too much wrapped up in his own thoughts and theories. The total effect denied to him the charisma necessary for dynamic leadership. On the other hand, he was regarded by friend and foe alike as well informed, keen minded, and brilliant. In private conversation, and in councils of government conducted over long periods of time, he was persuasive and effective.[53]

In other words, Madison's studiousness led him to be considered both brilliant and somewhat daft.

Typically, successful politicians are adept at making trade-offs. They may be genuinely devoted to a variety of ideals, but practical politics forces them to choose between them, emphasizing one over another. Madison had done the hard intellectual work of formulating "correct views" about virtually every aspect of government. However, he was not particularly willing to pragmatically order his ideals. Strictly limiting the United States' military establishment, deferring to Congress, and insisting that Britain discontinue its affronts on the high seas were all correct positions to him that he had come to carefully, even meticulously. Shading one to favor another might have proved practically beneficial. As it was, these three positions did not prove to be compatible. There was also an unrealized tension between his zeal for extending the "empire of liberty" and his normally pacific intentions that became apparent during the West Florida coup d'état.

It took Madison eight years as a member of the House of Representatives, eight years as secretary of state, and more than four years as president to understand that a republican nation would have to have a professional military to ensure that it would be treated well by world powers. Madison dropped his insistence on a small, amateur military establishment, and in doing so he came closer to grasping the necessity of pragmatically emphasizing some commitments over others to achieve them as best he could. For a student of Aristotle, as Madison was, this lack of attention to the best possible outcome—rather than attempting to produce an ideal outcome—is surprising. In formulating his new republican philosophy, Madison had consulted centuries' worth of theory and practice. The American system of government was a new form: it was only twenty years old when Madison became president. For one committed to the idea that "experience is the oracle of truth," this was precious little time to adjust. Madison was open minded enough to correct the flaws in his thinking, but realizing how he should do so took many years of hard experiences.

Madison was not impractical. The utilitarian philosopher Jeremy Bentham wrote a forty-one-page letter to the president early in his first term offering to write a complete body of laws for the United States. The letter went unanswered for nearly five years. Finally, in 1817, President Madison made his feelings known about the offer to the new U.S. ambassador to Britain, John Quincy Adams. Madison felt that the offer showed that Bentham had great "philanthropy" of character. Presumably having read some of Bentham's work, Madison also judged him to possess "capacity." Yet he also stressed that the philosopher "greatly underrates the task" he offered to perform.[54] Bentham's heart was in the right place, it was this philosopher's head that was the problem. Jefferson might have been enthused at Bentham's offer. It was, after all, virtually the same thing that Jefferson himself had attempted to do as a state legislator in the early 1770s. Madison turned Bentham down cold. This was not the judgment of a philosophic dreamer. It was the judgment of an eminently practical political architect, who had brilliantly succeeded in constructing a workable republic.

Chapter 5

WOODROW WILSON: KEEPING THE WORLD SAFE FROM PHILOSOPHY

I have conceived the (perhaps whimsical) purpose of combining Montesquieu, Burke, and Bagehot. Montesquieu often plays with his subject, but with a subtle mockery: he should play with it with the more manly, though equally pointed, humour—with the unflagging vivacity and the wide-eyed tolerant look straight upon life—of Bagehot. Both these masters in politics, however, lack the seriousness of Burke, his full-voiced eloquence, his ardent highstrung consciousness of the weight, the beauty, the delicacy of liberty. Combined, the three men stand for all that has force in political thought.
—Woodrow Wilson, memoranda for "Modern Democratic State," December 1885

What commends Mr. Lincoln's studiousness to me is that the result of it was he did not have any theories at all. Life is a very complex thing. No theory that I ever heard propounded will match its varied pattern; and the men who are dangerous are the men who are not content with understanding, but go on to propound theories, things which will make a new pattern for society and a new model for the universe. Those are the men who are not to be trusted.
—Woodrow Wilson, "Abraham Lincoln: A Man of the People," February 12, 1909

Presidents are ambitious people; many of them have wanted to wield political power from an early age. Woodrow Wilson was one of these. As a Princeton undergraduate Wilson made a pact with a classmate, Charlie Talcott, to gain power in order to advance the principles they held in common.[1] As a young man, he put aside his hope to be a politician for an academic career. Yet he never lost the burning ambition to be elected, and he pursued a course which allowed him to jump to a political career in his middle age. As president, Wilson reminisced that he had been preparing for the office since his undergraduate days.[2]

Wilson's ambition is hardly unusual for a president, but his view of how to pursue his political goals is strikingly unusual. Wilson remembered that in his undergraduate "covenant" to gain political power, he and Talcott had agreed "that we would acquire knowledge that we might have power."[3] The belief that knowledge could be translated into political power may be the most telling thought in Wilson's mental constellation. Wilson felt that success in a political career did not lie primarily in forging the right personal or group alliances or in crafting an effective policy platform, though he understood the importance of these things. Rather, he staked his chance to make a political mark on becoming a preeminent scholar of politics. Wilson, the only president to have earned a Ph.D., would parlay his academic reputation into a meteoric political career. He was confident that his studious or, as he called it, his "literary" approach to politics would make him a better president than those without that background.

The knowledge Wilson gathered in his academic path to the White House was not about policies so much as the operation of government institutions and the nature of political development. These are subjects of interest to political theorists. Yet Wilson consistently denigrated political theory as too abstract to be useful and too radical to be of benefit. His own political thought consisted of ideas borrowed from the thinkers whom he judged to have bucked this tendency. More conservative and practical were Edmund Burke, Baron de Montesquieu, and Walter Bagehot, among others. Wilson was not the brilliant formulator of a new philosophy. He did not claim to be. As he noted to himself, he had worked out a synthesis of these three thinkers' views. Wilson would be the voice who skillfully presented the views of these practical philosophers to the public in compelling narratives and stirring speeches.

Together the political thinkers from whom Wilson borrowed emphasized the primacy of public opinion in shaping a polity. Most of them stressed that because public opinion defines regimes, political change is inevitable—as opinions change, so will a nation's government. Yet opinion change takes place gradually rather than wholesale, typically building on the public's prior views. Leaders help to direct opinion change through their words. It is no accident that in the opening quote Wilson focuses on the *writing style* of Montesquieu, Bagehot, and Burke. If public opinion is the coin of the political realm, then to be a leader, one must be a skilled rhetorician and writer. If Wilson could make the opportunity arise through his public writings and addresses, he would happily become a "leader of men." By his early thirties Wilson was already confiding to himself the audacious question "Why may not the present age write, through me, its political autobiography?"[4]

As Wilson penned that line, he anticipated writing a book that he referred to as "The Philosophy of Politics." This would be his master work, which would cement his reputation as the foremost interpreter of American politics.[5] In this work he would present his synthesis of Montesquieu, Bagehot, and Burke. Though he was a prolific writer, Wilson never finished the book. In fact, he never produced anything more than drafts of a first chapter and a general outline. Something always got in the way. In mid-career he could make more money and reach more people by delivering public lectures and writing for a popular audience than by writing for an academic one. Next it was his elevation to the presidency of Princeton. Then it was his political career—first as New Jersey's governor for two years and then for his two terms as president of the United States. Even as president, Wilson expressed a desire to complete the work in his retirement. The massive stroke he suffered in 1919 put an end to that aspiration for all practical purposes.

We should not be too disappointed by the absence of his "Philosophy of Politics." The purpose behind the project was the application of well-considered ideas to political practice, something he could do even more readily as a politician than as an author. Furthermore, the reputation he had hoped to cement in writing "The Philosophy of Politics" was already secure. As it turns out, Wilson did not need to write the book to make the leap to politics and to gain the presidency. Had he written "The Philosophy of Politics" he probably would not have been elected in the first place because it would have taken time from meeting people and spreading his ideas in public lectures and popular writings. Furthermore, Wilson's other writings elucidate his political thought. Even though he never wrote his planned masterpiece, Wilson did realize his "ambition to become an invigorating and enlightening power in the world of political thought."[6]

Like Edmund Burke, Wilson was an antitheoretical theorist of politics. He possessed an antipathy to any abstract approach to politics intended to be applied across national boundaries. On the 100th anniversary of Abraham Lincoln's birth he praised the sixteenth president's learning in a public address, but he also stressed that Lincoln exhibited another kind of wisdom that he thought most studious individuals lacked. What set Lincoln apart was that he refrained from forcing what he learned into a theoretical pattern, which he might have imposed onto the world. Others who were knowledgeable did erect such theories which would create society anew. "Those are the men not to be trusted," Wilson intoned. Undoubtedly Wilson, then pondering a move from academia to politics, thought of himself in the same terms as Lincoln. He had been gaining knowledge to acquire power all his adult life. He was also mature enough to eschew theories. It was no wonder that he had been mentioned as a possible candidate for the Senate, or the governorship of New Jersey, or even the presidency of the United States.[7] Or so, at least, his antitheoretical political theory told him. In just four years' time the Princeton professor would be president-elect. At that time Wilson, imbued with a sense of his own destiny guided by Providence, must have felt that he had lived out his own ideal, to be America's "literary politician," who would formulate practical, not patterned, solutions to the challenges of the day.

The thinkers from whom Wilson borrowed frequently presented ideas compatible with each other, but they did not always do so. The fundamental tension in Wilson's thought is his combination of a devotion to Burkean gradualism with ideals of forceful leadership and cultural change inspired by Walter Bagehot. Emphasizing continuity and active leadership at once is an interesting and difficult combination. The stresses between these two commitments would manifest themselves both in domestic politics and in foreign policy. Many have observed that when he was president, Wilson abandoned his theoretical roots. At the very least, this is not how Wilson understood himself. He felt he was applying the same knowledge that had gained him power. However, the times he found himself in seemed to lead him to privilege leadership over gradualism.

"I Have a Passion for Interpreting Great Thoughts to the World"

Woodrow Wilson was probably dyslexic.[8] He did not learn to read until he was eleven years old, and as a result some family members thought of him as mentally defective when he was a boy. Wilson overcame his learning disability in extraordinary fashion, becoming a renowned author and essayist, but he always lamented his slowness as a reader. The disability had a significant impact on his professional life: Wilson did not read anywhere near as broadly as many of his academic contemporaries. Arthur Link, the editor of *The Papers of Woodrow Wilson*, relates that "he was a person of limited interests and narrow reading. Indeed, even in his own specialties of political science, constitutional law, and English and American history, Wilson was surprisingly poorly read."[9] Even so, from the time he entered Princeton in 1876 to the point he was selected as Princeton's first secular president in 1902, he had plenty of time to read and gain his orientation to politics from political theory. At the same time, he had none of the lust to devour political theory that John Adams had.

This disinterest made a good deal of sense to Wilson, because the great majority of what political theory had to offer was defective. Nor did he sift exhaustively through piles of archival material to do original research. Though his published output was prodigious and often well regarded, Wilson was not inclined toward original scholarship. Both his political thought and his writings consist mainly of borrowed ideas, adapted and updated, and more elaborately reasoned and eloquently stated than they had been in their original form.

Wilson's father, Joseph Ruggles Wilson, was a Presbyterian minister. Proud of his heritage, the Reverend Wilson subscribed to several British periodicals. These publications reflected the rabid Anglophilia of the day, and Tommy Wilson—Woodrow would not be known by his middle name until he was out of college—eagerly adopted the view that Britain possessed the best politics the world had to offer.[10] These popular publications echoed the thinking of the great conservative British thinkers in praising the moderation of British politics, its unfolding commitment to self-government and liberty, and the open debates which characterized its political institutions. Not surprisingly, the thinkers Wilson would come to admire most were the very authors whose ideas these publications popularized—Walter Bagehot and Edmund Burke. It was as if Wilson, after struggling to overcome dyslexia, attached himself to the first political theory that he learned, modifying his views only by deepening his explanations of it.[11]

The editors of *The Papers of Woodrow Wilson* call Wilson's first book-length essay, the unpublished "Government by Debate," "the fruit of an obsession for the reconstruction of the machinery of the American government along the lines of the British Cabinet system."[12] Other works relied heavily on borrowed ideas as well. An early essay, "Self-Government in France," was conceived of as an update of Tocqueville's commentary on his native country. In it Wilson suggests that French habits were not suited for democracy, just as Tocqueville (and not uncoincidentally Burke and Bagehot) had. The French wished to have democracy without the accompanying "habits of the heart"—Tocqueville's phrase—that would make it work. As a young man Wilson struggled to develop his own style. His sentence "New France is not yet completely builded; old France is not yet thoroughly cleared away" is unmistakably Tocquevillian, both in sentiment and in rhythm.[13]

Later works were more characteristically Wilsonian in style and substance, but they still relied heavily on the ideas of others. This was true of

Congressional Government, an application of Bagehot's ideas that no paper constitution literally defined a nation's politics because a nation's politics is always subject to slow evolution, and that open discussion was the most desirable feature of politics in advanced nations. Wilson judged that the federal government had departed from a democratic ideal by parceling out decisions to congressional committees, which generally operated behind closed doors. His comparative politics textbook, *The State,* borrowed extensively from a German series edited by Heinrich Marquardsen.[14]

Wilson recognized this tendency in himself—to borrow and publicize rather than to think anew—very early. When he was in graduate school, he related to his fiancee, Ellen Axson, "I have no patience for the tedious toil of what is known as 'research'; I have a passion for interpreting great thoughts to the world." As he conceived of writing *Congressional Government,* he wrote Axson that his "desire and ambition are to treat the American constitution as Mr. Bagehot . . . has treated the English Constitution. His book has inspired my whole study of our government."[15] Wilson's success, and even his innovation in applying Bagehot's ideas to the United States, is unimpeachable. *Congressional Government* started a robust conversation about the workings of American institutions that has lasted well over a century—an accomplishment which virtually no other scholar can boast. Yet even after his first book made Wilson a celebrated author, he had not changed his mind about scholarship. In 1893 he wrote to a friend, "I am not only not a scholar . . . I don't want to be one."[16]

This confession was not due to a lack of a sense of accomplishment on Wilson's part. Rather, it was a frank assessment of what he was doing. With the help of key thinkers he had identified the ideas which constituted a sound understanding of politics. Rather than write for academic specialists on some long-forgotten lacuna, he had decided to do something much more useful: inform the general public of these truths. This required him to speak and write for a popular audience. To scour Wilson's writings for groundbreaking original research is to not give credence to what Wilson himself hoped to accomplish. He set out to be and was more of an intelligent political editorialist, skillfully applying the ideas of innovative thinkers to present conditions. Without taking this approach and without a concerted effort aimed at reaching a popular audience, he never would have become president. His ideas, and by extension the ideas of his preferred political theorists, needed to gain currency with the public if he was to fulfill his life's mission.

The political thinkers whom Wilson patronized were ones that he deemed uncommon, in that they were practical rather than theoretical. Wilson explained to an interviewer in 1903 that "the philosopher was inclined to rationalize—to take his premise and then build up his theory, rather than to take his facts and make a generalisation." This produced a fatal tendency to overreach. In his address celebrating the centennial of Lincoln's birth he followed up his favorable assessment of Lincoln by saying that "the man who insists upon his theory insists that there is a way to the North Star, and I know, and every one knows that there is not—at least none yet discovered."[17] In public talks Wilson repeatedly offered the opinion that theories were too simple to be of use in a world that was very complex. Theories relied on rational thought. Political development was not rational. No matter how much anyone tried to make it rational, it could not be made so. To the New York City High School Teachers' Association Wilson related that "there is one sentence with which I always open my classes, a sentence quoted from Burke, in my opinion the only entirely wise writer upon public affairs in the English language. Burke says 'Institutions must be adjusted to human nature; of which reason constitutes a part, but by no means the principal part.'"[18]

Practical thinkers like Burke made generalizations, of course. But their generalizations were different. Their generalizations were not based on abstract premises; they were based on lived facts. They sprang from experience gained in particular contexts. Practical thinkers avoided assuming that what was learned in one context could be applied to others. The political philosophers Wilson included among those he admired and knew in greater detail than others are readily identified, because among his papers are lectures on them, lists of suggested readings which include their works, and frequent commentary about them.

In 1895 Wilson was asked to deliver a six-part lecture series in Brooklyn by the American Society for the Extension of University Teaching. He titled his series "Great Leaders of Political Thought." Wilson's selection of thinkers is instructive. He chose individuals with whom he most agreed. This being the case, the thinkers shared a good deal in common with each other. The six "great leaders of political thought" that Wilson lectured on were Aristotle, Niccolo Machiavelli, Baron de Montesquieu, Edmund Burke, Alexis de Tocqueville, and Walter Bagehot. The texts of these lectures have not been preserved, but newspaper accounts do exist. They indicate that Wilson borrowed heavily from his own previous lectures and that the content of these six talks was significantly more biographical than philosophical. Franklin William Hooper, who commissioned the lectures, was surprised by the paucity of philosophical content in them. Midway through the series he offended Wilson by noting the series' lack of intellectual rigor. In an otherwise apologetic letter, Hooper maintained that the lectures were "in my judgment addressed to a more popular audience than I had hoped they would be."[19] Hooper expected Wilson to be what he was not—a deep analyst of political theory.

With Hooper's assurance that the content of the lectures was to be solely determined by their deliverer, Wilson continued to focus on the personal side of his subjects in the remaining lectures. He could hardly have done otherwise. He had selected a group among whom interesting contrasts could be drawn, but only if one were truly versed in and devoted to the intricacies of political theory. This was not Wilson's interest. In between commenting on these figures' family lives, their travels, their friends, and their occupations, Wilson did what he intended: he elucidated certain key themes and ideas to the public—the themes and ideas shared by these six thinkers.

Each of these six theorists used an inductive method of analysis, gathering facts from history, often across political contexts, in order to draw more general conclusions. They each viewed politics as a natural extension of the society from which it sprang, dependent on its particular social character and its own unique public opinion. They resisted the temptation to advocate their preferred arrangements universally, recognizing that politics was not prone to rational construction but was fitted uniquely to each individual polity. They each focused on the dynamics of political change, with most stressing that positive changes in politics tend to be gradual.[20] Viewed in these broad terms, the political ideas of these six men reinforced each other and reinforced what Wilson had learned from his adolescence onward. Far from being deterred by Franklin Hooper's criticism, Wilson repeated this series in Tarrytown, New York, and Lancaster, Pennsylvania, in late 1895 and early 1896 without making any major changes.

Wilson took the writings of each of these six as independent confirmation that he had discovered the most important truths about politics. In reality, the relationship between these thinkers and the other sources from which Wilson learned was intellectually incestuous. To a significant extent, their ideas were similar because the later individuals had read and admired the earlier thinkers in the set. Wilson's approach to political theory was thus quite narrow, centering around relatively few thinkers, who had learned from each other. The Princeton professor did not read political theory to challenge his own views. He rarely even referred to any political theorists outside of this slim pantheon of six authors. Though he did not think of his efforts in these terms, when Woodrow Wilson read political theory, he desired to reinforce views he already held. Yet these six also had disagreements—disagreements that were masked by the substantial amount of agreement between them. Among these differences was an unresolved tension between Burke's observation that regimes advanced by a gradual organic evolution and Bagehot's hope that a polity would produce eloquent orators who would exert positive leadership.

Despite Wilson's ambivalence about most political theory, the discipline was particularly attractive to him because of one of its native attributes— its tendency to critique society as a whole. Before going to graduate school at Johns Hopkins, Wilson had attended law school at the University of Virginia and had practiced law for a year in Atlanta. The minutiae of case law were tedious and unsatisfying to him.[21] Winning cases did not satisfy his vaulting ambition. They were only small, private victories. He wanted to broaden his focus. His ambition was to figure out what made societies work well and then apply that knowledge to his own society. He had chosen law merely as the logical means of entry into politics, but the law was so tedious to him that he decided he had to find another way. Academia allowed him to take broad, ambitious cuts at society in his writing. Political theory offered many society-encompassing critiques. Though Wilson thought many of these critiques were defective, he would not abandon encompassing critiques altogether. Rather, he would find the *right* encompassing critique. Political theory indulged his natural penchant to think big.[22]

In lecture halls Wilson's skillful oratory won many converts. Scores of Princeton students thought of him as their best professor. As a teacher, Wilson was living out his own ideal of a leader who popularized the truths of political thought. His ambitious regimen of public lectures and his books soon helped him to become known outside of academia. While Wilson was president of Princeton, his political ambitions were stoked again and he felt that if the country were to hear his voice, its politics would be greatly improved. Like John Adams, Woodrow Wilson conceived of himself as a "translator" or popularizer of a correct political theory. He would not be its primary author, but he would publicize its valuable ideas and apply them in the political arena. These efforts were not impaired in the least by the fact that his analytical powers were relatively meager or that he looked past the finer points of all but a handful of political philosophers.

In fact, Wilson's willful ignorance of most political theorists helped him to create a useful narrative about himself. It was then, as it is now, unusual for an academic to enter politics. The era's kingmakers and average voters alike could be expected to have qualms about whether this transition could be made successfully. Could an academic, even a very successful one, succeed in high office, or would he be an impractical failure? Wilson understood their worries. In his standard lecture on Walter Bagehot, first delivered in the late 1880s, Wilson acknowledged that "practical politicians are wont to regard closeted writers upon politics with a certain condescension . . . dashed with slight traces of apprehension—or at least uneasy concern." Instead of countering this stereotype, Wilson embraced it, asserting, "Most fellows who live in libraries know little enough. . . . things are for the most part very simple in books—and in practical life very complex."[23] If Wilson were to make the unusual leap from academia to the White House, he would have to be an unusually perceptive academic. By publicly marking off other academics as impractical simpletons, Wilson gave himself a unique kind of credibility: he was more practical than they were—he had been able to buck the tendency to think like his fellow professors. Wilson not only gained his orientation to politics from political theory, he used his approach toward it to set himself up as a possible candidate for high office. In judging almost the whole tradition of political philosophy as unworthy of knowing, and in marking out other academics as impractical, he made the case for himself as an informed and practical "literary politician" who was worthy of people's confidence.

"I Want to Proclaim Myself . . . a Disciple of Edmund Burke"

April 27, 1912, was an unusual day in presidential history. Woodrow Wilson, who had spent less than two years as governor of New Jersey, was campaigning for the Democratic nomination for president, and having a candidate campaign for himself was still atypical. William Jennings Bryan had stumped for votes in 1896, but it was the campaign of 1912 more than any other which would change the old norm of "the office seeking the man" and usher in a new norm of presidential candidates actively seeking votes and offering their ideas to audiences. With the voluble Theodore Roosevelt and the fiery Socialist Eugene V. Debs in the race with the rhetorically oriented former professor, a new way to conduct campaigns was minted. But that April day in Boston was also unusual because of what Wilson said. In an almost unprecedented gambit in the annals of presidential campaign speeches, Wilson attempted to impress his audience by referencing a political theorist. He told the crowd, "I want to proclaim myself here tonight a disciple of Edmund Burke, who was opposed to all ambitious programmes on the principle that no man, no group of men, can take a piece of paper and reconstruct society."[24] Wilson knew himself. He *was* a disciple of Edmund Burke. No other president's political thought ever owed so much to a single individual.

In his writings and speeches Wilson repeatedly relied on a metaphor to describe nation-states, asserting that they are living "organic" entities. "Organicism" implied several different things to Wilson. First, each state is unique, like an individual—fundamentally different from every other state. Also, like living beings, each state constantly develops and changes. Typically these changes are so gradual that they are imperceptible to the casual observer. And just as a puppy does not turn into a goldfish, political change has a natural progression or logic of its own. Change occurs naturally, within a tradition, a tradition which prefigures the changes which will work and those which will not. A nation's traditions and its constituent parts—its individuals, its public opinion, its government institutions, and its informal arrangements—are inextricably linked and should work in harmony. This is Burkean theory in a nutshell. The organism metaphor is not Burke's, but it represents his thinking well and it was used by later Burkeans like Bagehot, as well as many other nineteenth-century thinkers.[25]

Wilson made these points repeatedly in a variety of writings. In *The State,* for instance, he titled one chapter "Society an Organism, Government an Organ."[26] The organs of a society must work toward shared purposes or the society is in trouble. In *Constitutional Government* he maintained that "it is difficult to describe any part of a great governmental system without describing the whole of it. Governments are living things and operate as organic wholes. Moreover, governments have their natural evolution and are one thing in one age, and another in another." In his standard lecture on Burke, Wilson related that "governments have never been successfully and permanently changed except by slow modification operating from generation to generation."[27] In the speech at Boston, Wilson employed Burkean organicism to criticize Socialists, who aimed to take a piece of paper (perhaps *Das Kapital* or *The Communist Manifesto*) and reconstruct society.

In *Reflections on the Revolution in France,* Burke had unleashed a devastating indictment of the French Revolution. Writing years before the Reign of Terror, he predicted that the movement was bound to fail because it attempted to change too much too quickly. To achieve "liberty, equality, and fraternity" the French revolutionaries hoped to set the influence of the Catholic Church, the monarchy, and the landed aristocracy at zero. To Burke the arrogance of these revolutionaries was appalling. These institutions had been the pillars of French society for centuries. No one could make the world over. No one could even make a nation over again with a plan produced on paper. Wilson heartily concurred, even campaigning on the issue.

Burke, Bagehot, and Wilson each strenuously opposed social contractarianism. This was not for its suggestion that there should be a mutual understanding forged between a people and its government. On the contrary, public opinion and government should be and normally are tightly linked. What they objected to was the contractarians' faith that they could rationally direct wholesale changes in government. To them, no successful society was built using the blueprint of a political philosopher. A society worked because its people had developed common habits and prejudices, and these habits and prejudices were reflected in their government. Contractarians attempted to exchange these habits for rationally chosen alternatives. The more radical of them, like Thomas Jefferson, wished to whisk away *all* habits and prejudices. This was an impossibility, of course, and the attempt itself would be dangerous. Even the United States was built around traditions. Wilson pointed out that "our own approval of the government under which we live, though doubtless conscious and in a way voluntary, is largely hereditary—is largely an inbred and inculcated approbation."[28]

Burke recognized that reforms are necessary—he had asserted that "a state without the means of some change is without the means of its conservation," but the key is to reform to preserve or to extend an already accepted tradition. This sentiment is echoed in Wilson's concluding sentence in *The State:* "The method of political development is conservative adaptation, shaping old habits into new ones, modifying old means to accomplish new ends."[29]

Most of these Burkean ideas had been repeated by Walter Bagehot, but Bagehot had added material to Burke which Wilson adopted. Burke's ideas on leadership had focused on the negative—leaders should refrain from offering ambitious, wide-ranging reforms. Bagehot aimed to say something more positive. He focused on what a leader should do. Leaders were to play a vital role in shaping public opinion. To be effective, a leader had to work within the prejudices which prevailed in a nation, but in doing so the leader could direct the people toward significant beneficial reforms. Bagehot wrote approvingly of the "oratorical statesman" who could simultaneously pay homage to tradition and push for progressive change through his words.

Unlike Burke, Bagehot was not content to endorse tradition. In fact, he found the practices of "primitive" societies problematic. Bagehot concluded that advanced societies are distinguished from primitive societies by the degree to which culturally predetermined views hold sway. In primitive societies cultural norms control almost all behavior. In advanced societies many matters are not culturally predetermined. They are open to political discussion. The greater degree of open-mindedness in advanced cultures allows "government by discussion" to take place. Authoritative decisions are made on the basis of these discussions, as in the British House of Commons. The more advanced a society, the more matters would be open for debate. In the most advanced societies, a great deal is up for discussion, yielding a substantial opening for positive leadership. These advanced societies are more successful than others because they are able to combine a devotion to custom, which brings stability, with innovation, which brings progress. In addition to his praise for the British system in this regard, Bagehot had commented that the American separation of powers did not facilitate valuable discussions. Wilson wrote this idea into *Congressional Government.*[30]

Wilson was never inclined toward cultural relativism. He was devoted to both democracy and Christianity. Bagehot's views served to justify the concept of the superiority of "Aryan" governments—the unfortunate label Wilson used for this type of regime in *The State.* Bagehot's thinking also suggested the superiority of the British government's practices over those of the United States, the idea that helped Wilson to become famous. *Congressional Government* touted the advantages of reforms which would encourage debate and facilitate leadership in American government. Wilson's early writings express frustration that there is no room for an "oratorical statesman" to coordinate activity in the United States. From where would such a person lead? From the (then) pitifully weak presidency? from the Senate? from the House? Throughout his academic career Wilson stressed that the Congress and the president should work together more closely to provide an opening to leadership. Bagehot's critique of the United States and his admiration for the British system, with its prime minister at the head of the House of Commons, was Wilson's direct inspiration.

While Wilson had mixed feelings about Alexis de Tocqueville, he nonetheless internalized a number of the latter's views. Like Burke, Tocqueville had recognized that a nation's "habits of the heart" define its life more than any formal constitutional structure. Constitutions are a product of a nation's habits. Tocqueville departed from Burke and Bagehot in his assessment of democracy. In both *Democracy in America* and *The Ancien Régime and the Revolution,* Tocqueville gave democracy his qualified endorsement. To him democracy was a gradual but inevitable international trend, whose origins stretched back at least seven centuries.[31] Wilson believed this too. The French thinker's description of democracy as a gradual, centuries-long development brought about more by happenstance than by a rational plan appealed to Wilson because it allowed him to embrace democracy without turning his back on Burke or Bagehot.[32] Tocqueville presented a conservative-friendly version of democracy: though democracy had great advantages, he stressed that it could not be pursued willynilly. Its development had to be gradual to be sustained, and checks on its unfortunate tendencies were vital. Wilson concurred, also accepting a key Tocquevillian concept: that a zeal for equality might destroy liberty.

Wilson's lecture on Tocqueville praised him for providing an argument against fanatical democracy, for quieting the fears of those who were afraid of democracy, and for "showing the solid qualities prerequisite to its successful establishment."[33]

The idea that a nation possesses an animating spirit, that its institutions are an outgrowth of its character, is not particular to Burke, Bagehot, and Tocqueville. Before them the idea was a pet theory of Montesquieu's. Montesquieu stressed that the animating spirit in republics is different from that in aristocracies or monarchies. Montesquieu's understanding that a nation's government and laws are an outgrowth of its spirit reinforced Wilson's conviction that the aforementioned thinkers were correct. Like Madison, Wilson lamented that so many Americans misunderstood Montesquieu's call for a separation of powers, as if he had called for the various branches of government to be "isolated island[s] of jealous power."[34] Wilson favorably referenced Madison's Federalist No. 47 to make the point that the branches of government can work together without violating Montesquieu's precepts. Good government requires such cooperation.

The earliest "realist" that Wilson admired was Aristotle. Wilson quoted him frequently, while at the same time understanding that their perspectives were very different in many ways. Aristotle was a kind of social scientist who collected "data" on every polity that he could. He was committed to understanding politics through comparative analysis. Wilson, though he did not engage in data collection himself, was also committed to understanding politics through comparative analysis. In his 1891 lecture titled "The Study of Politics," Wilson said that "to study one government alone is to understand none at all."[35] He could not have drawn general conclusions about organicism without knowing what had occurred in a variety of societies. Just as it is today, it was unusual in Wilson's time for a scholar of American politics to issue a comparative politics textbook, as he did with *The State*. The book shows that he wished to develop a comprehensive knowledge of politics in order to realize his ultimate goal of writing "The Philosophy of Politics." Comparative analysis also has the advantage of giving due credence to each state as a unique organic entity.

Wilson used Aristotle to pithily dismiss other theories. Instead of positing a hypothetical state of nature, or setting out the ideal of a philosopher-king, Aristotle had simply written that "man is by nature a political animal," which Wilson quoted in *The State*.[36] This statement cut through the fanciful abstractions which had been offered by others. In a practical sense, humans are inevitably shaped by their own communities, and in those communities each political animal needs to reconcile with the other political animals. Aristotle believed the best way of doing this was in a mixed constitution. As we have seen in earlier chapters, this was an idea reiterated by many subsequent thinkers. Wilson was committed to democracy rather than the mixed constitution. However, he squarely acknowledged the necessity of accommodating interests to produce a "common good." Humans possess self-interest. The aim of politics should be to temper that self-interest for the good of all. As he put it in a 1908 speech to business leaders in Chicago, "If you want to save this country . . . forget your own interests and think awhile on the public interest."[37] Wilson's speeches are filled with earnest calls to subordinate selfish interests to the public interest, a characteristically republican view stretching back at least to Aristotle.

Wilson's contact with contemporary academics also shaped his thinking. The editors of *The Papers of Woodrow Wilson* state that while in graduate school "at the Johns Hopkins . . . [Wilson] had absorbed both [Professor] Herbert Baxter Adams's and [Professor] Richard T. Ely's disdain for theoretical and general historical, political, and economic writing unsupported by evidence, and their emphasis on the origins and organic evolutionary development of institutions."[38] Adams was known for his "germ theory" of institutional development, which posits that American institutions originated with European institutions but that they had gradually diverged from them by slow, organic growth.[39] While Adams's training had been in Germany, these views were sufficiently reminiscent of Burke and Bagehot to harmonize with Wilson's outlook. Even though the main contours of Wilson's political thought were essentially set by the end of graduate school, fellow political science professors also contributed to his understanding. The writings of Henry Jones Ford and James Bryce in particular convinced Wilson that there was significant leadership potential in the presidency, without the need to resort to the constitutional amendments he had suggested in *Congressional Government*.[40] Frederick Jackson Turner, who had been a fellow student at Johns Hopkins, convinced Wilson of the significance the frontier played in American development and that its closure represented a new era in American political life.

Wilson was far more interested in social and institutional dynamics than in economic theory or international relations. However, he was impressed by the ideas of a variety of thinkers who welded these two subjects together, like Adam Smith, John Stuart Mill, and John Bright, who had been a member of Parliament. They had touted the benefits of international trade, not just because it would increase wealth, but also because it would increase understanding across national borders. Walter Bagehot had stressed the benefits of increased international contact too, but these economic theorists had explored the issue from a different angle. It was a common belief of nineteenth-century liberals that as democratic institutions spread throughout the world and as trade and commerce drew nations together, the peoples of the world would gradually acquire a better knowledge of their naturally harmonious interests and would become increasingly willing to act in accordance with them, until eventually . . . all nations would observe the same standards of reasonableness and good will.[41]

Thus it was that Wilson favored lowered tariffs, a position which had always been favored by southerners who wished to trade their agricultural commodities abroad. Wilson's reasoning was, however, based on something larger than the cash that trade would bring to his native region. He was convinced that increased trade would promote understanding among nations, resulting in less war, and democratizing improvements around the globe. There was a tension between this view and the conviction that each nation was a unique organic entity. Yet Wilson knew that Burke was a product of his own time—a time with significantly less international contact than in Wilson's time. Commercial ties between peoples would continue to grow, and this would produce political dividends in the form of development and democratization.

Those wondering what a Wilson presidency would bring could find substantial clues in his approach to and understanding of political theory. In domestic politics he could be expected to advocate the increased coordination of government institutions, to facilitate that coordination himself from the presidency, and to refrain from making radical policy proposals. In foreign policy he would favor free trade, democratization, and the autonomy of nations. There were recognizable tensions that he would have to work out in practice. It remained to be seen how Wilson would increase coordination of American politics from above without radically departing from long-accepted political practices. How he would exert substantial leadership without altering indigenous traditions, both at home and abroad, was an open question. And his promoting market economics and democratization abroad without meddling in the politics of other nations would be a challenge. These tensions would require choices that Professor Wilson had not yet made, but his varied borrowings from political theory had given him great confidence that he understood politics as well as anyone. In the words of Robert Alexander Kraig, "Woodrow Wilson came to the presidency with more intellectual preparation than anyone since John Quincy Adams."[42] While he had scrupulously avoided deep consideration of specific issues, he had very much lived out his own ideal. In short, by 1912 he had gained knowledge to wield power as America's literary statesman.

Making the World Safe for Burkean Gradualism

Wilson's presidency was the most active to its time, with the exception of Lincoln's. The federal government of 1913 did much more than the federal government of 1813, offering many more opportunities for Wilson to put his worldview into practice than his early counterparts had. Wilson's vaulting ambition also ensured that the federal government would do much more in 1921 than it had when he took the oath of office just eight years earlier. This is a rather curious record for one who had so assiduously labeled himself a conservative throughout his academic career. In domestic politics Wilson reversed his stance on regulations and regulatory commissions. Having complained of them as a step toward socialism as late as his gubernatorial race of 1910, he endorsed many of them as governor and as president. Any explanation of how Wilson's ideals contributed to his policies must also address apparent contradictions in foreign policy. Why did this champion of the self-determination of nations order more incursions into foreign territory than any other president ever had? How could a committed Burkean lead a crusade for a wholly unprecedented collective security apparatus in the form of the League of Nations? Wilson had answers to these questions. His answers are not entirely satisfying, but they do teach us about the relationship presidents may forge between the theory of politics and its practice.

Wilson's understanding of politics centered around institutional dynamics, leadership, and political development, not policy. Even as he made the transition to elective politics, his ideas about what policies to endorse were ill formed. The leaders of New Jersey's Democratic Party machine who recruited him to run for governor knew about this fuzziness, and privately they celebrated it. Wilson's professions that he opposed regulation suited them just fine.[43] If the governor did not know the issues, so much the better—this ignorance would help him follow his limited-government principles. But as Wilson applied himself to the governorship, he found that inaction simply would not do, because inaction favored the wealthy. To be true to his value that a statesman must adjust policies away from particular interests and toward the common good, Wilson became a "progressive," to the surprise of New Jersey's Democratic Party leaders.

The story of Wilson's political journey from 1908 to 1913 is a complicated one that we will never fully understand. At the very least, however, it is clear that Wilson did not believe that he betrayed his own principles in taking a progressive turn.[44] Though Wilson had earlier emphasized his dislike of regulation, even suggesting that it was contrary to the American spirit, his Burkeanism had never been in service of a "stand pat" conservatism.

He always knew that the statesman who would conserve a tradition had to look for and endorse reforms. The New Jersey bosses had not scoured his writings sufficiently to understand this side of Wilson's political thought. Nor, apparently, had they found out how much of an emphasis he placed on using executive leadership to promote the common good. For his own part, Wilson had not discouraged their misunderstanding of him when the possibility of his attaining high political office was at stake. He accepted the gubernatorial nomination provided he would have a free hand to act as he saw fit. That Wilson exacted this promise from party leaders in New Jersey indicates that he was already contemplating moves of which they would not approve. With a clear conscience Governor Wilson proceeded to disappoint them by borrowing much of the progressive agenda that had already been implemented in Wisconsin, Oregon, and California.

As we have seen in his Boston speech, during the 1912 campaign for president Wilson did not hide his connection to political theory. Of that contest John Milton Cooper notes that "for the only time except perhaps for Jefferson's first election in 1800, a presidential campaign aired questions that verged on political philosophy."[45] Wilson's speeches typically did not refer to Burke, Bagehot, or any other theorist, however. The practicing statesman was under no obligation to lay bare all the internal gears of his machine. What he did stress was the importance of embracing reform to safeguard democratic rule. In 1912, Wilson judged the United States to be at a point where substantial reforms were required to preserve the American tradition. By thinking himself placed at a particularly critical point in time, Wilson was able to reconcile to his own satisfaction Burke's organicism with Bagehot's emphasis on active leadership. American politics was in a position where the president had to lead a substantial reform movement to preserve the American tradition of democratic rule for the common good. Wilson's election reinforced his sense that he was the spokesman for and guardian of the American spirit.

When pressed, President Wilson acknowledged that his political thought required him to adjust to developing circumstances. In a 1916 meeting with a group which disliked increased military preparedness, Wilson responded in a revealing manner: "I think in such affairs as we are now discussing, the circumstances *are* the logic. I remember a sentence of Burke which was something to the effect, 'if you ask me wherein the wisdom of a certain policy consists, I will say that it consists of the circumstances.'" *Saturday Evening Post* correspondent Samuel G. Blythe reported that in an extended interview Wilson "showed me why a writer was wrong who said he could not be a progressive Democrat if he admired Edmund Burke, and explained his liking for Burke and quoted much from Burke's orations."[46]

Unfortunately, Blythe did not get more specific, but Wilson likely repeated the "reform to preserve" mantra to the reporter. In general, Wilson concluded of the presidency that its "chief advantage . . . is that you can get a hearing for things you have thought all your life." Though many others have not seen it this way, Wilson felt that he was true to his long-standing principles as president, "endeavoring to coordinate political theory and practice in order to improve the health of the polity."[47]

On a range of policies, but particularly in labor relations, Wilson's reform efforts were directed at righting the balance between the interests of labor and capital. He would have preferred to see the captains of industry acting responsibly without government prodding. They had the obligation to be "public men" committed to the common weal. If they would not make the common good their primary consideration, however, then it was the statesman's obligation to implement reforms which would allow capitalists to make profits while laborers made fair wages in safe conditions. For these reasons Wilson came to support progressive legislation which protected miners, seamen, and child laborers, despite having some qualms about their constitutionality. He also supported the establishment of the Federal Trade Commission to investigate unfair business practices and endorsed the prosecution of trusts. The sheer amount and scope of legislation advocated by Wilson in the area of labor relations might be enough by itself for some to think that the president was not a Burkean conservative. Significantly, this is not an assessment that Wilson entertained. He believed he was reforming to preserve a state dedicated to democratic principles and the common good.

Wilson advocated the reduction of tariffs and succeeded in having Congress enact them in his first weeks as president. Besides bringing the benefit of increased trade and prosperity, the reduction of tariffs would increase competition. This would, Wilson believed, blunt the damage done by domestic monopolies—a reform well within the American spirit. Even the Federal Reserve Act was understood as an effort to balance the interests of corporations and average individuals in a way which served the common good. A central bank would help to ease credit, aiding middle-class Americans who had been harmed by the tight credit policies of the private banking system.[48] Almost all of these economic measures became law in a form very close to Wilson's wish. As suggested by William Diamond in his *Economic Thought of Woodrow Wilson,* "what the student had learned and the professor had thought and taught, the President tried to practice," even if it meant getting more comfortable with regulation than he had been before he was a politician.[49] Wilson proudly announced that these efforts reclaimed the American democracy for its people. Privately these policies satisfied his Burkean impulse to preserve the American tradition, his Bagehot-inspired desire to lead, and his republican devotion to the common good.

In foreign policy, Wilson was filled with good, if self-righteous, intentions. In the Americas he was determined to depart from the heavy-handed gunboat diplomacy which had been used to appropriate the Canal Zone during Theodore Roosevelt's administration. Wilson floated the idea of a pan-American nonaggression treaty in 1913, but with Latin American nations wary of U.S. intentions, the proposal went nowhere. Wilson probably should have learned more from this rebuff than he did. However, even without the treaty, Wilson hoped to promote goodwill in the hemisphere, along with democracy and stability. The pursuit of all three simultaneously would prove impossible.

A 1913 coup in Mexico brought Victoriano Huerta to power, and he proceeded to dissolve the Mexican legislature in an attempt to exert dictatorial power. Wilson's diplomatic efforts to mediate a return to constitutional rule failed, and he subsequently sent American naval forces to the vicinity of Veracruz, "the main entry point for arms shipments to Huerta."[50] An affront, the detention of several Americans by Huerta's men, led to a battle for the city of Veracruz. The Americans won the battle and occupied Veracruz, and Huerta was soon deposed.

This incursion was not a development foreseen or wished for by Wilson. Nevertheless, he was the one who made the decision to send troops into a foreign land. His justifications were several: Huerta had seized power illegally; the detained military personnel had been taken in violation of international law; and absent intervention, Mexico as a whole faced civil war. Wilson went to great pains to deny that he sent in the troops to appropriate territory or smooth the way for corporations to exploit Mexican resources. He pledged the same things in 1916, when 10,000 troops were ordered into northern Mexico to catch General Pancho Villa, who had raided a town in New Mexico.

Wilson saw no contradiction between these actions and his political thought. This was not colonization, which Burke and Wilson explicitly objected to. Nor was it a war of conquest or an act of aggression. Because Wilson felt the United States had no selfish motives and the incursions were small, he was convinced that he was respecting Mexican sovereignty and the ability of its people to determine their own course.[51] In the aforementioned interview with Samuel Blythe, the president stressed the Burkean point that the Mexican people would have to build their own institutions from the bottom up. He would not impose a government on them. He compared Mexico to France at the time of its revolution. To Wilson this meant that the traditional order had been torn asunder. "The old order is dead," he said. The United States was allowing the Mexican people to reestablish a republican tradition "which shall have its foundation on human liberty and human rights."[52]

It may have been presumptuous of Wilson to set these goals for Mexico. Certainly many of the Mexican people felt Wilson was meddling in their affairs. With good reason they might have pointed out that in sending troops into Mexico, Wilson had contradicted his Burkeanism. But again, this is not how Wilson understood himself. To this charge Wilson would protest that his administration's actions were nothing like what the British had done in India or what they had done in the American colonies, for that matter. He proceeded on the assumption that if Burke could have removed the French revolutionaries from their position of power in 1789, he would have done so. Think of how much anguish France would have been spared if their violent revolution had not been allowed to move forward. Wilson was removing the Mexican equivalent of the French revolutionaries in both 1913 and 1916, allowing the Mexican people to try their hand at restoring their own indigenous government, consonant with their institutional traditions.

Bagehot had stressed that increased international contact would be good for "primitive" governments because they could develop more quickly into deliberative regimes which reflected open-minded public opinion. As long as the United States did not set up a government for the Mexicans, Wilson felt he could aid them in fostering political development. By exerting leadership while allowing Mexicans to determine their own course, he felt he had been true to both Burke and Bagehot. In encouraging them to adopt a democratic form, Wilson was also being true to his commitment to democracy.

But Wilson's self-justifications only go so far. This was a serious misstep for one who acknowledged the primacy of public opinion and supposedly respected the indigenous views of each nation's populace. Wilson should have better understood the Mexicans as they understood themselves. A Burkean conducting foreign policy owes other nations no less.[53] Wilson also sent troops to Haiti and the Dominican Republic to restore order in chaotic situations. As with Mexico, in these situations he felt that he was giving these nations a chance to reestablish indigenous traditions at a time when their own political traditions were being torn asunder. Temporarily, American troops did bring stability to these island nations, but intervention failed to produce sustained democracy. Nor did it produce gratitude among their people. As in Mexico, "benevolent motives . . . tempted the Americans to intervene where they were not wanted and where they did not understand the situation."[54] The tension between active international leadership favoring democracy and national self-determination seemed to be resolved by Wilson in a way that favored leadership.

The most significant foreign policy event which occurred during Wilson's administration was American entry into World War I. After keeping a tenuous neutrality for nearly three years, the United States fought in order that the world "be made safe for democracy." At the heart of Wilson's thinking both in staying out of the war and later in entering it was the eventual establishment of an international collective security apparatus. Wilson proposed a "league of nations" which would ensure the territorial integrity of nation-states even before American entry into the war. The phrase "league of nations" was not Wilson's. It was coined by a Cambridge University classicist named Goldsworthy Lowes Dickinson, who published an article in a late 1914 issue of *Atlantic Monthly* titled "The War and the Way Out." Thomas J. Knock relates that the article "had enormous intellectual and moral appeal" to Wilson.[55] In 1919 the president worked tirelessly to establish the League of Nations and to ensure that it would arbitrate international disputes. As a last resort, it would guarantee the territorial integrity of member nations against foreign aggression. But how could such an unprecedented global institution doing such unprecedented things be squared with Wilson's professed nation-state-respecting conservative gradualism?

The answer is that to Wilson, collective security was a way to guarantee that political development in each nation-state could proceed unmolested by outside forces. In other words, the League of Nations would allow each nation's organic growth to proceed undisturbed. In a January 1917 address to the Senate on future terms for peace, Wilson proclaimed, "I am proposing, as it were, that the nations should with one accord adopt the doctrine . . . that no nation should seek to extend its polity over any other nation or people, but that every people should be left free to determine its own polity, its own way of development, unhindered, unthreatened, unafraid, the little along with the powerful."[56] In Wilson's mind, the absence of a League of Nations allowed states to interfere in each other's domestic politics, disrupting their organic growth. The League would prohibit that interference.

This understanding was predicated on two big assumptions. The first was that the League could actually prevent nations from meddling in the domestic politics of other nations, even as the transfer of goods and people across borders accelerated. The second was that the League itself would be a neutral force, not affecting the domestic politics of states in any way. It was as if Wilson believed that this new institution could be at once very powerful but also "politics-less," effectively leaving all internal decisions to sovereign nations. Wilson expressed this idea in the conclusion of his Senate address: "I am proposing that all nations henceforth avoid entangling alliances which would draw them into competitions of power, catch them in a net of intrigue and selfish rivalry, and disturb their own affairs with influences intruded from without. There is no entangling alliance in a concert of power."[57]

Stunningly, Wilson conceived of the abrupt adoption of an international security institution, an unprecedented global action, as a way to make the world safe for Burkean gradualism in each individual state. If each state could be guaranteed that outside powers would not control its domestic institutions, then Wilson's hopes for progress toward self-government could be realized in many more states. His efforts from 1917 to 1919 were not a repudiation of his Burkean ideals but a quixotic quest to fulfill them, pursued concurrently with the hope for gradual democratization that he shared with Tocqueville and Bagehot.

Wilson's application of theory to practice in the area of institutional dynamics is more straightforward than his odd Burkean internationalism. He significantly altered the relationship between the presidency and Congress by serving as an active coordinator of his party's activities in both houses. On April 8, 1913, Wilson became the first president since John Adams to address Congress in person. In a short speech delivered to a special session that Wilson convened to pursue economic reforms, he began by saying,

> I am very glad indeed to have this opportunity to address the two Houses directly, and to verify for myself the impression that the President of the United States is a person, not a mere department of the Government hailing Congress from some isolated island of jealous power . . . that he is a human being trying to co-operate with other human beings in a common service.[58]

In total, Wilson addressed Congress directly twenty-seven times, more than any other president. These speeches were covered extensively in the press and served to concentrate public attention on the president's agenda and on his preferred solutions. Though his speaking style was usually understated and the addresses short, Wilson was acting like his parliamentary heroes, Prime Ministers Gladstone and Pitt. More to the point, he was living out Bagehot's ideal of the "oratorical statesman," who would lead "government by debate." In so doing he "recreate[d] the presidency in a way that permanently changed the character of the institution" and permanently changed interbranch relations to something much closer to his ideal than American practice had previously seemed to allow.[59]

Wilson also served as his own legislative liaison, actively lobbying members of Congress in a way that no president had done before. He came to Capitol Hill even when not scheduled to deliver a formal address, becoming the first president since Lincoln to use the President's Room in the Capitol. As Daniel Stid describes it,

> At the Capitol, the White House, and over the direct phone line that Wilson had installed between the two buildings, the president was continually conferring with legislators, working with the Democratic committee chairs and floor leaders . . . marshalling a consensus among the various factions of his party, and buttonholing undecided Democrats before key votes.[60]

Before the disastrous midterm election of 1918, Wilson consistently succeeded in maintaining Democratic unity to pass legislation. These were self-conscious attempts to get the American system to function in a more coordinated manner, the ideal he had learned from Bagehot and which he had written about for thirty years. It was an audacious project—one that not even his ambitious and hyperactive predecessor Theodore Roosevelt could conceive of. The effort was predicated on his Burkean understanding that no nation's constitution is static and the relationship between a nation's institutions is not fully defined on paper.

On the occasions when Wilson's proposals were stymied in Congress, he turned to the American people for support. The most famous of these appeals was his western trip to argue in favor of the League of Nations. This effort ended in tragedy, with Wilson's physical collapse and subsequent stroke. In preceding years speaking directly to citizens had worked for the president. These efforts acknowledged public opinion as the mainspring of a nation's politics, the idea emphasized in his "Great Leaders of Political Thought" series. Wilson's actions showed that he believed public opinion could be substantially driven from above. This "top-down" dynamic is reminiscent of Bagehot and Machiavelli rather than of Tocqueville and Burke. Even so, Wilson convinced himself that he was leading the public to embrace the reforms which would safeguard traditional values. In the process, he made "Americans think of the White House as the center of government more than they had ever before."[61]

The last two years of Wilson's presidency were marred by the tragedy of severe illness. New initiatives in government were on hold after the president suffered a massive stroke on October 2, 1919. The stroke affected Wilson's mind as much as it did his body. A loss of recall, irritability, increased stubbornness, and an inability to reason abstractly were evident to

those allowed to see the president. To the last, Wilson continued to quote
Burke and Bagehot, and kept recommending that people read them and
follow their advice.[62] However, these were only the vestiges of his former
political thought. The higher brain functions required to pursue political thought in practice had essentially collapsed. In the commentary on
Wilson's illness written by Dr. Bert E. Park, M.D., in *The Papers of Woodrow
Wilson* is the assessment that the president was no longer able to deal in the
abstractions required to successfully pursue his own conception of the job.
Without the ability to think abstractly there is no political theory—even
for one who emphasizes its more practical side. In essence, a vital portion
of Wilson's person was gone after his stroke, and with it his distinctive
political thought, replaced by an encompassing self-righteous moralism.
Self-righteous moralism had always been a part of Wilson's worldview,
and tinges of this tendency were to be found in Bagehot, but his primary
influences in this regard did not come from political philosophy, but from
a combination of his proud Presbyterian heritage, the British tracts which
his father imported, and his deeply inculcated ethnic pride.[63]

Conclusion

Wilson's political thought was accompanied by a messianic sense of
self, an assumption of white/Anglo superiority, and an ethic of Christian
duty. These combined to convince him that his country's future and then
the world's salvation were dependent on the substantial reforms he envisioned. These attitudes make it tempting to apply Kendrick Clements's
assessment of Wilson's foreign policy to his entire presidency. Clements
argues that Wilson "was seduced by the possession of great power" into
abandoning his theoretical commitments to self-determination and the
evolutionary development of nations. "Ironically, his experience suggested
that his original analysis of the evolutionary nature of democracy, before
he experienced the great temptations of power, was more accurate than
his later opinions; the scholar was wiser than the statesman." Arthur Link
makes this same point more generally, contending that Wilson's "political
thought [after 1909] was so radically different from his earlier thought that
it must be considered apart and as a unit in itself."[64]

This thesis of a radical disjuncture in Wilson's political thought has the
distinct disadvantage of ignoring Wilson's own understanding of what he
was doing. Wilson did not conveniently ignore Burke while he was president. Nor did he downplay that thinker's influence on him. Instead he
insisted that he was acting like a good Burkean should. The president continued to use phrases and to voice thoughts characteristic of that particu-

lar brand of conservatism. That he did so raises important points about presidential political thought. First, political thought does not exert a pull on a president that is independent of one's personality or one's prejudices. Political thought works in combination with them to produce some tangible result. Wilson's background and his character made Burke appealing to him. His ambition and his attachment to other thinkers contributed to how he understood Burke. Other presidents committed to Burke would have acted differently. Wilson's Burkeanism was a particularly ambitious kind, focused on promoting democratizing reforms and self-government in all nations.

This is not to say that Wilson could shape Burke to the point of meaninglessness. However, it does raise a second point: when a political theorist is admired by a politician, that theorist's work is inevitably reshaped through interpretation and adaptation. Wilson was not simply applying Burke's principles to the "real world." He was applying his own understanding of Burke to the real world. Wilson did not lose his principles when he found himself in a position of power—rather he applied a unique interpretation of Burke when he found himself in a position of power. A case might be made that Wilson misunderstood Burke. Or the claim can be made that he was unwise in the ways he attempted to apply Burkean ideals to practice. The assertion that he left his principles behind in 1913 is much less defensible.

Third, despite his profession to be a disciple of Burke, Wilson incorporated into his political thought others' ideas which did not fit comfortably with Burke's. Burke was agnostic about the traditions of other nations. He would not judge them. Wilson was not agnostic about these things. Nor were the other thinkers he admired, like Bagehot, Tocqueville, and Aristotle. They each possessed a vision of what good government looks like. They hoped that other nations would come to embrace the form they endorsed. If Wilson could use his authority to be a catalyst for democracy and the politics of the common good, he would do so. In fact, he could not have admired Bagehot as much as he did without attempting to be an active leader. The criticisms of Clements and Link are predicated on the belief that Wilson was a unidimensional Burkean. Wilson himself may have given the impression that he was at times, but in reality he was not. He may have emphasized leadership (Bagehot) and democratization (Tocqueville and Bagehot) to the point that Burkean values became secondary. However, if he were not still steeped in Burkean values he might have used the provocative incidents that occurred between the United States and Mexico to start a full-scale war to appropriate territory. President Polk had done so. Wilson wanted to avoid the creation of an American empire because he knew from his reading of political theory that generally empires do not work. The understanding of politics that he developed through his acquaintance with Burke helped him to avoid that temptation at the very time the United States became a global superpower.

In a quest to understand how presidents apply political theory to practice, it is not enough to find that a president admired certain thinkers. We have to know the specific ideas adopted and how those thinkers' ideas were interpreted. Additionally, particular events induce reactions from a president which are logical but unexpected. This was the case with Wilson in both domestic and international settings. Simply noting that Wilson was a Burkean is not particularly helpful; examining what kind of Burkean he was and how he fit this "master's" ideas with the views of the other thinkers he admired is.

A familiar dichotomy of blame and praise played out in the public persona of Woodrow Wilson. His chosen profession and his bookish understanding of politics led his proponents to argue that he was particularly wise. James Bryce's observation about Wilson's prospects quoted at the end of Chapter 1 is a case in point. By contrast, Wilson's nemesis in 1912, Theodore Roosevelt, cast "aspersions on 'Professor Wilson' and his 'academic theories.' . . . Such imputations of impracticality . . . constituted the arrows most frequently flung against Wilson for the rest of Roosevelt's life."[65]

Academics, and political theorists in particular, are often accused of being out of touch. One might conclude from this that a devotion to political theory would make it harder to break into politics. Surprisingly, writing in this relatively abstract field aided Wilson's real-world ambitions. Instead of delving deeply into particular policies and commenting extensively on contemporary political figures, Wilson's theoretical approach granted him the luxury of distance that many others did not have. John Milton Cooper notes that Wilson "was a detached observer who, when he was nearly fifty, made his first foray into political engagement."[66] As a political theorist, Wilson had alienated few in the "real world." His vague reformist conservatism allowed him to tailor his message to appeal to a broad variety of individuals, influential and otherwise. The few people he had alienated in his professional life were professors. They were fairly easily caricatured as stodgy protectors of elitist privilege, a story which helped to burnish Wilson's own populist credentials. In 1912 conditions were right for a professor acquainted with political theory to become president. This career path will always be unlikely. But enough professors have been elected to Congress to prevent us from concluding that a political scientist could not be elected again. As I write, the United States has a former law professor as its president, after all, and one who has given serious consideration to political theory.

Chapter 6

Franklin Delano Roosevelt: A First-Class Trimmer

In the words of the great essayist, "the voice of events is proclaiming to us. Reform if you would preserve." I am that kind of conservative because I am that kind of liberal.

—Franklin Delano Roosevelt, campaign kickoff speech in Syracuse, September 29, 1936

Our first question is this: what makes for the greatest good of the greatest number?

—Franklin Delano Roosevelt, speech at Oklahoma City, July 9, 1938

At first blush it would seem that Franklin Delano Roosevelt would be a most unlikely case study for this subject. Famously pragmatic and not much of a reader of books, Roosevelt exhibited a lack of attraction to political theory that was palpable. In this respect he is the polar opposite of John Adams and James Madison. FDR also has a reputation as something of an intellectual slouch. He earned "gentlemen's C's" at Harvard College when it most fervently catered to a moneyed elite, and he complained to friends that none of his classes there had been interesting.[1] Nor did he distinguish himself as a scholar at Columbia Law School.

During his convalescence from polio, FDR tried his hand at writing, beginning several book projects only to have each of them stall in its initial stage. He began to write a book about American political history in 1924. In this, as in so many other things, he wanted to follow in the footsteps of his distant cousin Theodore, but he quickly learned that he could not replicate the elder Roosevelt's dogged determination with the written word. The project was abandoned while still in its first chapter.[2] It is no wonder that the scholarship on Roosevelt repeats Oliver Wendell Holmes Jr.'s half indictment over and over: FDR possessed a "second class intellect, but a first class temperament."[3]

Clearly Franklin Roosevelt used his temperament to great effect as president, but the evidence suggests that he also used his intellect in the way that is at issue here—the shape of his presidency was informed by political theory. His knowledge of political theory was sparse and his public display of it was very limited, but theoretical understandings of politics were indeed reflected in his rhetoric and in the way he dealt with public policy. Still, a wholesale reassessment of the thirty-second president is not in order. He *was* an indifferent student, he *did not* much enjoy reading books, he *was* highly pragmatic, and he *did* chafe at theories. However, none of this prevented FDR from finding and practicing his own chosen theory of politics. One need not have a first-class intelligence to gain something from political theory. Someone generally hostile toward political theory can still borrow from it and embrace certain axioms about politics. A politician can also find meaning in rejecting certain political theories. FDR did these things. His approach to political theory may have been different from Adams's and Madison's, but that doesn't make it any less real. In fact, for a practicing politician of the modern era, this casual, utilitarian approach is much more normal than making a study of political philosophy. Furthermore, among the presidents who have made some connection to political theory, it should be clear that there is no typical way of doing this.

Most commentators, even those who had a long and close association with Roosevelt, seem to be at a loss in explaining his decision making or his seemingly variable fealty to his stated commitments. "Pragmatic" is a word often used to describe Roosevelt—and this word is often used in an uncomplimentary fashion. To put it more bluntly, FDR seems inconsistent or insincere to many. His prolific biographer, Kenneth S. Davis, relates this frustration openly. Roosevelt always seemed to keep his options open, putting off making clear-cut, irrevocable decisions, and he seemed to enjoy being devious.[4] That there was a first New Deal and a second New Deal has become a widely accepted truism, a testament to FDR's flexibility but also to his lack of a master plan or a philosophy of governance.

Columbia professor Rexford G. Tugwell, one of the so-called Brains Trust advisers of the 1932 presidential run and later a prolific FDR commentator, was both fascinated and puzzled by his subject. Tugwell called Roosevelt a conservative at heart, but he also felt that the president wanted far more sweeping reforms than those he proposed to Congress. Another of these Brains Trusters, Raymond Moley, described FDR as only half pragmatic: he was very receptive to a wide variety of new ideas, but he was deficient in the skills of logic and judgment required to success-fully scrutinize their workability.[5] These assessments are representative of many others. FDR's progressive commitments—to internationalism, to democracy, to human rights, and to economic security—are not hard to identify or even difficult to line up behind. But those who value these things also tend to be frustrated by this president's seemingly highly vari-able pursuit of them.

The first FDR quote in the epigraphs above offers as much of an expla-nation for this vexing quality as the president himself was ever to give. "In the words of the great essayist . . . 'Reform if you would preserve.' I am that kind of conservative because I am that kind of liberal."[6] The great essayist was Thomas Babington Macaulay, a mid-nineteenth-century member of Parliament, historical essayist, and rector at the Uni-versity of Glasgow. Macaulay's philosophy of politics paired seeming op-posites: reform to preserve.

Macaulay worked out a distinctive approach to politics called "trim-ming." Trimmers had commitments, but these commitments were always to be tempered by the things which made politics work: compromise and accommodation. Politics, Macaulay noted, is prone to the expression of extreme views. Zealous reformers gain their reputation by how ardently they trash the status quo. Equally zealous "Tories" gain their reputation by taking a hard line against reform. These groups divide into parties which engage in wars of words. These wars of words can easily end in real war. Trimmers are the responsible characters of politics who understand that neither extreme is realistic or desirable. They reject all pat philoso-phies. They stand at a distance from all uncompromising extremism. They favor moderate, incremental progressive reform, which effectively mutes the revolutionaries' appeal, and gives the lie to the conservatives' claim that reform is inherently problematic. Trimming in politics averts disaster. FDR understood himself to be a trimmer.

This is, of course, not all there is to be said of him. It does not reveal much about the substance of his commitments. Besides being a trim-mer, Roosevelt brought to the nation a vision of Christian democracy. He thought that all citizens should be treated with a dignity befitting their status as God's favored creation. Domestically this dictated widespread individual freedom, the universal right to participate in politics, and a basic level of economic security for all citizens. A vague but firmly inter-nationalist "good neighbor" foreign policy extended the Christian ethic across borders. That the United States (and FDR himself) did not come close to fully living up to these ideals confirms one of the lessons of trim-ming: a nation *never* fully realizes its stated ideals. The operative question for the trimmer is not whether an ideal has been achieved, but whether the nation has made incremental strides toward it.

Not one to draw fine intellectual distinctions, Roosevelt thought Christian democracy could be expressed just as easily in Benthamite terms as in biblical ones. In a 1938 speech in Oklahoma City, he proclaimed that "during these past six years the people of this Nation have definitely said 'yes' . . . to the old Biblical question, 'Am I my brother's keeper?'" Moments later he offered the classical utilitarian formulation that "our first question is this: what makes for the greatest good of the greatest number?"[7]

The original utilitarians conceived of their project as being distinctly at odds with traditional Christianity, which seemed to them to admire an other-worldly asceticism. Many Christians railed against the early utilitarians for espousing a philosophy of hedonism. But in FDR's mind, Christianity, democracy, freedom, and happiness were all of a piece. The United States could stride toward all of them by choosing the proper policies. This progressive vision entailed the rejection of two extremes: laissez-faire capitalism on the one hand and socialism (or communism) on the other. When quizzed by reporters about his own outlook, Roosevelt answered with a classic trimmer's response: "I am going down the whole line a little left of center."[8] Guarded about so much in his life, FDR in these words spoke honestly about the position he took and the most effective way to reform to preserve.

FDR trimmed between the most widely articulated, or at least the most ardently proclaimed, philosophies of the 1930s. This general outlook did not exactly give him a great deal of specific direction about policies, however. For that, FDR sought help, often from academics. In 1932, he commissioned Moley, a Columbia economist he barely knew, to put together a team which would brief him on the economic problems of the day and the possible solutions to the Great Depression. Moley brought in many academics. Two besides Moley became trusted advisers: Rexford Tugwell and Adolf Berle. This Brains Trust and the others who spoke with the president throughout his twelve years in office brought significant insight to FDR.

In embracing Macaulay's trimming, FDR found an antitheoretical political theory in much the same way that Wilson had been served by Burke. This outlook simultaneously appealed to his practicality and his sense that politics could do some incremental good in a fallen world. Luckily for FDR, in the 1930s and 1940s there were two extreme ideologies readily apparent to the public, laissez-faire capitalism and state socialism, to which he could offer a moderate alternative.

"Siren Voices That Offered Glib Answers"

While he read briefings as president, skimmed several newspapers every day, and kept up an active correspondence, FDR did not read many books during his political career.[9] Several contemporaries who worked closely with him while he was president do not recall Roosevelt *ever* reading a book, quite a feat for someone who amassed a library of more than 15,000 volumes. The chronicler of his presidency for the University Press of Kansas series, George McJimsey, confidently concludes that FDR "read no serious books of fiction, history, or social analysis."[10]

FDR wanted his information presented in smaller units, and he preferred learning through conversation to learning through the printed page. Davis describes him as being "possessed of an intellect that was broad but shallow" and explains that he "collected facts and ideas as he did stamps and naval prints, letting them lie flat, distinct, separate in his mind, never attempting to combine them into any holistic truth. Indeed, he shied away from generalized thinking and abstract ideas."[11]

Given this mental terrain, it is unsurprising that FDR was not well acquainted with political theory. Only rarely did he mention a theorist by name, and when he did, the reference was invariably negative. In general, he mistrusted theories as a relevant source of wisdom. Like Wilson, he thought that they approached complex reality in an overly simplified way. They were alluring, but they ultimately did not explain as much as they claimed to. Nor did theories solve as much as they promised. Recognizing this mistrust is important. Mistrust is very different from indifference. FDR did not exactly ignore political philosophy or remain entirely aloof from it—he rejected it as doctrinaire (with the expenditure of surprisingly little intellectual energy). In general it is fair to say that Franklin Delano Roosevelt defined his thinking in reaction against political and economic theory.

When asked by a reporter about his philosophy, the president replied dismissively, "Philosophy? I am a Christian and a Democrat—that's all."[12] His own mistrust of the theoretical went back at least to his undergraduate days at Harvard. FDR's C average was not due to a lack of intellect as much as a lack of interest. It is only a slight exaggeration to say that in his frequent letters home "there is not one word about [the] content" of his classes. "He had found them all dissatisfying, he would tell his roommate in his final year."[13] Given the stellar faculty on Harvard's staff at the time, including Frederick Jackson Turner, William James, and George Santayana, this remark probably tells us more about FDR than about Harvard.

Roosevelt remained somewhat estranged to Harvard University through-out his life. Its graduates tended to oppose his politics, but there was more than this to his ambivalence. Even as president, FDR still seemed to think that his education was less valuable than it should have been, likely be-cause he felt his professors' theories did not square with real-world expe-rience. This is all the more surprising given that nearly all classes at the time were electives. James MacGregor Burns quotes Roosevelt saying, "I took economics courses in college for four years, and everything I was taught was wrong." The one philosophy course he enrolled in he dropped after three weeks. Davis notes that, because of the all-elective policy, "the curriculum he chose to follow had grave deficiencies as preparation for a life of intelligent awareness in twentieth-century America."[14] FDR prob-ably already thought of philosophy as useless overthinking when he en-tered Harvard. No mandatory course in it would have likely changed his mind. But the elective curriculum enabled him to take this view forward into adulthood unchallenged and fully intact.

His devaluation of Harvard was reinforced by the academics he consult-ed during the 1932 campaign. During his discussions with FDR, Tugwell made an effort to reconstruct what Roosevelt had learned about economics and law as an undergraduate. Tugwell found that the candidate retained a good deal of what he had been taught. However, the Columbia economist also concluded that FDR's knowledge was significantly out of date and of absolutely no use in solving the crisis of the Great Depression, and Tugwell told him so. FDR and Tugwell disagreed widely about the desired level of centralized economic planning in an advanced economy, with the latter fa-voring more and FDR less, but one of the things which brought the two together was their shared negative assessment of his college education.[15]

Though FDR freely consulted with academics and intellectuals, he also distrusted them. He found that many of them were devoted to purity at the expense of practicality. They could afford to take an ideal position be-cause they did not have to deal with political reality. Roosevelt chided Tugwell, saying that *he* was teaching the professor about politics while the professor taught him about economics. In their partnership with FDR, the Brains Trust had an understanding: the advisers would present useful ideas to Roosevelt, and the president himself would assess their political feasibility. In this way Roosevelt insulated himself from discussing how he would determine which of their ideas he would champion, and he gave the distinct impression that he favored many more of their proposals than he could possibly implement.

Roosevelt also complained that intellectuals "never allowed a politi-cian the least leeway."[16] John Dewey frustrated FDR most of all. Dewey had gained international fame for his philosophy of pragmatism, but he would not join forces with the New Deal, the political movement dedicated to pragmatism through the use of "bold, persistent experimentation."[17] Instead, Dewey attempted to organize a third party that would challenge Roosevelt from the left. Its lack of success did not prevent Dewey from being a thorn in FDR's side. Nevertheless, the president fully appreciated the delicious irony of an academic who suggested that value comes from what works attempting the quixotic task of founding a political party from scratch and failing. Undoubtedly Roosevelt thought that was exactly what an academic theorist would do.

Since those in the academy could take positions regardless of their real-life consequences, they were particularly prone to doctrinaire positions. Many in the academy thought that the adoption of some version of socialism was inevitable. Howard Zinn reminds us that "Marxism was in the air all around" in the 1930s. The president consistently rejected it, confident that in the long run a regulated free market would prove to be the better path. He wryly observed that many professors "were going to squirm when the economy was righted and they had to find a way back home from Moscow."[18]

Speaking at the International Student Assembly of 1942, FDR offered as plain a lesson in political thought as he could. He blamed the world-wide depression for the popularity of theory-based visions. Because of the depression, many young people "were tempted to seek some simple remedy . . . for all the problems that beset the world. Some listened to alien, siren voices that offered glib answers to all the questions they asked."[19] With the United States already in the war, Roosevelt took care to directly mention only one of these foreign philosophies, fascism, in this speech. Nevertheless, he had frequently expressed similar sentiments about communism and socialism. They were "foreign ideologies" or "isms," a label he used frequently and dismissively, to describe the philosophies which he rejected because of their glib rigidity.

Roosevelt was consistent in his rejection of theories of economics and government. He was confident that he possessed a more beneficial and realistic approach than did his opponents. And yet, as I will explain in the next section, this "anti-theory" was its own theory of politics, with a long history and an intellectual provenance that FDR himself recognized, at least to some extent. Fully explaining this theory was not something that Franklin Delano Roosevelt was prepared for—politically, but probably psychologically as well. He needed to consider himself more practical than others—and this meant drawing a line between his own understanding of politics and "theories," which were for others and were foolish and impractical. His attitude toward political thought is reminiscent of that of Edmund Burke and Woodrow Wilson, whose theory of politics was to denounce theories. This is a paradox, to be sure, but the recognition of a paradox does not necessarily diminish the value of a position.

Because of his background FDR was wary of being thought of as an effete, overeducated "squire of Dutchess County." In the New York state senate he had made his name as a Democratic opponent of Tammany Hall. By taking on the Tammany bosses he had gained a favorable reputation as a reformer, but there was a price to be paid for doing so. The New York City–based political machine attempted to portray their upstate, estate-raised and Harvard-educated opponent as an out-of-touch intellectual. There was a hefty dose of irony in an anti-intellectual Harvard-hater's being criticized as an intellectual who was closely allied to his alma mater. However, FDR realized that the charge might be taken seriously by the farmers and factory workers whom he would rely on for political support. Even as late as the 1932 campaign FDR was being portrayed as a "scholar-gentleman" who was not really capable of championing the plight of the common man during the Great Depression because "he has just read about him in books."[20] Explicitly discussing political theory would have hindered FDR's attempt to identify with common people, so he scrupulously avoided naming political and economic theorists, except to make occasional negative references. In the 1936 campaign kickoff at Syracuse, FDR alluded to Macaulay, but did not mention him by name. When FDR did mention Macaulay's name, as he did in a speech of August 18, 1937, it was to criticize his elitism.

Over and over in his speeches, particularly after 1935, Roosevelt congratulated the American populace on being more intelligent about politics than they had ever been in the past. This might seem to be a throwaway line—a small bit of flattery uttered by a politician ingratiating himself to the public. But FDR's view of theories makes this observation take on meaning. In earlier times the American populace had been swayed by "isms." The alluring simplicity of laissez-faire had dominated the Gilded Age and had reemerged with a vengeance in the 1920s. With FDR's election, the American people had come to embrace the more complicated antitheoretical view which animated the New Deal. There were no simple, doctrinaire answers in politics or economics. Public policy had to be shaped by gathering facts about a particular matter, formulating a plan to achieve some concrete goal, vetting its political feasibility, and then moving forward with an experiment in public policy. If the first attempt at doing this did not succeed, one needed to reevaluate and tack anew. The world was a complicated place, after all. Governing was inevitably a process, a process which was not compatible with pat answers and the theorist's impatience for compromise, or indeed for anything which did not go his way.

Along the way, FDR would receive a good deal of help from advisers. He consulted hundreds of experts both within government and outside of it to help him formulate policies. The earliest presidents had turned to "canonical" books for inspiration. Other sources of political wisdom were rare. Few policy analysts worked for the federal government before the New Deal. The academy was in its infancy in the nineteenth century. With universities firmly established by the 1930s there were hundreds of experts waiting to be consulted. There were also government employees whose job it was to gather facts relevant to the dilemmas government faced. Their information more than the canonical works of political theory would contribute to FDR's attempt to keep moving the country forward a little left of center.

"I, Too, Am a Philosopher"

To the twenty-first-century ear, FDR's speeches quite often sound trite, the relic of a more troubled but simpler time. Democracy, Christianity, and security—economic and international—are main Roosevelt themes. Rhetorically, stories, metaphors, and analogies abound. Tugwell noted that FDR was addicted to clichés. But alongside the truisms were self-conscious attempts to describe an outlook—Roosevelt himself typically balked at describing it as a philosophy. He usually offered one speech per campaign devoted to his outlook and at other times he interlined his stories and clichés with generalizations about his political thought. These snippets are easy to miss in the large corpus of FDR rhetoric, but they do exist. The thirty-second president did not need to write a book to articulate the essence of his thinking, and he was probably incapable of doing so if he tried. Yet there is more to FDR's political thought than at first meets the eye.

Since FDR found himself in the rejection of theories, it is important to explain what he rejected and how he did so. The Democratic campaign of 1932 was crafted to get the electorate to focus on the failings of incumbent president Herbert Hoover. In this effort, Roosevelt suggested that Hoover was an unrepentant advocate of laissez-faire. Hoover's writings, including the slim book which described his political philosophy, *American Individualism,* make clear that he was not a free-market zealot. Instead of drawing a finer (and more accurate) distinction between his own more aggressive and Hoover's less aggressive approach to government regulation, Roosevelt portrayed his opponent as the possessor of an extremist philosophy inspired by Adam Smith.

In his pathbreaking nomination speech, Roosevelt asserted that the average American had been "forgotten in the political philosophy of the Government of the last years."[21] Earlier he had accounted for the reason this happened in a speech at Oglethorpe University. This speech is best remembered for the line "the country needs . . . [and] the country demands bold, persistent experimentation." Less well remembered is its critique of doctrinaire economics. The law of supply and demand dictated that the economy would right itself. "Whatever elements of truth lie in it, it is an invitation to sit back and do nothing; and all of us are suffering today, I believe, because this comfortable theory was too thoroughly implanted in the minds of some of our leaders, both in finance and public affairs." FDR had risen above his education in these "economic laws." Hoover and his associates had not.[22]

Many Republicans would counterpunch by suggesting that FDR was preparing a path for socialism. Initially Roosevelt's protestations to the contrary were mild. "I am not speaking of an economic life completely planned and regimented," he said at a Jefferson Day dinner in 1932. He added, "I plead not for a class control but for a true concert of interests." Later in the campaign he parried by noting that when he was a state senator "a lot of us youngsters . . . were called radicals. We were called Socialists" simply for favoring a workman's compensation law. These charges, already two decades old, were stale and dubious. FDR was not a socialist any more than he was a free-market absolutist. He stood between or above the two.[23]

In 1936, FDR reassured the public by saying, "I have not sought, I do not seek, I repudiate the support of any advocate of Communism or of any other 'ism' which would by fair means or foul change our American democracy." By his fourth campaign for president, he turned the charge to his advantage. In a speech delivered by radio on October 5, 1944, FDR complained that "political propagandists" were again using the red herring of communism to describe the social measures of the New Deal. Roosevelt suggested that twelve years into his presidency these charges were particularly hollow.[24]

Whether it was laissez-faire capitalism on the right or socialism on the left, Roosevelt believed that they both failed because of their simplistic approach. Laissez-faire types placed more faith in the anachronistic theoretical writings of Adam Smith than they did in reality. In a radio address to the Young Democratic Clubs of America, FDR offered the observation that "you and I know that this modern economic world of ours is governed by rules and regulations vastly more complex than those laid down in the days of Adam Smith or John Stuart Mill. They faced simpler mechanical processes and social needs." Massive corporations did not yet exist in these theorists' time, and these entities created a wholly new economy which was unforeseen by them. He continued by saying that "facts are relentless. We must adjust our ideas to the facts of today."[25] That meant throwing out the trite philosophies of yesteryear in favor of a more nuanced and flexible approach.

The facts also mitigated against communism and socialism. They too were alluring in their simplicity. However, their simplicity threatened to do violence to reality. Transferring control of all enterprise to the public sector would stifle freedom. It would attempt to fix things which did not need fixing. In an address on Constitution Day in 1937, FDR referred to communism as "a pseudo-science of economic organization."[26] American admirers of fascism also threatened to submerge freedom in favor of the state. Fascism's emergence strongly reinforced FDR's understanding that pragmatic moderation was an indispensably necessary counterpoise to extremism.

The failure of these theories to square with facts was a problem, but it was not the most pressing one. The most pressing problem was that theories were dangerous. Those who were dazzled by theories were causing great harm because they were programmed not to compromise. The ideologies they espoused were all-or-nothing propositions. The socialists wanted government to own the means of production entirely. There was no middle ground. Laissez-faire advocates wanted the market to work its magic without any government intervention. There was no middle ground for them, either. As FDR saw it, the adherents of either of these ideologies would not compromise. To those who led the socialist and free market parades there was to be no intelligent, selective governmental regulation of the type FDR championed. Nor would partial government ownership of sectors of the economy, like electrical utilities, be acceptable.

The president described his own pragmatism as a counterweight arrayed against both extremes. As he put it in an address recommending the regulation of utilities, "I am against private socialism of concentrated private power as thoroughly as I am against governmental socialism. The one is equally as dangerous as the other; and destruction of private socialism is utterly essential to avoid governmental socialism."[27] This was a skilled rhetorical linkage of two radically opposed ideologies; but what they had in common, extremism, was more important to FDR than their differences. The headlong pursuit of "private socialism," the term he was using for laissez-faire, would backfire and produce Leninist "governmental socialism." FDR suggested that he was saving capitalism from the excessive zeal of its own partisans. The Republicans' more market-oriented approach did not promise to do the same.

Franklin Roosevelt's political thought was not just about rejecting philosophies; he adopted a positive political theory as well. Without fully articulating it to the public or even to his advisers, FDR was a trimmer in
the mold of Macaulay. The familiar tools of the president's politics were
to be found in Macaulay: a rejection of theories as extreme, the search for
a pragmatic middle way that mutes others' extremism, judgments on a
case-by-case basis for each policy proposal, and the conservation of familiar values through reform.

Today Macaulay is not well remembered. However, he was well known
in the latter half of the nineteenth century. In Parliament Macaulay faced
some of the same issues as FDR, including whether the government
should intervene in the marketplace for humanitarian reasons. Both politicians answered with a qualified yes. In May 1846 the House of Commons debated the "Ten Hours Bill," which proposed to prohibit employers
from having children work more than ten hours in a day. Macaulay tried
to stake out a judicious middle ground, saying,

> I hardly know which is the greater pest to society, a paternal gov-
> ernment, that is to say, a prying, meddlesome government, which in-
> trudes itself into every part of human life, and which thinks it can do
> everything for everybody better than anybody can do anything for
> himself; or a careless, lounging government, which suffers grievances,
> such as it could at once remove, to grow and multiply, and which to all
> complaint and remonstrance has only one answer: "We must let things
> alone: we must let things take their course: we must let things find their
> level." There is no more important problem in politics than to ascertain
> the just mean between these two most pernicious principles.[28]

Macaulay did not possess the joie de vivre of FDR, but along a variety of
dimensions, they took strikingly similar positions. Macaulay stressed that
those who think government involvement can solve every problem are
misguided. He too was critiquing socialists along with various other utopians. He thought that those who opposed all regulations were equally
unrealistic, and ultimately inhumane. Finding the mean between these
two extremes was vital and required exercising judgment on a case-by-
case basis. To Macaulay, that judgment was the most important part of
politics. He had it, and those he opposed did not (or at least did not exercise it in public). If this middle ground were found, the nation could
progress; if not, there would be danger.

Edmund Burke had first articulated the idea that "a state without the
means of some change is without the means of its conservation."[29] Ma-

caulay ran with that idea. FDR did too, stressing that "what we are doing today is a necessary fulfillment of old and tested American ideals." While his living quarters were being renovated, Roosevelt compared the New Deal to what was occurring at the White House: the old familiar form was being retained, but renovation adapted the old structure to modern times. There were those who perceived the New Deal as a revolution in government. FDR countered that it was not a revolution, but an *evolution*.[30]

Macaulay felt that writers could affect politics as profoundly as politicians. In his five-volume *History of England* he arranged facts to make his point: extremism is dangerous and politicians need "to recognize the wisdom of trimming as a way of maintaining consent for a constitutional regime which combined liberty and order."[31] Macaulay felt that the author who succeeded in winning converts was worthy of the title "philosophical historian," and he worked hard to be one.

FDR's handwritten opening to his never-completed history of the United States drips with the same aspiration. In the few pages which are extant, FDR goes to pains to set himself apart from other chroniclers of American history. The textbooks have it wrong, he says: it is absurd to think that Henry Hudson was the first person to find "Hudson's Bay." The Americas were not founded by explorers. They were founded instead by an age and its people.[32] Only when common people had the audacity to dream about making a better life was the American continent truly discovered. America and democracy were discovered together. With a political career seemingly precluded to him because of his paralysis, for a brief time FDR aspired to be the philosophical historian of democracy—one who would interpret events to celebrate (his version of) American democracy—a role inspired by Macaulay's understanding of what was at stake in the writing of history.

This aspiration to "teach reality" did not fade, despite FDR's successful reentry into elective politics. The president frequently offered the image of himself as a teacher—one who had great truths to disseminate. When he did so, he channeled Macaulay. In a 1940 campaign address at the University of Pennsylvania, the president related that "it is the whole duty of the philosopher and the educator to apply the eternal ideals of truth and goodness and justice in terms of the present and not terms of the past."[33] His speech suggested that he was this kind of educator. He was not the philosophical historian in 1940, but he was the philosophical politician, teaching the public about the need for moderation and reform in the continuing pursuit of democracy and social justice.

In a Jackson Day dinner in the same year, he told his audience that in his job "there is the philosopher's satisfaction of trying to fit that particle of truth into the general scheme of things that are good and things that are bad for the people as a whole."[34] Though he did not specifically reference Macaulay, this is a clear allusion to him. Macaulay's self-professed hope was to find particles of truth and to fit these particles into a narrative that would make clear to the reader what was good and what was bad in political and social life. In this Macaulayesque sense, and in this sense only, did FDR consider himself a philosopher: he had a practically useful outlook that could help the nation move incrementally closer to its democratic and Christian values.

Macaulay urged politicians to think simultaneously about long-term ideals and what was possible to achieve in the short term. This theme shines through in a 1939 letter that FDR wrote to Theodore Dreiser. The president had his eye on both long-term goals and short-term practicalities: "I, too, am a philosopher and try to think in terms of a century as well as in terms of this week and next."[35] That he wrote this and described a "philosopher's satisfaction" in doing his job strongly suggests that Roosevelt knew that trimming was his philosophy. FDR was not simply fed phrases reminiscent of or referring to Macaulay by speechwriters. Someone with such a strong bias against an "ivory tower" mentality would have rejected them as inauthentic impositions if they did not describe his own outlook. FDR knew he was a trimmer, possessed of an antiphilosophical philosophy.

If there were many points of similarity between Macaulay and FDR, there were also many points of disagreement. Unlike Macaulay, who intentionally held himself aloof from political parties when he was in Parliament, FDR was a committed Democrat. Macaulay was a lukewarm Christian, who feared extremism in religion as much as he did in politics. FDR was a committed, if a vague, left-leaning Christian. Macaulay was far more dour than Roosevelt and often felt driven by a fear of immediate civil strife and even civil war. The Briton also applied his philosophy of moderation to his preference for political institutions. He favored the mixed constitution, as exemplified by Britain's House of Lords, House of Commons, and monarchy. FDR thought that this preference was elitist and championed democracy, hence the latter's explicit criticism of "modern Macaulay's" in a speech of August 18, 1937.[36]

FDR's knowledge of Macaulay may have been secondhand. His fifth cousin Theodore likely recommended him to FDR. TR knew Macaulay well, admired him greatly, and believed that he himself took a similar approach to politics. Consider the following quote from a private letter: "Of all the authors I know[,] I believe I should first choose him [Macaulay] as the man whose writings will most help a man of action who desires to be both efficient and decent, to keep straight and yet to be of some account in the world." TR read Macaulay's *History of England* through a number of times, including during the 1904 campaign. The books in FDR's collection written by Macaulay, like almost all of FDR's books, are unmarked, but if nothing else, as a young adult Franklin likely got a lesson in Macaulay's thinking from "Uncle Ted."[37]

To this general outlook was added a utilitarian gloss. FDR employed Jeremy Bentham's phrase "the greatest good for the greatest number" frequently in his years as president. The inspiration was probably Rexford Tugwell, who had considered himself a second-class citizen at Columbia University because he was assigned to teach a general "Western civilization" course. Preparation for this course had required him to read up on philosophy and intellectual history. Tugwell felt this preparation deepened his own critique of classical economics, and he recommended the main ideas of the utilitarian Bentham to FDR.[38]

FDR's Chicago convention speech in 1932 framed the choice to voters using Bentham's phrase: "Ours must be a party of liberal thought, of planned action, of enlightened international outlook, and of the greatest good for the greatest number of our citizens." After being reelected to a third term, he greeted the Economics Club of New York by saying, "You and I know that in order to maintain our American system of private initiative and enterprise, it must function as a system that will do the greatest good for the greatest number. It is only by keeping our economy socially conscious that we can keep it free."[39] Macaulay did not feel that trimming and Bentham's aggressive reform movement (being championed in a modified form in his generation by John Stuart Mill) were compatible. FDR's democratic bent and his vague use of Benthamite language served to reconcile the two, at least to his satisfaction.

Roosevelt was also informed by a variety of academics. The Brains Trusters provided him with the facts that invalidated glib theories. FDR met with many members of the business community who pleaded with him not to intervene in their sector of the economy. They endorsed the free market even when regulation would seemingly benefit them, and FDR delighted in marshaling information which exposed their ideologically driven ignorance.[40] Moley, Berle, Tugwell, and others brought FDR data which helped to explain what was happening in the Great Depression. These advisers had policy suggestions, and FDR determined which of them to use.

In a theoretical sense the most important academic influence on FDR seems to have been one of his teachers at Harvard, Frederick Jackson Turner. Roosevelt frequently offered a thumbnail sketch of Turner's "frontier thesis" to explain why a democratic government that had historically done very little regulating had to give way to a government that regulated a good deal. For example, in the Commonwealth Club Address of September 1932, FDR paid nameless homage to Turner by pointing out that "there is no safety valve in the form of a Western prairie to which those thrown out of work . . . can go for a new start."[41] Turner himself had stressed that the first age of American development was over and a new one was at hand, in which government might play a much larger role. FDR concurred, following the foregoing observation with the suggestion that "the day of enlightened administration has come." Turner's suggestion that the closing of the frontier would fundamentally transform the American approach to government helped FDR to dismiss his opponents as the fossils of a discarded age.[42]

FDR's mind, which has often been portrayed as a rather barren field, was not so uninteresting after all. He was not a deep thinker, nor did he read political philosophy with interest or care. Yet he made important connections between political theory and political practice. The most important of these connections involved Macaulay, whose views prefigured FDR's wariness toward philosophies. The laissez-faire capitalism of Adam Smith and the collectivism of Karl Marx and later socialists provided FDR with the foils against which he defined himself. They were the siren voices that offered glib answers. FDR genuinely thought that he took the harder path. Because of its endorsement of compromise as a key political value, trimming is not something that a politician can easily admit to. Roosevelt had the political gifts of vagueness and discipline—only occasionally did he refer in roundabout ways to the inspiration for his political thought. Doing this often helped him politically, but it also exacted a toll on his reputation, as frustrated advisers wrote their memoirs and those disappointed by moderate reforms wrote their histories.

Pluralism a Little Left of Center

Unlike many other philosophies, trimming does not readily lend itself to concrete suggestions about policy. In this respect FDR was more like John Adams, who had gained from political theory an understanding of how institutions should interact, than he was like Thomas Jefferson, who found a policy program in Enlightenment political theory. Trimming offers only a relative orientation. The trimmer seeks a way to position himself in relation to others—to moderate, to seek compromise, and to oppose doctrinaire solutions. This may make its connection to the "real world" less dramatic or less clear than is the case with other philosophies, but there is good reason to believe that FDR practiced what he had referred to in speeches.

This is not to suggest that FDR's positions were necessarily consistent or even clearly thought through. Into the 1930s he was giving speeches which opposed government centralization. During the 1932 campaign he promised to cut federal expenditures by 25 percent and to balance the budget while providing increased economic relief. All of this did not add up to a coherent vision. Trimming may be a unique philosophy, however, in that it tries to encompass a degree of inconsistency. The trimmer must reconcile the opposite views which are contending for domination of a particular policy arena in a reactive manner. Like any politician's, FDR's thinking changed through time. However, his reactive outlook made him more flexible than many others. He was less encumbered by specific policy commitments because he knew he might have to, depending on events, tack in a different direction. He comfortably tacked between opposing ideas or combined them, often frustrating others while doing so.

Raymond Moley describes a case of this frustration in *After Seven Years,* a book the disappointed Brains Truster wrote to prevent a third Roosevelt term. High tariffs had been enacted by Republicans in the early 1920s, and by 1932 these tariffs were often being cited as a cause of the Great Depression (goods were available, but they would not move because of the high prices). Many Democrats favored lowering trade barriers. However, two schools of thought emerged about how this should be done. Senator Cordell Hull proposed an immediate, across-the-board reduction of duties levied on goods coming into the United States by 10 percent. Others favored negotiating bilateral reductions through treaties, requiring both the United States and another nation to lower their barriers simultaneously.

As he was involved in the preparation of Roosevelt's Democratic Convention speech in 1932, Moley felt that Roosevelt would have to choose between the two. He asked the candidate for guidance about what he should write for the nomination speech in Chicago. What FDR said to Moley dumbfounded him: "Weave the two together."[43] Roosevelt wanted Moley to stake out common ground by pairing the two seemingly incompatible options. In this way Roosevelt attempted to avoid losing support from advocates of either alternative. He also kept his options open by not firmly committing himself to either.

This was not exactly trimming between ardent ideologies, but it does offer an accurate picture of how Roosevelt preferred to proceed in making policy. Forcing others who opposed each other to find common ground was a model of policy formation employed by FDR in a number of different settings. Tugwell relates that FDR himself avoided making specific proposals about agriculture. Instead he asked all relevant stakeholders to gather together with employees of the Department of Agriculture, including Tugwell, and work out a preferred solution to the problem of slack agricultural commodity prices, threatening them not to enact anything if they could not come to an agreement.

Farmers, cooperatives, wholesale buyers, consumers, and manufacturers of agricultural goods came together to request that the president support what Tugwell had advocated from the beginning: a voluntary program that paid farmers to keep acreage out of production.[44] This request became the centerpiece of the Agricultural Adjustment Act. Politically this was an astute move, because whatever these various stakeholders agreed to was bound to become law. It also avoided extremes. AAA did not rely on the market to correct itself, nor did it require that the government dictate to farmers what they could grow or how they would grow it. Despite thinking that "conflicting policies ... existed somehow side by side in Roosevelt's mind," Tugwell proudly acknowledged that "AAA and the Hopkins relief efforts were the most effective of all the New Deal initiatives."[45]

FDR tried to proceed similarly in industrial policy. What Roosevelt meant when he said that "the National Industrial Recovery Act was drawn with the greatest good of the greatest number in mind" was that it sought to enact solutions that were agreeable to producers, laborers, trade associations, and consumers.[46] The stakeholders in different sectors (e.g., textiles) were asked to gather to work out a code that would help solve the problems in their sector. The nature of the code was largely up to the stakeholders, but the government guaranteed that businesses would be protected from most antitrust suits while labor would be guaranteed the right to organize. More than 500 such codes were written. These did not work anywhere near as well as the set-asides of the AAA, and much of the NIRA was invalidated by the Supreme Court in 1935. Nevertheless, the codes were an attempt to address the problems of industry in a voluntary fashion by forcing those with opposing points of view to come to an accommodation.

This effort at trimming paints the Court-packing controversy of FDR's second term in a new light. Undoubtedly this was a significant political misstep for FDR in that it seemed like he was tampering with the traditional constitutional balance of power to favor the executive. As he saw it, however, the Court was dominated by a set of ideologues, the holdovers of previous regimes. They did not just possess outmoded views, they were philosophical reactionaries who used their theories to stand squarely against compromise and moderation. They struck at the New Deal precisely because they had an ideology, and they made no bones about justifying their decisions using that ideology. It would take an adjustment in the membership of the Court to successfully trim and moderate. FDR could easily identify individuals who took a more pragmatic and flexible approach to what the federal government could do, and he proposed expanding the Court's membership to allow moderation, as he saw it, to prevail.

In his analysis of Roosevelt's presidency, George McJimsey stresses that "pluralism" was the animating ideal of the Roosevelt administration. Government would not dictate but it would coordinate, facilitating problem solving by bringing various parties together. Roosevelt employed this pluralistic model among his advisers, in domestic politics, and internationally. In the White House he frequently told his subordinates to work out an agreement among themselves before coming back to him. He attempted to remain above the fray of domestic politics by having others formulate voluntary, pluralistic policies. He was also typically a firm internationalist, and he envisioned the collective security apparatus of the United Nations—a global variant of pluralism.[47]

FDR's approach to politics was pluralistic, to be sure. In fact, the concept of pluralism, which was popularized by political scientists in the 1950s, grew out of theorists' observations of the New Deal. Labeling New Deal programs pluralistic is entirely accurate, but it risks being circular, limiting its explanatory value. Adding FDR's connection with Macaulay's concept of trimming acknowledges his preference for pluralism while at the same time offering an explanation for *why* Roosevelt acted the way he did—an explanation that the president himself acknowledged, though vaguely. His was not just a response to the growing complexity of society, where there were multiple groups interested in any issue or policy. Nor was it only a strategy designed to keep himself above the political fray. It was a self-conscious approach designed to forge moderate, consensual solutions that would preserve the free market while promoting regulated economic security. As McJimsey points out, lowest-common-denominator policies of suspect workability were a frequent result. At the same time, FDR did not proceed immoderately, and he did not allow the country to proceed immoderately in its time of crisis.

Social Security legislation was framed by a blue-ribbon committee. The Committee on Economic Security consisted of various government officials, professors, and experts headed by the University of Wisconsin's Edwin E. Witte. The president offered only general guidelines to the committee. He wanted the legislation to provide income for those of retirement age, unemployment insurance, and income security against "all major hazards which lead to poverty and dependency." He envisioned the program as a cooperative one involving both the federal government and the states, and he wanted the program to be funded by its own separate tax. Witte tried to get the president to elaborate on these suggestions, but found that he would not.[48]

Through the legislative process, Roosevelt was unconcerned about details, but he tried to make sure that the legislation was comprehensive in its scope, covering all possible economic dislocations. This was cornerstone legislation to FDR—a permanent solution to the problems created by heartless markets, but which would simultaneously preserve the vibrancy of free enterprise. If it worked, the attractiveness of the revolutionary movements which promised to remedy these same ills by the drastic means of the application of some theory would wither. After Social Security was enacted FDR suggested to audiences that that was what had actually occurred. He had helped save capitalism from its own excesses. In doing so he saved the nation from socialism. There is every reason to believe that FDR believed his own claim.

In international affairs, Roosevelt offered up the United States as a "good neighbor," and he was a firm internationalist during his twelve years as president.[49] Long an advocate of the League of Nations, FDR was the primary architect of the international security apparatus designed into the United Nations. This was pluralism on an international scale—and it was a vision that could only be put into place after the trauma of World War II. Roosevelt came to the office hoping to meet other nations, particularly those in the Western Hemisphere, halfway in the realm of foreign relations. Three distinct aspects of FDR's foreign policy warrant commentary here: his good neighbor policy, his approach to the Soviet Union, and his relations with Nazi Germany.

The content of the good neighbor policy was vague, and intentionally so. Since the trimmer finds his way in reaction to the views of others, FDR did not have a detailed blueprint for the shape of U.S. foreign policy when he took office. After decades of invasions and interference on the American side, Roosevelt wanted to signal that his administration would act differently and more positively, by considering more seriously the views and interests of those outside the United States. The Roosevelt administration pledged not to interfere with the internal or external politics of other nations and abrogated the treaty with Cuba that allowed the United States to send troops into Cuba to promote stability. The effects of this policy were most tangibly felt in Haiti, where the presence of U.S. troops was ended in 1934 after nearly two decades. The good neighbor policy was a logical international outcome of the ethic of trimming. It promised that dialogue and compromise would be the norm rather than unilateralism and armed response—even in the Western Hemisphere.

What Roosevelt aimed to do with the Soviets—and was at least somewhat successful in doing—was to blunt the hard, ideological edge of communism by drawing the U.S.S.R. into the community of nations. This effort presumed that there were substantial pragmatic elements among the Soviet leadership. Leninist state socialism was already a major step away from Marxist utopianism, a concession to political reality. If the Soviets were willing to compromise Marxist orthodoxy to set up a state, might they not be willing to compromise away more of their doctrinaire positions for the good of their nation? One of Roosevelt's first diplomatic actions was to have the U.S. government recognize the Soviet Union for the first time and exchange ambassadors. Recognition would strengthen the hand of moderates and weaken the position of the doctrinaire global revolutionists. In normalizing relations, the people of the Soviet Union would have to come to grips with the existence and permanence of the United States with its free market.

Formal recognition and the exchange of ambassadors came with side agreements. To gain recognition the Soviets had to agree not to advocate a communist revolution in the United States. They also had to promise that they would not make any effort to support communist organizations in the United States. More than seven decades later, these might seem like minor concessions, but that would underestimate the strength of the communist movement in the United States in the 1930s and the revolutionary zeal of many Soviet leaders. In proposing the Soviets as a permanent member of the U.N. Security Council with veto power, FDR attempted to integrate them further into the family of nations. This move seemed warranted in 1945, given the monumental sacrifices of their people in the successful alliance against the Nazis. The arrangement clearly did not work as Roosevelt had hoped, however.[50] Nevertheless, it was an effort to blunt the potential radicalism of Soviet Communism by integrating the Soviets fully into an international security regime that would protect the community of nations.

Roosevelt treated the threat from fascism differently. He recognized at an unusually early point that Nazism and its fascist cousins in Japan and Italy posed a threat to global security. FDR judged that there was no moderate element in them to appeal to, and he did not try to do so. Hitler and Mussolini provoked in him the trimmer's dislike of uncompromising extremism. There was to be no working with them, and he would do what he could to keep their sphere of influence from expanding. In their disputes, he backed Britain and the other constitutional democracies of Europe as moderate counterpoints to aggressive fascism. Roosevelt spoke out against fascist aggrandizement well before the beginning of World War II. When war did break out in Europe the neutrality carved out by the administration was explicitly antifascist. Roosevelt had made up his mind that he would back Britain and other democracies in Europe at the risk of going to war with extremists, even if this move was at odds with 150 years of American history and threatened to set at naught the warning to "beware entangling alliances."

Sam Rosenman, whom Roosevelt entrusted with the editorship of his public papers and addresses, summed up his boss's approach to politics as follows: "If being a progressive means the willingness to advocate change in order to meet changing conditions, that was the very foundation of Roosevelt's political thinking. The dictum of Macaulay, 'Reform if you would preserve,' was one of Roosevelt's maxims, which he quoted frequently and observed always."[51] FDR was president at a time when navigating between ideologically driven extremes made a good deal of sense—and it was an orientation made familiar to him by "the great essayist" Thomas Babington Macaulay, whose tack he turned toward the Benthamite mantra of seeking "the greatest good for the greatest number."

Conclusion

In recent decades FDR's reputation has dimmed. The generations which knew him well have receded into history and the New Deal coalition has lost its vibrancy. Hard scrutiny of Roosevelt's presidency has found it wanting in certain ways, as the assessments of partisans have given way to the more measured critiques of historians. Part of his legacy is an administrative state which is often unwieldy and frequently frustrates reform. More of those who are middle-aged or older now tell young people that Ronald Reagan's policies "won the Cold War" than tell of how FDR's policies saved the nation from socialism or "solved" the Great Depression, though this may be changing as I write.

Among our sober second looks at FDR we should include a look at his political thought. He was pragmatic, but he was not simply aimless or conniving. His approach was frustrating to many, but there was a method behind it. As in one of his beloved hobbies, sailing, he had a destination in mind but he rarely moved directly toward it. The winds of politics rarely blow in exactly the right direction. Roosevelt did not read widely in political theory like John Adams; he did not formulate a political theory with strikingly new elements, as had Thomas Jefferson; he was not meticulous and imaginative as was James Madison; he was not even doggedly determined like his former boss Woodrow Wilson. FDR was not an intellectual titan, but he did not need to be to be a trimmer.

FDR adds breadth to our understanding about how political theory and practical politics interact in the hands of a president. A president need not be well read in political theory to adopt an outlook from it. A president can define his politics in reaction against the theories of others. A president might ascribe to a theory that he does not fully describe to the public because doing so might exact a political cost or because he is not intellectually prepared to articulate it at length. Because of its nature, when a president adheres to a philosophy of pragmatism there will likely be many hurt feelings and disappointments among supporters. And a related point is that we can fail to recognize a theoretical orientation even when it is present.

Moderation and compromise have always been a part of American politics. They were built into the United States' constitutional structure. The politician who climbs the ladder of ambition to its highest rung in the United States cannot possibly be where he or she is without having made many compromises, both personal and political. In modern American government, from FDR forward, this is particularly the case. Modern government does so much, and the changes that a president can make are only piecemeal and incremental. Knowing political theory does not necessarily make it harder for a president to deal with this reality. In the cases of Wilson and now Roosevelt, we have seen that these presidents' acquaintance with political theory *described for them how to be pragmatic.* Thus the danger that Daniel Boorstin describes in *The Genius of American Politics* must be rephrased. It is not political theory in general that threatens to blind politicians and the public to pragmatic outcomes. At most, only some particular political theories do this.

A key form of judgment that a president must possess is the ability to distinguish when to hold fast to principle and when to choose compromise. In the main, FDR's philosophy of trimming, consistently choosing compromise in the creation of policy, was politically effective and frequently appropriate. Yet at times there is also something inappropriate about embracing compromise as a value from the beginning. It threatens to undermine those things which should not be compromised away. FDR negotiated this difficulty well when it came to Nazism. He recognized that there was to be no compromise with it because its adherents would never be content with compromise. He did not do as well with this dilemma when it came to other matters, such as race in the domestic sphere. The trimmer's wariness of substantial reform meant that the nation's racial policies were held hostage by recalcitrant forces during Roosevelt's tenure. What little progress African Americans made during the New Deal was not attributable to any courage or moral leadership displayed by FDR. It would take Harry Truman to show such courage, to move the nation forward.[52]

From Franklin Delano Roosevelt's speeches one often gets the impression that he is tilting at straw men. Through four campaigns and more than twelve years in office, he skewered the heartless forces of laissez-faire economics, as well as utopian socialist ideologues. All along FDR portrayed himself as the responsible moderate, pointing out the follies of these two courses, assiduously avoiding either of these extremes, and going down the whole line a little left of center. This could be viewed as effective propaganda—finely honed stagecraft by a master of political image making. But is it propaganda if the person saying it really believes what he is saying?

Chapter 7

BILL CLINTON: FLIRTATION WITH THE SOCIAL CONTRACT

One of the things I've learned in all trade cases is that it once again reaffirms the wisdom of the Italian Renaissance political philosopher Machiavelli, who said—I'm paraphrasing here, but this is almost exactly right—he said, there is nothing so difficult in all of human affairs as to change the established order of things. Because the people that [might] win will always be uncertain of their gain; whereas, the people who will lose are absolutely sure of what they are going to lose.

> —Bill Clinton, speech to farmers and students in Seattle, December 1, 1999

Earlier this year I said we should reserve any surplus until we save Social Security first. We have done so. We should take the next step and act now. It is more than an opportunity; it is a solemn responsibility—to take the achievement of past generations, the Americans who, according to President Roosevelt, had a rendezvous with destiny, and to renew the social contract for a new era.

> —Bill Clinton, speech opening a conference on Social Security, December 8, 1998

Every president who has been interested in political philosophy has approached it in a unique way, has internalized a distinctive set of ideals from it, and has applied these ideals in ways that are original to him. Bill Clinton is no exception. Clinton's intellect has frequently been analyzed, and patterns have emerged. Clinton reads prodigiously, he is a polymath who enjoys substantive discussions—sometimes to the point of a fault—and he likes to split the difference between options or avoid stark choices if he can. How these intellectual tools were applied to political theory has been woefully underexplored, which is remarkable since Clinton chose to study political theory while he was a Rhodes scholar at Oxford University.

At the very least, acknowledging Clinton's acquaintance with political theory is necessary to understand what the president felt animated him. Clinton believed that he possessed a coherent, philosophically driven understanding of politics. He also came to realize how difficult it was for him to convey to the public that he had a coherent governing philosophy. Early in his presidency he observed to Larry King that "the thing that has surprised me most is how difficult it is . . . to really keep communicating what you're about to the American people. That to me has been the most frustrating thing" about being president. This feeling did not subside in subsequent years. Speechwriter Michael Waldman describes Clinton as frustrated that he was not being given credit for having "a well-developed governing philosophy . . . far more than most presidents" while he prepared for the 1998 State of the Union Address.[1] At the end of his second term, Clinton lamented to Joe Klein that he had not succeeded in communicating his "coherent philosophy." Elsewhere I have demonstrated that Clinton's sporadic articulation of his political thought was a barrier in getting the public to understand his public philosophy.[2] Clinton possessed a worldview that was informed by political theory, but the public did not realize it, in large part because he talked about it only at strategically beneficial times. His political thought was built around concepts from political theory with which most Americans are unfamiliar, which further hindered his ability to communicate except by using the most general of terms.

In his public addresses Clinton mentioned political theorists often. He typically did so very briefly and to make a specific point, as in the quote about trade above in which Clinton paraphrased Niccolo Machiavelli. The passage referenced is from chapter 6 of *The Prince*. The verity introduced there is that political leaders who hope to effect significant changes face great difficulty. Those who stand to lose are advantaged by current arrangements and perfectly aware of the stakes. They fight tenaciously against new rules and regulations. Meanwhile, those who might gain from change are not only disadvantaged by the current state of things, they are unsure what the future will bring. They do not fight for reform as hard as their opponents fight against it. Clinton would repeat this idea in public many times during his presidency, applying it across a range of issues, referencing Machiavelli each time.[3]

Chapter 6 of *The Prince* is a particularly important section of that pithy book. It describes the leaders whom Machiavelli deems to be "most excellent." These leaders are "armed prophets" and include Moses, Romulus, and Theseus. These armed prophets attained political power with great difficulty because they had to destroy old regimes in order to do so. They achieved their positions through the force of arms, and instituted new "modes and orders"—sometimes translated as "rules and regulations"—in place of the old, by which the reformed state is successfully governed for an extended period.[4] These are the figures who Machiavelli notes overcame the dynamic that Clinton mentions.

Clinton's affinity to this portion of *The Prince* is interesting for several reasons. Successful politicians typically protect their images with great care. When it comes to mentioning political theorists in speeches, quoting Machiavelli throws caution to the wind, as his writings were on the Papal Index for centuries and he is still acknowledged by many as a "teacher of evil." Bill Clinton is the only president who made frequent public references to Machiavelli.[5] The way which Clinton referenced Machiavelli did not deeply implicate him in the Florentine's political thought, however. He did not proclaim himself to be a "Machiavellian" like Wilson proclaimed himself to be a Burkean. Yet an astute listener might still wonder what the president who quoted Machiavelli during the day was capable of at night. And if that president agreed with *The Prince*'s observations about the difficulty of change, might he not also be tempted to agree with the book's advice about what to do about it? Might not the commander in chief of the most potent military force in world history be tempted to bring change as an "armed prophet" who would establish a new regime?[6]

If Clinton was *not* tempted in this way, the choice of the quote is interesting because it accepts Machiavelli's main observation but flouts his advice about what to do. If a leader wants fundamental change and does not use arms, Machiavelli asserts that he will be "ruined." Chapter 6 even gives an example of such an "unarmed prophet" who came to ruin: Father Girolamo Savanarola. Savanarola, the monk known for presiding over bonfires which were used to burn "vanities" like portraits and books, succeeded in changing the tone of Florence's politics for a time. However, he came to a violent end in 1498, when he was burned alive on a pike. If Clinton knew this chapter well, its use served to justify his own integrity to himself: he would fight the hard battle for change, but he would do so without the force of arms. He would face constraints the leaders of old never did. He would push for reform against the odds, because it was the right thing to do.

The reference to Machiavelli is indicative of the unique way that Clinton used the ideas of political theorists. In referencing a thinker, Clinton almost inevitably tied the thinker's ideas to something very specific. In this case it is trade policy. Machiavelli did not have much to say about free trade, an issue at the center of political discourse during the late twentieth century but not in the early sixteenth century. Yet Clinton applied Machiavelli's truism to it in a logical way. The industries and workers which benefit from protectionism fight hard against free-trade agreements. The great majority of people might benefit from them, but not knowing what their benefits will be and not feeling a personal stake in the fight, they do not do much to support free trade. It was up to Clinton to champion this issue, against the odds, or so he thought, anyway.[7] When individual thinkers were named and quoted by Clinton, as in the case of Machiavelli, they served as a kind of intellectual window dressing. They did not inspire the actual policy at hand.

The primary programmatic influence on Clinton's thinking was not Machiavelli or any other particular thinker. Rather, it was political theory's venerable tradition of the social contract. Clinton's own sense of the concept did not neatly correspond to any particular thinker's version of it, but was an amorphous amalgamation of traditional and contemporary ideas. Drawing vaguely on sources from John Locke to John Rawls and Robert Reich, Clinton found that the contract metaphor was almost universally applicable to his preferred policies. In general, Clinton melded a traditional way of thinking about the social contract, as an understanding between citizens and their government, with a more contemporary treatment of contractarianism as a set of incentives that individuals have to engage in cooperative behaviors. Additionally he grafted a concept of historical development onto his contractarianism. Inspired by his Georgetown University instructor Carroll Quigley and Yale University's Stephen Skowronek, Clinton stressed that to maintain a democracy, new social contracts had to be forged at regular intervals.

The quote at the opening of this chapter describes Social Security as a social contract. Clinton would come to describe a myriad of programs as contractarian, including Medicare and Medicaid, international-trade agreements and worker-retraining provisions, efforts at racial reconciliation, education policy, human rights, welfare, and debt relief in developing nations. These were the policies which made Clinton a "New Democrat." Many have offered a cynical interpretation of this label, which Clinton took for himself, as if it merely meant splitting the difference between conservative and liberal positions to gain an electoral advantage. Undoubtedly there was calculation behind the phrase. However, there is more to it, which can be discerned when examining his thinking through the lens of political theory. Clinton rejected an "Old Democrat" ethic, which he suggested stood for a government providing benefits to citizens without any attendant obligations on their part. He also contrasted this view with "Reagan Republicanism," which emphasized that government should get out of the way so that individuals could succeed (or fail) on their own. By contrast, Clinton was enamored of policies which provided the kind of reciprocal benefits that a contract offers to its respective parties. Government would provide benefits to citizens as long as they worked to better themselves. The nation would benefit, socially and economically, from these responsible citizens. In the pursuit of these policies, and in the administration of a thickened government with thousands of existing programs and millions of employees, Clinton made daily compromises in advancing this vision. These compromises muted the impact of his political thought, but did not preclude its existence. Nor did they render Clinton's contractarian vision meaningless.

"An Intellect That Can Stand the Pressures of Political Life"

There has been so much written about Bill Clinton that it is strange to suggest that scholarship about him is just now emerging from its infancy. The interpretations provided by journalists, political operatives, and pundits will slowly give way to assessments by historians and political scientists, as has been the case for other presidents. In the short term, the challenge for scholars is to make assessments from a documentary record that is spotty. Much of what was written and spoken by early presidents is lost forever; the challenge with a recent president like Clinton is different. Much of what Clinton wrote and thought is preserved, but has not been made public. Anyone can go to *The Papers of Woodrow Wilson* and find Wilson's love letters, his lecture notes, and even excerpts from his college notebooks. Comparable items exist for Clinton, but the great majority of these documents have not been released. Nevertheless, we can get some sense of his approach to political theory by examining what he has said about it and what has been discovered through interviews of those who know him.

Clinton is an avid reader. As president he tried to set aside several hours a day as "alone time," a healthy portion of which was used for reading. Acquaintances marvel at the speed with which he reads. Thus it is no idle claim that despite a sometimes wavering interest in his academic work as a Rhodes scholar, Clinton remembers that he "read hundreds of books" in his time at Oxford.[8] As president he set a goal of reading, or at least skimming, several books per week. Much of what he reads is fiction, but he is also very interested in history, and he has read extensively in the social sciences. In *Intellectuals and the American Presidency*, Tevi Troy reports that while Clinton was president "most of the books he read were current" and that he regularly solicited prominent professors for suggestions about what to read.[9]

Clinton's reading of political philosophy began as an undergraduate at Georgetown University. The Jesuit liberal arts curriculum in place during Clinton's time there allowed no electives during the first two years and was heavily tilted toward an understanding of the history of Western civilization. In the mid-1960s Georgetown still relied heavily on the *ratio studiorum*, the late sixteenth-century outline for Jesuit instruction, which prescribed a "philosophical course . . . at least three years long" with an emphasis on reading Aristotle.[10] In *My Life*, Clinton reports a number of intellectual experiences at Georgetown which relate to political theory. He read Kant, Hegel, and Nietzsche. One of the highlights of his first semester was Professor Quigley's lecture on Plato, in which Quigley denounced the ancient Greek as a fascist. Clinton delivered a class presentation on Joseph Schumpeter's *Capitalism, Socialism, and Democracy* and dropped out of a course called "The Theory and Practice of Communism"—not because of its content, but because of his adoptive father's terminal illness. A senior-year paper of which Clinton was particularly proud examined "the legal and philosophical roots of the conscientious-objection allowances" in several nations.[11]

When Clinton submitted his application for a Rhodes scholarship in his senior year, he told the selection committee that he had chosen Georgetown "to prepare for the life of a practicing politician." He proceeded to ask "the committee to send me to Oxford 'to study in depth those subjects which I have only begun to investigate,' in the hope that I could 'mold an intellect that can stand the pressures of political life.'" This idea sounds vaguely reminiscent of Woodrow Wilson's covenant with Charlie Talcott. But instead of the Wilsonian formula of gaining knowledge to wield power, the young Clinton viewed learning as something to steel himself against the "pressures of political life." Apparently Clinton thought of political philosophy as something which might give a practicing politician a compass, pointing to worthy commitments in a world filled with temptations to do the wrong thing. Looking back on this application, Clinton judged it to be "a bit strained and overdone, as if I were trying to find the kind of voice in which a cultivated Rhodes scholar should speak."[12] He did not, however, refute its understanding of the role of political philosophy.

At Oxford, Clinton quickly realized that he had been placed in the wrong program. The "politics, philosophy, and economics" track, known by the acronym PPE, was not for him. This was not because the subject matter was heavily tilted toward political theory. Clinton switched programs because he "had covered virtually all the first year's work in PPE at Georgetown." He continued to study political theory in another program, supervised by the Polish émigré and Hegel scholar Zbigniew Pelczynski. Among Clinton's seminars was one on pluralist democratic theory, another was on "the relevance of scientific theories to strategic planning," and a third had him read Thomas Hobbes and John Locke. Clinton found the seminar on pluralism boring. It led him to conclude that "I am at root not intellectual, not conceptual about the actual." He did not, however, take the next step to conclude that political theory was of little worth—a step that we have seen others take. He came to prefer Locke's ideas to Hobbes's, and contractarian thinking remained with him as an enduring intellectual enthusiasm.[13] Clinton emerged from his two years at Oxford a bit sheepish for not having produced scholarship as deep or as meaningful as his friends Strobe Talbott and Frank Aller. Compared to their self-styled curricula on Russia (Talbott) and China (Aller), Clinton had emphasized breadth rather than depth and theory rather than comparative politics.[14] In the long run this choice would not be an impediment to him but an advantage. It meant that he departed Oxford having read eclectically about politics, including a good deal of political philosophy, which he proceeded to borrow from and use in his political career.

Perhaps the most famous networker ever, Clinton made many connections with academics and intellectuals, both in the years before he became president and while he was in office. He consulted fellow 1968 Rhodes scholar Robert Reich frequently as he climbed to political prominence. The Harvard University professor would later become Clinton's first secretary of labor and a somewhat conflicted memoirist of the Clinton administration. Clinton's path to the presidency was forged with the help of the Democratic Leadership Council, a forum for New Democrats who envisioned themselves moving beyond the New Deal coalition and presenting a viable ideological alternative to Reagan Republicanism. The DLC and its affiliated think tank, the Progressive Policy Institute, was a second home to several academics, including the political theorist William A. Galston, well known for his reconciling of liberal and communitarian ideals. Galston would play an integral role in crafting Clinton's campaign message in 1992.[15]

Relatively few members of the DLC ended up with jobs in the Clinton administration, and many were unhappy at the level of influence they wielded—an indication of the DLC's weakness within the Democratic Party. Several, including Galston, did find jobs in the Clinton White House, however. In addition to having responsibility over policy projects like a national service program, Galston coordinated roundtable sessions between the president and members of the academy, a task later assigned to Sidney Blumenthal in Clinton's second term. The roundtables meant that Clinton brought more professors into the White House than any other president. He got to know some of the participants quite well, and he regularly consulted academics about the "state of the union" before delivering his annual address to Congress. Troy argues that Clinton did not take much intellectual direction from these meetings. This may be true, but for a reason that Troy does not acknowledge: Clinton already possessed a worldview informed by political theory. The academics did not move him much except insofar as he could integrate their ideas into his preexisting view and accomplish in practice what they suggested.[16]

This was not enough to satisfy some of the participants of the academic roundtables, like communitarian political theorist Benjamin R. Barber. Barber's book about his experiences as an academic adjunct to the Clinton White House is titled *The Truth of Power*. The book stresses that "although Clinton enjoyed our company and reveled in our ideas, he took his political cues from politics and the polls."[17] A theorist who is particularly ambitious in his normative aspirations, Barber has a point, but the point does not carry the great weight that Barber intends it to. Clinton did make frequent concessions to public opinion and majority sentiment in Congress. A case in point concerns one of Barber's ideals: a universal national-service program. When Galston suggested that a national-service program be part of the Clinton platform for the 1992 campaign, Clinton eagerly agreed, touting its benefits in stump speeches across the nation. In 1993 that campaign theme met the realities of governing. Never having envisioned the program as anything but voluntary, and therefore far from universal, Congress passed a significantly scaled-down version of what Clinton suggested. The president signed AmeriCorps into being, but AmeriCorps was not on the scale that Barber wanted. However, it *is* a public-service program—and arguably the most that Clinton could get out of Congress. Its size was a concession to political reality. Given the large budget deficits of the time and Clinton's outsider status within his own party, it is difficult to imagine another result, except in thought. Among the professors brought to the White House were Alan Brinkley, Theda Skocpol, Amy Gutmann, Amitai Etzioni, Michael Sandel, Richard Rorty, Cass Sunstein, and Jane Mansbridge, all of whom are either political theorists or whose work has significant theoretical implications.

Several of the presidents featured in this book have drawn stark lines within political theory, delineating what is useful from what is problematic or dangerous. Adams did this when he venerated the tradition of the mixed constitution and dismissed the strands of the Enlightenment, which were more democratic; Jefferson felt that the ancients were not worth reading, while modern, "scientific" Enlightenment thought offered the true path to human happiness; Wilson rejected all of political theory except for the few thinkers whom he deemed to be realistic, like Burke and Bagehot. Bill Clinton did not and would not make such categorical distinctions. He would find value in many views, and he would synthesize disparate ideas. Zbigniew Pelczynski noted this tendency of Clinton's at Oxford. He told David Maraniss that "what suited Clinton was the longer form [of essays], laying out all the different lines of thought and synthesizing them rather than independently developing his own line of thought." Journalists also remarked on Clinton's intellectual eclecticism and his tendency to reconcile opposing ideas.[18] Many report the frustration of Clinton confidants, who would believe that the president agreed with them, only to discover that he also agreed with others whose ideas they believed were incompatible with their own. The president sought to reconcile ideas where others felt a choice had to be made.

In terms of political theory, Clinton's intellectual eclecticism meant that he found value in the social contract without feeling a necessity to choose between versions of it. Clinton could admire and embrace both Locke and Rawls, a combination that would strike many political theorists as difficult. Barber's frustration with Clinton is understandable, but it is less a result of cynical maneuverings on Clinton's part than of their incompatible approaches to political theory. Barber sees stark distinctions and the necessity of making clear choices and pursuing one option to the exclusion of the other. Clinton does not. In *Strong Democracy: Participatory Politics for a New Age* Barber famously stresses the incompatibility of liberal contractarian politics with communitarianism (he calls the former "politics as zookeeping").[19] To Barber, communitarian values should *replace* the liberal contractarian tradition, not be grafted onto it. Reconciling the two is futile to him—a sure way to fatally compromise the benefits promised by an invigorated communal life. With a personality inclined to harmonizing disparate views and smoothing over controversies and a job in which these traits are significant assets, Bill Clinton did not see a necessity for citizens to choose between self-advancement and a commitment to community. He felt he could successfully combine liberal social contractarianism with communitarianism.

This tendency was reinforced by Galston, who stressed that the liberal-communitarian distinction had been overdrawn. With Galston's counsel, Clinton saw no difficulty in taking communitarian suggestions—like the national-service initiative—and happily welding them to a preexisting liberal contractarian worldview, without pausing to consider that others, like Barber, might not consider these ideas compatible. The result was a fascinating admixture of ideas employed ad hoc, issue to issue, making it difficult for the public—and the political theorists Clinton consulted—to understand where he was coming from and leading the few who recognized his use of themes from political theory to not take him particularly seriously.

Clinton reveled in the details of policy. As governor of Arkansas and then as president he was both hands-on and knowledgeable across an impressive range of policies. Someone with this kind of interest in detail often has difficulty moving between the "micro level" of policy and the "macro level" analysis that political theory typically requires. One thinks of speechwriter James Fallows's indictment of Jimmy Carter: Carter's problem was that he thought fifty different things but believed no one thing, and thus there was no overarching direction to his presidency.[20] By contrast, Clinton showed great facility in moving back and forth between a theoretical outlook and specific policies which fit within that outlook. Clinton's nomination-acceptance speech in 1992, for example, masterfully wove policy commitments around the theme of the "New Covenant," a label Clinton developed with the help of DLC staffer Bruce Reed to describe his unique vision of the social contract.[21]

The speech explained how the New Covenant was "a solemn agreement between the people and their government, based not simply on what each of us can take but on what all of us must give to our nation."[22] He proceeded to explain how benefits received from government were to be linked to responsible behaviors in economic policy, education, welfare, and health care. The fuzzy, eclectic nature of Clinton's contractarianism may have facilitated his moving between the general and the specific, but this is a skill that is unusual in a practitioner of politics who is theoretically inclined. If Carter had trouble moving from the specific to the general, Woodrow Wilson was challenged in moving from the general to the specific. Compared to Clinton, Wilson had little idea of how he would apply his theoretical ideals in practice as he campaigned for the presidency in 1912. Wilson would formulate his applications of theory to practice on the fly as president, with intriguing results. Clinton's policy preferences were typically better synchronized with his theoretical understandings than were Wilson's, and therefore more consistent. When he disappointed hopeful backers, it was on an issue-by-issue basis—unlike Wilson's turn to progressivism, which disappointed his political sponsors wholesale.

Bill Clinton was well read in political theory and well connected with many of the academics who shaped the discipline in the late twentieth century. He acknowledged political theory's value, thinking of it as something which might elevate politics above naked self-interest. His approach to its ideas mirrored his own personal tendencies: he tried to find common ground and synthesize various views, even when others felt that there was little common ground to be had. Clinton had a talent for moving from abstract theory to a set of preferred policies. However, as we will see, he often failed to effectively articulate his theoretical outlook, and frequently set it aside because of various political pressures.

Regime-Cycle Contractarianism

In Chapter 3, I pointed out that Thomas Jefferson was not interested in writing a work of political theory. His devotion to science and his feeling that what he embraced was commonsensical mitigated against such an endeavor. Jefferson's beliefs may have even made him incapable of writing such a work, despite the fact that he had read and internalized a good deal of political theory. This does not suggest that his political thought is uninteresting—or without impact. On the contrary, Jefferson's reluctance to deeply analyze his own political thought makes the analysis of it all the more important. Bill Clinton is similar to Jefferson in this regard.

Clinton's explicit references to individual political theorists were always brief. As in his paraphrase of Machiavelli, he usually referenced a specific quote from a thinker's writing. He did not explore the position for more than a few sentences or spell out its implications in depth. Another favored reference, to Alexis de Tocqueville, illustrates the point. A typical telling went like this: "I believe fundamentally in the common sense and the essential core goodness of the American people. Don't forget that Alexis de Tocqueville said a long time ago that America is great because America is good; and if America ever ceases to be good, she will no longer be great."[23] Clinton included this same idea, told almost verbatim, in at least eight of his public speeches. The reference is not without meaning, particularly if one is acquainted with Tocqueville, but it is exceedingly vague. The comment is related to the distinctive ideas that make Tocqueville a notable voice in political theory, but it is told without any of the depth required to make it more than an offhanded truism. Nor does it offer much direction in terms of desired policies. The reference seems intended to grant an intellectual heft to his remarks. Almost all of Clinton's references to specific theorists served this purpose. They demonstrate a certain respect for political theory, and at the same time, they are a calculation that dropping the name and an idea of a political theorist will be politically useful.

Undoubtedly this tendency was partly due to the rhetorical realities of the late twentieth century. Tocqueville had intellectual currency in the 1990s, but devoting paragraphs to how his ideas might be applied contemporaneously would have risked losing any modern audience.

However, this does not fully account for why someone who had read scores of books and thousands of pages of political theory never discussed particular thinkers at length in any of his available writings or speeches. Over 100 speeches Clinton delivered as president used the terms "social contract," "social compact," or "New Covenant." He used these terms without ever speaking extensively about them conceptually or linking them to the individuals whose vision of the social contract inspired him. It is as if the ideas Clinton gleaned from political theory did not need to be explained. Clinton loves to talk and is highly intelligent, yet he would not and maybe could not write at length about social contractarianism except to explain how specific policies fit with this ideal. The practical result is that it is a challenge to pinpoint the individuals from whom Clinton borrowed, though it is not difficult to show that he employed this concept used by many theorists. It was the idea or the metaphor of the social contract which resonated with Clinton more than any particular version of it.[24]

Traditionally, a social contract has been understood as an agreement that binds citizens together in a political community or creates a government. Rousseau, Locke, and Kant are among the "civil contractarians" who argue for some kind of preferred arrangement between citizens and government. A major variant, prevalent among contemporary theorists, suggests that the social contract is a shared understanding among citizens who voluntarily pursue enlightened self-interest. These "moral contractarians" believe that enlightened individuals will "adopt constraints on their behavior in order to maximize benefits."[25] Government may be involved in this process, but it need not be. Most of these later authors were, in some way, inspired by the revival of the contractarian tradition by John Rawls, whose *Theory of Justice* was published in 1971. Bill Clinton read both civil- and moral-contractarian theory, and he used contractarian language to refer both to a desired arrangement between citizens and government and to cooperative relations among citizens.

When Clinton used the term "New Covenant," he always included the government as a contracting partner. For example, in a speech at Georgetown in June 1999 Clinton noted, "I asked the American people instead to embrace a new way—something I called a New Covenant between America and its government; an agreement with the citizens and their government that we would jointly pursue opportunity for all Americans, responsibility from all Americans, and a community of all Americans." In an April 1995 radio address he said that "what I call the New Covenant [is] a partnership between Americans and their government that offers more opportunity in return for more responsibility."[26]

Clinton was in law school when *A Theory of Justice* came out, and he read it soon after it was published. When presenting Rawls with the Congressional Medal of Freedom in 1999, Clinton described himself as being "moved" by the book. Clinton said he became captivated by the idea that "a society in which the most fortunate helped the least fortunate is not only a moral society, but a logical one."[27] Rawls's social contract asks individuals to imagine that they do not know anything particular about themselves (gender, race, athletic ability, etc.). Because people are risk averse about their life prospects under these conditions, Rawls suggests that people will "maximin," or maximize the position of the class of people who are least well off. They will also agree only to inequalities which have a positive effect on the least well off. Thus, Rawls's contractarian vision is predicated on a collective display of enlightened self-interest. Government is involved, but the more important step is establishing a unanimous prior agreement among citizens about a society's ethical parameters.

Rawls's view of justice is most compatible with the policies of an advanced welfare state. Clinton did not share a similar enthusiasm for Scandinavian-style politics. However, he folded into his political thought the moral-contractarian ideal first inspired by Rawls: self-interest properly pursued yields mutual benefits for all. Self-interest and cooperation could be made partners and individuals did not have to choose between them. Clinton therefore included in his understanding of the "social contract" and "social compact" an element of cooperation among citizens. For instance, at a DLC event in 1997 Clinton emphasized that

> it is up to us—to all of us—the generation of the computer revolution, to craft a new social compact for a new economy, a new understanding of the responsibilities of government and business *and every one of us what we owe each other.* It is up to us to make sure that our people have the strength, the skills, the security, the flexibility we need to reap the rewards of the 21st century.[28]

The italicized phrase suggests the kind of voluntary cooperation of the moral contractarians. John F. Harris reports that at the end of his presidency, Clinton was "enthralled" with the book *Nonzero: The Logic of Human Destiny,* written by Robert Wright. *Nonzero* stresses that "the instinct for social progress [is] inherent in the human species, and that progress is achieved by human interactions that are not zero-sum propositions." The imperative for the modern world was to promote relationships and social endeavors in which all sides win.[29] The reason the president was enthralled by *Nonzero* was not that its message was a revelation to him, but that it meticulously argued the "moral-contractarian" point that he had believed in at least since law school: self-interest rightly pursued yields cooperation and prosperity rather than strife and exploitation.

It is this assumption that allowed Clinton to graft several communitarian themes onto a contractarian frame with the aid of William Galston. If the most effective way to pursue an agenda of self-interest is through cooperative behavior, then the American people would not have to choose between the individual protections provided by the liberal state and the benefits of community—they could have both at the same time. Clinton touted the national-service program's benefits to the nation, but he simultaneously suggested that service would be attractive to individuals because it would be a valuable credential and would help pay the costs of their college education. This confluence of self-interest and communal behavior also informed Clinton's approach toward race. At a Democratic National Committee event at which he elaborated on his vision about how to "preserve the social contract," Clinton related,

> It is a selfish thing to want every American, without regard to their race, their neighborhood, their background, or where they start out in life, to have a good chance to make it. That is a selfish thing to feel, because if they don't, then they're a drag on your future. And if they do, then they're contributing to your future.[30]

With this understanding, fostering racial harmony is not so much a matter of convincing people with widely disparate cultural histories to respect each other. Instead, racial justice would be effected as soon as people realize that it is in their self-interest. Racial fair play is part of a desired social contract, something that every American owes to every other American. Clinton stressed, however, that this is not a difficult obligation to fulfill, because the collective success of people from each race is beneficial to all others. He used the same argument about education: increasing spending on education is in everyone's self-interest.

On many occasions and in numerous policy areas Bill Clinton called for sacrifice and responsibility. It was, however, sacrifice and responsibility without a hard edge, for these admonitions were radically tempered by the promise that such actions were actually in the subject's best interest, which simultaneously coincided with the public good. This is a striking assertion about how human interaction can work. It holds out the promise that if people understand their self-interest correctly there will be virtually no zero-sum actions and almost no disputes over what individuals should do and what public policy should aim at.

Regardless of the phrase used, "social contract," "social compact," or "New Covenant," the concept consisted of an arrangement of mutual benefit to the contracting partners. Typically a specific policy or set of policies was offered up along with the phrase. Regardless of the contracting parties mentioned, none of the references elaborated greatly on the concept. Nor did the president mention any particular political theorist that an interested citizen could read in order to enhance their understanding of the idea. Clinton never even mentioned that the social contract was an idea borrowed from political philosophy. He simply used its language to describe what he wanted to effect, hoping that the public would respond favorably.

Clinton's campaign speeches in 1992 were filled with specific policy suggestions. The contractarian gloss that Clinton put on these programs made his political thought notable. Benefits would be tied to the performance of socially redeeming behaviors. Clinton summarized his thinking in a speech at Notre Dame University in this way:

> When I think of how I want to help change America during the next four years, I want, most of all, to restore the link between rights and responsibilities, between opportunities and obligations: the social contract that defines what we owe to one another, to our communities and to our country, as well as what we are entitled to for ourselves.[31]

Policies which took the form of mutually beneficial transactions were the ones which Clinton hoped would define his legacy.

Much of Clinton's distinctive approach to politics had been articulated by Robert Reich. Clinton's ongoing friendship with Reich acquainted him with Reich's quasi-contractarian view of "human capital" best expressed in *The Work of Nations: Preparing Ourselves for 21st Century Capitalism.* In this book, Reich notes that the United States is in a critical time of transition. National borders are decreasing in importance. The divide between those with "intellectual capital" and those without it is widening. A college education or technical skills are required to succeed in the new "information age." National success in the new global economy requires government to facilitate advanced education or training. The United States government should invest in building the intellectual capital of its citizens. The "fortunate fifth" (the label Reich uses to describe those in the highest quintile of earnings) should pay the most in taxes, as they benefit most from the growth of intellectual capital. Trade barriers should come down as unskilled workers in developing nations could produce goods requiring unskilled labor while the United States developed a new economy centered around high-skill and information-oriented jobs.[32] Clinton used these ideas and folded them into the New Covenant's "benefits in exchange for responsibility" ethic.

Political development has often been of little concern to those in the social-contract tradition.[33] Ever the eclectic in intellectual matters, Clinton seems to have attached an understanding of how political history works to his social contractarianism. The phrase "New Covenant" implies the existence of an old covenant, and in Clinton's view the old covenant still in place when he assumed the presidency began during the New Deal.[34] The New Deal had itself once been a new covenant which modified a previous social contract forged during the Progressive Era. Clinton identified five different eras in American politics, each with its own distinctive "covenant."[35]

Clinton's thinking about political history was influenced by two scholars who had commented extensively on the importance of periodic renewal in politics. In *My Life* Clinton relates that "two of [Georgetown Professor Carroll] Quigley's insights had a particularly lasting impact" on him. The first was that civilizations become "institutionalized," meaning that through time structures and practices originally designed to benefit most of society become the tools of "vested interests more committed to preserving their own prerogatives than to meeting the [socially beneficial] needs for which they were created." The second was that Western civilization possesses a uniquely resilient set of animating ideas, including that human beings are basically good, that there *is* truth but no mortal fully possesses it, and that through hard work tomorrow can be made better than today. Quigley called this set of ideas "future preference," and future preference granted Western civilization its unusual resilience, its creativity, and the impetus to periodically overcome institutionalization.[36]

In *The Politics Presidents Make: Leadership from John Adams to George Bush,* Yale's Stephen Skowronek stresses the periodicity of presidential power. Presidents are empowered at the beginning of a "regime cycle," defined by a critical election, and the presidency's capacity for leadership wanes as that partisan coalition advances in age.[37] Even though Skowronek concludes that this cycling had probably come to an end due to the substantial "thickening" of the federal government, which has made it harder to change, Clinton believed that the United States was ready for a new regime cycle which would supersede the New Deal and refresh American democracy. Policies which had outlived their usefulness and been captured by special interests would be replaced by policies which worked for the people.

Neither Quigley nor Skowronek is typically characterized as a political theorist. However, in Clinton's hands, the idea of regime cycles became inextricably linked to democratic theory. A democracy could not survive without periodic renewals.[38] The New Covenant was to be such a renewal.

Quigley's stark juxtaposition of optimism (we can renew our civilization) with pessimism (it is going to be an uphill battle against selfish interests, and once a renewal is accomplished it immediately starts being co-opted) became characteristically Clintonian. Clinton believed that "institutionalization" was peaking just as the world was rapidly changing from an industrial economy to an information-based one. In order to remain the world's economic, political, and moral leader, the United States would have to break the hold of vested interests on public policies. Forces beyond the ken of one generation alter conditions so fundamentally that policies which promoted democracy in one era may hinder it in the next. A democratic nation needs to effect a kind of "regime-cycle contractarianism," with new social contracts forged in the aftermath of critical elections to short-circuit the self-serving forces of institutionalization, thus preserving democracy. Upon his election, Clinton ambitiously hoped to effect the transition to a new social contract that preserved old values.

"What Is the Nature of the Social Contract Now?"

While President Clinton consistently used the shorthand slogan that he associated with his New Covenant ("opportunity, responsibility, and community"), his explicit use of the terms "social contract," "social compact," and "New Covenant" was sporadic. A search for these three phrases among the thousands of documents posted to the Clinton Foundation website reveals that the bulk of Clinton's use of them came at three critical junctures. Contractarianism was stressed during the 1992 campaign, then it was reintroduced as the House Republicans tried to implement their Contract with America in early 1995, and finally, Clinton made frequent mention of these phrases during the Monica Lewinsky scandal.[39]

The uneven use of contractarian language corresponded to changes in political context. As a candidate running his own entrepreneurial campaign in 1992, Clinton was relatively free to define himself as he wished. In transitioning from campaigning to governing, he had to take into consideration the views of the members of Congress with whom he would be working. Since only a small fraction of Democrats identified with the DLC, this dictated muting the themes he had emphasized during the campaign. Additionally, Clinton needed to address a pressing issue first, deficit reduction. Though he succeeded in cajoling a deficit-reducing budget out of Congress in 1993, new programs that would have been part of the New Covenant would be scrapped, postponed, or radically scaled back. Clinton's political thought did not fundamentally change after he won the 1992 election, but the context in which he operated did.

The signature effort of 1994—trying to put together a majority coalition in favor of universal health care—required Clinton to court many Democrats who were indifferent or even hostile toward the DLC-inspired agenda. In pressing for health care Clinton did not emphasize that government would provide a benefit in exchange for responsible behavior. He simply promised the benefit.[40] In short, the choice to focus on deficit reduction and then on health care in the first two years of Clinton's presidency demoted the pursuit of contractarian policies. Clinton reemphasized contractarian themes in response to the Republicans' stunning election victory in the first half of 1995 to demonstrate that he offered a viable alternative to the thinking associated with the Contract with America. When he went back to working with Congress on specific policies, his contractarian rhetoric receded again. As he faced the crisis of the Lewinsky scandal, Clinton reintroduced contractarian phrases, probably as a means of demonstrating to the public that he offered them a serious alternative to "the politics of personal destruction."

Clinton used contractarian terms outside of the three junctures outlined above, but not with much frequency. Subordinating a full articulation of his political thought to his attempts to knit together winning coalitions was a strategic choice. It served Clinton well in many individual policy fights, but that came at an overall price: the appearance of a lack of consistency, which led observers not to take the New Covenant seriously. Sidney Blumenthal's semiofficial account of the Clinton presidency, *The Clinton Wars,* asserts that this practice had a devastating effect on Clinton's reputation. Because Clinton offered a new way of thinking and embraced fundamental change across a range of policies, forging coalitions to pass legislation required "constant improvisations." Clinton had few consistent legislative partners. His policy preferences often crossed traditional party lines, catching even members of his own party off guard. These shifts "made it easy to criticize [Clinton] as an unprincipled, shambling huckster, and to see in his stumbles profound flaws" rather than conveying an image of him as someone with a coherent set of ideals, even though in the abstract he did have a theoretical ideal in mind.[41]

In his first year in office, Clinton signed the North American Free Trade Agreement (NAFTA) into law, relying more on Republican votes in Congress than Democratic votes. Clinton was a devout free trader, though he consistently suggested that trade agreements had to include environmental and worker safeguards in signatory nations. Clinton was not just concerned about the workers in China or Mexico, which may not have had such safeguards in place. He also suggested that the agreements obligated the United States government to emphasize job retraining for its citizens who would be displaced. The benefits of more commerce and cheaper products came with the attendant obligation of retraining workers at home for high-skill, high-paying jobs. Thus at the bill signing for NAFTA, Clinton stated that while expanded trade was universally beneficial, "we have an obligation to protect those workers who do bear the brunt of competition by giving them a chance to be retrained and to go on to a new and different, and, ultimately, more secure and more rewarding way of work. In recent years, this social contract has been sundered; it cannot continue."[42] Clinton had reluctantly decoupled his worker-training proposal from NAFTA to obtain the latter's passage. In an era of large deficits, broad Congressional support for retraining never materialized, severely disappointing Secretary of Labor Reich. Nevertheless, a modest retraining program for displaced blue-collar workers did become law in the wake of NAFTA. A more ambitious proposal was sacrificed to deficit reduction. Reich's influence could also be seen in the shape of the 1993 budget agreement, which raised taxes on those who had the most success in the new global economy, individuals making $200,000 per year or more.

Clinton's approach to domestic poverty embodied the "opportunity for responsibility" model as well. "Changing welfare as we know it" was one of the most familiar refrains from the 1992 campaign. Clinton identified welfare as a flawed "old covenant" policy which resembled a handout. His preferred reform aimed at encouraging work and the development of job skills. Initially the Clinton administration allowed individual states to implement "workfare" programs. A new national workfare policy was signed into law in 1996. With the Republican takeover of Congress, a cross-party coalition was required, the substance of which upset many Democrats. Clinton was not able to cajole Republicans into accepting the level of funding for job training or day care that he sought. Nevertheless, the program was a substantial reform which promised a benefit contingent on participation in job-training programs and finding actual employment.

After the 1995 Republican takeover of Congress, many of Clinton's references to the social contract had an altered emphasis from those offered up in 1992. Clinton turned his primary attention from developing a New Covenant for a new age to making sure that the desirable aspects of the "old" social contract were not bulldozed by the "Republican Revolution." Clinton most frequently described Social Security, Medicare, and Medicaid as part of an existing social contract which he would prevent the Republicans from slashing, but he included other items too. Early in the 1995 budget impasse, Clinton staked out his position by saying,

We can work this out, folks. The only thing I won't do—I will not do this—I will not let balancing the budget serve as cover for destroying the social compact: for cutting back on education, wrecking the environment, or undermining our obligations to help protect our children and treat our elderly people decently, because it is not necessary to balance the budget.[43]

After the 1994 election, Clinton still hoped for a New Covenant, but he also employed the phrases "social contract" and "social compact" as a shorthand description of the existing programs that he would veto any fundamental changes to. The American people had invested in Social Security, Medicare, education, and the environment. Clinton was determined to see that government would guarantee American citizens a good return on their investment.

In this same way, Clinton urged other nations either to preserve existing social contracts as they were or to extend the social contracts which protected their citizens. This was particularly the case in developing countries. In nation after nation during his second term, Clinton encouraged inhabitants to think about government in his preferred terms. In South America, for instance, Clinton reported that "the Venezuelans . . . understand that they can't preserve their democracy in a free market economy unless they try to strengthen the social compact. They've got to figure out a way for more people to do well and they've got to figure out an intergenerational strategy that not only supports education for children but protects the environment."[44] In several conferences on the "Third Way" in politics, Clinton posed questions that were, for him, fundamental. These included the Reich-like dilemma "how do you make the most of the economic possibilities of the global information economy and still preserve the social contract?" and he encouraged discussants to consider the question "what is the nature of the social contract now?"[45]

Though the term is normally applied exclusively to domestic politics, Bill Clinton used "social contract" in international settings. Under Clinton's leadership, the United States government and multinational actors like the World Bank were to deal with other governments and their citizens in a way that promised benefits in return for certain desired behaviors. In his international valedictory speech delivered at the University of Warwick, Clinton triumphantly suggested, "We have embraced the global social contract: debt relief for reform. We pledged enhanced debt relief to poor countries that put forward plans to spend their savings where they ought to be spent, on reducing poverty, developing health systems, improving educational access and quality." From the Mexican debt-crisis bailout to Russia's admission into the World Trade Organization, Clinton conceived of international agreements in the transactional terms of a contract.[46] The United States and transnational organizations would offer benefits to developing nations not for free, but in exchange for responsible behaviors. Traditional political theory had defined the contract as what brought a nation into existence or what legitimized an existing national government. Even Rawls's new contractarianism was firmly rooted in the nation-state paradigm. Clinton's loose, eclectic approach to the concept allowed him to apply it in an unorthodox way—to international politics and relations between states.

The Crime Bill signed into law in 1994 embodied New Covenant thinking. Federal money was made available to local governments for a broad array of activities which would reduce crime, from drug-treatment programs to neighborhood-based policing to enhanced extracurricular programs in schools. In contrast to federal grants, which were made automatically or by formula, the Crime Bill's money would be distributed primarily on the basis of competitive proposals, which rewarded programs that promised to achieve the best results. Clinton enjoyed pointing out that funding for the program came from reductions made in the federal workforce (a happenstance necessitated by the PAYGO rule, which was part of the 1990 Budget Agreement). These reductions in the federal workforce were part of the "reinventing government" initiative headed up by Vice President Al Gore, a fellow member of the Democratic Leadership Council. The term "reinventing government" was partly inspired by the book of the same name written by David Osborne and Ted Gaebler. The book provided numerous examples of how government could be made to work well if efficiencies were introduced and goal-oriented designs implemented. True to form, Clinton worked these ideas into his contractarian worldview, maintaining, "We want a government that offers opportunity, demands responsibility, and shrinks bureaucracy, one that embodies the New Covenant I've been talking about."[47] The reinventing-government initiative also aimed to reduce bureaucratic tangles by discarding counterproductive regulations and streamlining paperwork. These initiatives were designed to produce a government that would be more effective at upholding its end of the bargain that was the New Covenant.

In almost every individual case Bill Clinton's policy commitments were not extraordinary. Yet the set of policies that he backed was very unusual, as was often remarked by those who wondered if there was any coherency or principle to his thinking. While many speculated that Clinton assembled his commitments based on electoral concerns, a more careful accounting of his language suggests that his outlook was animated by a vague but encompassing contractarian vision with deep roots in political philosophy: governments should offer benefits for those who perform socially and economically beneficial behaviors. In short, President Clinton hoped to produce a set of policies which would encourage citizens and nations to engage in productive and socially responsible behaviors which were in their enlightened self-interest. This required overturning old policies which created perverse incentives and exhorting citizens to conceive of their self-interest in the more sophisticated, cooperative manner of the moral contractarians. This was his attempt at a "Third Way" in politics, an alternative to the more familiar orthodoxies of the day: the preference for a minimal government among Reagan Republicans and for a government which promised handouts to all among liberal Democrats. As Clinton put it in his 1995 State of the Union Address, "The old way of governing around here actually seemed to reward failure. The New Covenant way should have built-in incentives to reward success."[48]

In this same speech Clinton declared that "the era of big government is over." This, rather than his return to the contractarian theme of the New Covenant, was what grabbed headlines. As a result, the speech was almost uniformly misinterpreted, worrying Democrats and leading columnists to speculate that Clinton was capitulating to the Republicans. However, taking Clinton's regime-cycle contractarianism seriously puts a very different gloss on that speech and his subsequent efforts to reemphasize the New Covenant. Clinton understood the 1994 election as a watershed event in American politics. To him it marked the definitive end point of the New Deal regime cycle. Clinton's acknowledgment that the era of big government was over was the closest he could come to telling members of his own party that it was time to abandon New Deal politics and embrace his progressive, contractarian alternative. Ironically, he saw the Republican takeover of the House and Senate as a second chance to get the American people to rally behind the New Covenant, which would redefine the Democratic Party.

At this endeavor Clinton never quite succeeded. A variety of things got in the way: the American people's unfamiliarity with the concept of the social contract, the cynicism of the late twentieth-century American press, Clinton's eagerness to find common ground with others, and his inability to discuss contractarianism in anything but pithy phrases or a few well-crafted sentences. In concert, all of these prevented Americans from understanding and believing that Bill Clinton possessed a governing philosophy.

Conclusion

Bill Clinton was roundly condemned by his political opponents for lacking consistency and acting on the basis of expediency, but he was also blamed for this by many of his political partners, including Robert Reich, Dick Gephardt, David Gergen, and Dick Morris. A number of presidential scholars also stress Clinton's lack of a philosophical compass.[49] Ascribing Clinton's political success to his ability to split the difference between opposing viewpoints and his "slickness" in moving from one position to the next became a kind of folk wisdom lent credence by these criticisms.

A few journalists and academics have argued in a revisionist vein. Thomas B. Edsall contends that as a candidate Clinton successfully combined "cultural conservatism with economic populism," a potent mix which gained him the White House before he abandoned the first half of that equation in 1993 and 1994 to favor more traditional Democratic constituencies.[50] Ronald Brownstein notes that "Clinton synthesized an approach to expanding opportunity that was both effective and politically popular" by employing both "carrots" and "sticks," incentives that rewarded desirable behaviors and discouraged undesirable ones. He maintains that Clinton was not a "poll-driven opportunist who abandoned traditional Democratic priorities for a cynical centrism" and that the retrospectives which find him to be this kind of politician are not accurate.[51] Joe Klein emphasizes in *The Natural: The Misunderstood Presidency of Bill Clinton* that Clinton "arrived in Washington with a coherent, sophisticated political vision, which he pursued rigorously, quite often in ways that were politically inexpedient in the short term." "By any fair accounting, Bill Clinton was running a very serious presidency— and yet his administration, as portrayed by the political community in Washington, seemed trivial, juvenile, a circus," wrote Klein.[52] Political scientist Robert F. Durant argues that Clinton did possess a core set of beliefs centering around "opportunity, responsibility, and community." These authors and a few others stress that the politics of the Clinton era reflect Clinton's deeply held values.[53]

What should be added to these reflections is that Clinton's political thought had an almost wholly unappreciated intellectual provenance. Clinton rooted his governing philosophy in social-contract theory, one of political philosophy's most important concepts, and he possessed an informed sensitivity to historical development gained from academic works. His frequent references to political theorists like Tocqueville and Machiavelli demonstrate that he valued political theory. He borrowed on their intellectual currency.

At the same time, Clinton, like any president, faced numerous contextual challenges which mitigated against pursuit of his preferred political thought. Clinton found that the separated system required him to cooperate as much as to lead.[54] His attempt to fundamentally reform policies butted up against a thickened government whose other actors were generally outside of his control. The massive deficits that he inherited, a party caucus whose majority disliked many of his ideas, and a resurgent Republican Party which had the upper hand in Congress for six of his eight years as president all hindered Clinton's ability to make the New Covenant a reality. These things even seemed to limit his willingness to articulate his political thought. The visions he occasionally spun, of a fundamental transformation of American politics, were not only grand, in the context he faced they may have been unrealistic. Clinton typically displayed a level-headed sensitivity to political context, but this sensitivity came at a significant price—it fueled the misconception that he lacked an ideological rudder.

Clinton never offered a deep vision of the social contract—perhaps because to him there was no great depth to plumb. He had simply found a commonsensical idea that he applied to practice in many different policy arenas. The result worked for him politically. He was able to get millions to hear the term "social contract" and to identify with the slogan "opportunity, responsibility, and community." Yet this lack of depth came with a cost. He did not succeed in teaching the public to embrace the concept of the social contract deeply. Political theory requires more precision and depth of articulation than Clinton mustered in public—and more detail than the American public is currently accustomed to hearing. Any contemporary president with an interest in political theory will face this dilemma. Acquainting the public with political theory in sufficient detail to get them to accept its ideas risks losing most of them. The challenge is to balance articulation with resonance. Clinton emphasized resonance over depth; yet if he had chosen depth he may not have been as successful as he was. Even with the difficulties Clinton faced, he succeeded in fashioning many policies with a contractarian stamp which have had a significant impact on American politics, even if none of the top two or three things Clinton will be remembered for are policies in the contractarian mold.

A contemporary president with an understanding of and a set of commitments informed by political theory is on the horns of a dilemma. Aggressively advancing that understanding is likely to alienate many with whom you need to work. On the other hand, if a governing philosophy is only sporadically articulated, few will take it seriously. Bill Clinton's solution was to shuttle between frequently articulating his theoretically inspired view and voicing only muted generalities about the kind of policies he preferred. Given the difference between his campaign rhetoric and how he articulated his ideas during much of his presidency, it seems that his campaign wrote a theoretical check which he could not cash as president.

Like John Adams, Bill Clinton was not devoted to any particular thinker from political theory. Instead, each of these two was devoted to a concept. Adams's mixed constitution focused on institutions. This was a more concrete and specifically defined concept than the one which Clinton lifted from political theory, and it helped Adams understand how to do the job. The concept that Clinton appropriated was more policy oriented. A devotion to social contractarianism, at least as he understood it, helped Clinton to critique existing policies and to formulate new ones. What is remarkable about this is that it bears little resemblance to the more traditional social contractarianism embraced by James Madison. To Madison the social contract was the agreement made by the American people to adopt the Constitution and pursue politics within its parameters. Clinton's use of the social contract was more vague, but it was also more capacious, encompassing the policies which the American people had come to expect from their government and any other mutually beneficial reciprocal arrangement which could be envisioned. Clinton also acted differently from any other president in the way he referenced political theorists, frequently using them as intellectual window dressing in speeches. Had he gone into greater depth about their ideas, he might have served as a more effective "teacher in chief," but this would have been a gamble because of its potential to alienate or bore.

President Clinton demonstrated that a contemporary president can still have coherent political thinking inspired by political theory. Political theory is not merely something that once had meaning, in the days of the founders, but has since lost its relevance. Clinton found that he could readily apply his favored concept from it to generate or justify many specific policies. Useful political ideas can come from many different places. Traditionally, one of those places has been political theory. Currently there is more political theory and more meaningful political theory being written than ever before. If politicians of yesteryear were willing to consider its ideas, then why not the politicians of today? Bill Clinton did, and his presidency would have been vastly different had he not.

Conclusion

DEAR MR. PRESIDENT

I beseech you Gentlemen, are not we the Writers of Politics somwhat a ridiculous sort of People? Is it not a fine piece of Folly for private men sitting in their Cabinets to rack their brains about Models of Government? Certainly our Labors make a very pleasant recreation for those great Personages, who, sitting at the Helm of Affairs, have by their large Experience not only acquir'd the perfect Art of Ruling, but have attain'd also to the comprehension of the Nature and Foundation of Government.
> —Matthew Wren, *Considerations on Mr. Harrington's . . .*
> *"Commonwealth of Oceana"* (1657)

To say that a man may not write of Government except that he be a Magistrat, is as absurd as to say, that a man may not make a Sea-chart unless he be a Pilot. It is known that Christopher Columbus made a Chart in his Cabinet, that found out the *Indys.* The Magistrat that was good at his steerage never took it ill of him that brought him a Chart.
> —James Harrington, reply to Wren

As evidenced by Wren and Harrington's exchange, we have been arguing about whether political theory is of any real value for centuries. Unfortunately, this argument has not often progressed much beyond the blanket accusation that theorists (or professors) have little or no real-world experience and therefore cannot offer valuable suggestions, and the equally weak counterargument that those who have studied something systematically have greater expertise and therefore offer more valuable advice than those who have not. This book attempts to move this argument to a more realistic and nuanced understanding of the relationship between political theory and political practice by looking at real evidence in the cases of six presidents who possessed an outlook derived from political theory.

A brief recapitulation is in order. There is a latent but important dispute revolving around the value and usefulness of presidents' having an acquaintance with political theory. James Bryce believed that someone with this kind of knowledge might be able to govern in a way which transcends doling out patronage and satisfying group interests, even though in the presidency's late nineteenth-century incarnation he was by no means optimistic that such a person could gain the office. Kenneth Thompson articulates a similar point: we rely on presidents to offer a coherent public philosophy; without a theoretical understanding of politics, a president is unlikely to do this well. Other scholars disagree. Richard Neustadt stresses that the presidency is "not a scholar's job." Once someone becomes president, what we most often associate with political theory, ideal scenarios and long-range plans, gives way to strategic bargaining and the need to pragmatically "ride events." Being savvy at these latter two is far more important than possessing a theoretically inspired plan. Daniel J. Boorstin went significantly further than Neustadt, suggesting that by its very nature, political theory tends to become a dangerous obsession. He believed that politicians espousing a theory of government should be scrupulously avoided.

The cursory look at presidents in Chapter 1 indicates that a healthy percentage of them have had some acquaintance with political theory. An in-depth examination of such figures promised to grant insight into how theory and practice interact in the hands of a president and to help sort out these various claims. Thus we have become acquainted with six presidents along three dimensions related to political theory: how the individual approached political theory—including his attitudes about its value, what he read in the field or knew about it, and how he sorted what was valuable in it from what was not; the ideas the individual internalized and the thinkers he admired or ones he disliked and oriented himself against; and the impact that this array of interests, disinterests, enthusiasms, and antipathies had on the subject's presidency.

We have seen that John Adams was virtually obsessed with political theory, reading it constantly throughout his adult life and believing that it possessed answers to the question of how to order politics. He placed faith in the venerable tradition of the mixed constitution, which he found to be the only manner of ordering institutions which would produce a stable government. This commitment induced a very specific response from him when he was president: Adams felt compelled to chart his own way, exerting judgments independent of the legislative branch. At a critical time in the nation's history, Adams chose to keep the nation out of an unnecessary and possibly debilitating war strongly favored by his sup-posed political allies, the congressional Federalists. This course harmed Adams's political career, costing him reelection in 1800. Adams was aware that this consequence was likely and chose to act in accordance with his theoretical commitments anyway.

The beneficiary of Adams's choice was Thomas Jefferson, whose ap-proach to political theory was deeply ambivalent. He blithely dismissed almost the whole tradition of political philosophy as problematic ratio-nalizations of privilege. By contrast he favored a modern, "scientific" approach to politics that he found among the thinkers of the latter En-lightenment. Jefferson aspired to whisk away the detritus of the old phi-losophies—heavy-handed, government-imposed aristocratic privilege. His ambition was to replace this with a minimalist, tiered democracy in-spired by various thinkers but ultimately of his own contrivance, which would dramatically increase human happiness. At this endeavor he was a qualified success. He significantly reduced the government establishment, he enshrined liberty as the highest civic value in the United States, he became a pivotal figure in the history of popular government, and he ex-tended the territory over which these values held sway. However, in doing so he also extended executive power, disrespected cultural differences, and created incentives for other nations to bully the United States—very serious side effects.

Jefferson's ally James Madison was much more meticulous in his ap-proach to political theory than his predecessor, and more of a realist. He read extensively in political theory to figure out actual solutions to par-ticular real-life problems. He was frequently skeptical of the theoretical ideas which were most widely accepted. His research was directed at finding truer solutions than those offered up by the conventional theo-retical wisdom of the day, and he contributed significantly to the theory of republican government while engaged in shaping his nation's course. Difficult times did not lead him to compromise the vision that a repub-lican government safeguards the rights and civil liberties of its citizens and continues to be dedicated to the rule of law. Madison was committed to many of the same values as Jefferson, and the set of commitments he formulated included executive deference to the legislative branch, a mini-malist military establishment, and an insistence on the rights of neutrals in foreign policy. Each of these positions was well thought out, but they did not complement each other well because the pursuit of each of them threatened the chances that the others could be effectively realized. It took Madison years to fully acknowledge this problem. In the meantime, the United States was put in jeopardy by the War of 1812. Yet Madison's theoretical nature has been used by some to portray his presidency as a whole as a failure, which is an unwarranted leap. The irony is that these commentators use a theory to judge Madison: the theory that presidents should not be theoretical and that they will fail if they are.

Enter Woodrow Wilson. Wilson was the only president to have earned a Ph.D., and his work in political science led him to the consideration of many political theorists, whom he typically approached with suspicion. Very early in his academic career, even while still in college, Wilson embraced the ideas of antitheoretical theorists like Edmund Burke. Through graduate school and in his career he found a network of authors with mutually reinforcing ideas which helped to shore up the views which he had already developed. He felt that these authors were far more practical than nearly all other political philosophers. By studying them and by applying their ideas to the American setting he believed he was a "literary politician," uniquely suited to be president because he was less theoretical, and thus more practical, than other academics, and simultaneously more systematic, principled, and wise than other politicians. When he did jump to politics from academia, he seemed to have to figure out on the fly how his favored ideas might best be applied. The result was a much more aggressive set of policies than expected, including the somewhat theoretically paradoxical effort of making the world safe for Burkean "organicism" in each nation by means of a global security apparatus.

Wilson's assistant secretary of the navy would be elected to the presidency in 1932. Like Wilson, Franklin Delano Roosevelt had a keen distaste for political theory. Unlike Wilson, FDR had little tolerance for study or for writing. Accordingly, his knowledge of political theory was very limited. Yet FDR did embrace the thinking of the British essayist Thomas Babington Macaulay, who stressed the need for flexibility, accommodation, and compromise in the creation of all government policies. Roosevelt's political rise occurred when socialism was in vogue. Many thought of it as the inevitable future of politics. It was staunchly resisted by others who were vociferously committed to the free market. These starkly drawn alternatives, state socialism and an unfettered free market, induced Roosevelt to stake out a moderate position between them, advocating economic regulation and moderate reforms which paid due consideration to all relevant stakeholders and which would preserve the American tradition of liberty and free enterprise, tamping down on extremist visions in the process.

Bill Clinton studied political theory as an undergraduate at Georgetown University and while he was a Rhodes scholar at Oxford University. His experiences produced a lifelong enthusiasm for the concept of the social contract, an idea which stresses that the best political arrangements are reciprocally beneficial. Unlike the best-remembered social-contract theorists, who tend to carefully outline the parameters of the concept, Clinton did not bother to make such fine distinctions. He attached a concept of political development to the social contract, used its phraseology as a rhetorical device, and employed it to describe a wide range of policies where citizens who acted responsibly and cooperated would be rewarded for their behavior. His articulation of the idea of the social contract varied drastically by context. At certain critical junctures he strongly emphasized this aspect of his thinking to the public, while at other times he shied away from articulating it. This may have been appropriate given the changing contexts he faced, but it also made many observers wonder whether his commitment to the idea was solid. Clinton quoted political theorists with regularity, using them as intellectual window dressing in speeches. He also invited many academics, including political theorists, to the White House. Some helped craft policies, but the most ambitious among them came to be disappointed that Clinton's level of commitment to their preferred theories did not match their own.

Political Theory and Presidential Performance

These six presidencies span two centuries and represent a wide range of achievement. As judged by the periodic rankings compiled by Arthur Schlesinger and Arthur Schlesinger Jr., Adams and Madison tend to be ranked "below average," while Jefferson, Wilson, and FDR are routinely judged to be "near great" or "great." Ranking between these figures, toward the higher end, is Clinton. While these rankings are rightly treated with a good deal of caution, it is fair to conclude that a president acquainted with political theory can prove to be anything from a failure to a great president. No universal pronouncement about how an acquaintance with political theory will affect presidential performance seems valid. There is no good reason to offer up either a blanket condemnation or a universal endorsement of a theorizing president.

A more nuanced understanding must recognize that it is the content of the theory espoused and its appropriateness to the times that are the keys to its effect on performance in office. Careful attention to how theory and practice interact also leads to a reassessment of presidential performance. Ever since performance rankings were invented, they have privileged a certain model of presidential effectiveness which emphasizes leading Congress or exerting the presidential will to effect change. This unfairly discounts such things as Madison's refusal to muzzle free speech and the press during the War of 1812, or John Adams's principled resistance to the Federalist warmongers of the late 1790s, or even FDR's facilitation of policy creation by locking stakeholders in a room and appearing to be aloof until they came to an agreement. There was much more than strategy or weakness behind these acts. There was a preferred political philosophy, heeded not unthinkingly, nor as a way to cultivate popularity and favor, but as a way of governing properly in a republic. These presidents' understanding of what was to be done has hurt their reputations but helped them to do the right thing.

That the specific *content* of a president's theoretical application to politics had far more to do with his performance than that he attempted to apply theory to practice poses a challenge to each of the generalizations of the authors cited above. The assertion that theoretically inclined politicians are obsessive and dangerous does not receive validation here. A president dedicated to a particular political theory may insist that he is correct and may be very resistant to compromise (though probably no more so than other presidents). This was the case with John Adams. The result of Adams's stubbornness, however, was not the kind of conflagration which Daniel Boorstin warns about. Rather, it was precisely the opposite: Adams's theory-bolstered stubbornness enabled him to resist the push to declare war on France, which a less principled Federalist would not have had the ability to do. The tenacity with which Jefferson and Madison held to their "Quaker" foreign policy was more dangerous for the United States than Adams's stubbornness, but not for the reason Boorstin offers. The third and fourth presidents were anything but quick to go to war because of their theory-based confidence. If anything, their stubbornness was employed in keeping a peace of very dubious quality. The *content* of their political thought was the problem in a world not yet ready to respect the United States—not their commitment to understanding politics with the help of political theory.

With the exception of Thomas Jefferson, none of the six presidents treated here can be accurately described as ideologues. The three twentieth-century presidents covered in this book—Wilson, FDR, and Clinton— were quite pragmatic, giving the lie to Boorstin's contention that those acquainted with theory will inevitably be ideologues. Bill Clinton was also, famously, a compromiser. If anything, he seemed to be too ready to compromise rather than being insufficiently willing to do so. His acquaintance with and enthusiasm for social-contract theory did not produce a dogmatic approach to politics, but was compatible with a very flexible one. This is not what Boorstin would have predicted from an Oxford-trained political-theory student.

Wilson and FDR challenge Boorstin's thesis on a deeper level. They were dedicated to something that Boorstin does not acknowledge: beginning with Burke, there is an "antitheoretical" tradition within political theory. Burke's approach to politics was to eschew theories as dangerous, precisely the approach which Boorstin advocates. Since Burke's is a systematic orientation toward politics which purports to be broadly applicable across time and place, it is a theory, if a paradoxical one. That Boorstin never acknowledged the existence of this strain of political theory, which does precisely what he wishes to accomplish, is glaring because of its embodiment in two key presidencies of the early twentieth century. FDR was committed to moderation and compromise as fundamental components of good politics, things which Boorstin ignores as possible building blocks of a theory of politics.

When we consider Richard Neustadt's suggestion that the presidency is not a scholar's job, it should be remembered that he was writing of the presidency only at "midcentury." As he was writing *Presidential Power: The Politics of Leadership* (1960) during the waning days of the Eisenhower administration, it may have been true that the presidency was not a scholar's job. But Neustadt himself noted that his pronouncements were not to be taken as a description of the entire history of the presidency. Thus, without any contradiction to Neustadt, one can confidently say that early in U.S. history, the presidency *was* a scholar's job. After George Washington and before Andrew Jackson, voters selected several of the most learned and innovative political thinkers in the land, including John Adams, Thomas Jefferson, and James Madison. This will probably prove to be a unique time in American history. Nevertheless, in individual cases dotted through history, the presidency is likely to be a scholar's job again. It may be no coincidence that after a presidency perceived by many to have been a failure because of the lack of intellect of its principle, the American people have again made the presidency a scholar's job—if that is not an improper label to put on someone who was president of the *Harvard Law Review* and a law professor at the University of Chicago.

Another episode where the presidency was a scholar's job was during Woodrow Wilson's presidency. Other scholars, like J. William Fulbright and Newt Gingrich, have been elected to Congress and have received serious mention as presidential contenders. These exceptions to the idea that scholarship and politics do not mix suggest that Neustadt was too quick to dismiss political theory as irrelevant or something of a hindrance. With Wilson, in particular, the American public intentionally made the presidency a scholar's job for eight years.

By almost all accounts, Wilson did very well in the job before his stroke. Neustadt does not address the issue, but how would he account for this occurrence? Was Wilson able to successfully ride events and bargain despite being a scholar? If so, then the assertion that the presidency is not a scholar's job seems unnecessary. Were the conditions Wilson faced substantially different than those of the presidency at midcentury, so that the office could be successfully occupied by a scholar in 1915 but not in 1950? This seems a more likely response, but a close examination of Wilson's years as president would suggest that he had to respond to events and work with Congress every bit as much as did FDR or Truman or Eisenhower. Was Wilson not really a scholar? Wilson made this assertion about himself, of course, and if this is the case then there are plenty of "nonscholars" in the academy who would probably make very fine presidents. This definitional trick might resolve the irony of Neustadt's advising presidents from his office at Harvard University. The Harvard professor might not have considered himself a scholar—at least not one typical of Harvard. However, this concession can only come at a cost: Neustadt's blanket assertion fails to have much meaning. Unfortunately, we will never know how Richard Neustadt would have answered these questions—his dismissal of scholars as presidents is too brief and too suggestive to speculate on, and he is no longer here to elaborate.

Within a year after *Presidential Power* was published, Arthur Schlesinger Jr. was made a special assistant to the president by John F. Kennedy. Presidents ever since have made connections to the academy.[1] Most academics consulted and hired by presidents have been policy analysts. But there have been political theorists who have been consulted as well, including William Galston, whom President Clinton hired in 1993, and Cass Sunstein, who advised Clinton and is now a part of the Obama administration. Even if the presidency is not a scholar's job, it is a job whose occupant has ready access to scholars and the resources required to hire academic help, including political theorists, if he or she is so inclined.

Contrary to the views of Boorstin and Neustadt, no warning should be issued against the appearance of political theory in the White House, for it has already frequently been there and it has often acquitted itself quite well. However, an avid interest in political theory is certainly not a prerequisite for the job, nor is it inevitably useful to a president or the country. The president who is considered the best by the most people, Abraham Lincoln, seemed dismissive of political philosophy to his law partner, who liked to read it. At the same time, Lincoln did possess a theory of politics that guided his decision making through a very difficult time. It was a theory built upon logic, inspired by Euclid more than by traditionally consulted works of political theory. Presidents without a deep knowledge of political theory can probably be great presidents or failures in office—or anywhere in between. However, even if a president does not know political theory, it is likely that he or she has theoretical views about politics. Theories are not things that are reserved to professors or authors. People use theoretical ideas every day in their approach to life. So the operative question is not whether or not presidents possess theories, but what theories do they possess? This question begs for several follow-ups, including where did they get their theories? how will they be applied? and are they appropriate to the situation? Additionally, we must acknowledge that a president's acquaintance with political theory need not be particularly deep to grant him an orientation. With this acknowledged, are Bryce and Thompson onto something in suggesting that a president would be helped by knowing ideas from political theory?

Thompson suggests that by elevating the public debate, a president who is attuned to political theory can repair the public's anemic faith in government and reduce contradictions in government policies. He particularly commends the early presidents who "worked to construct their own coherent philosophies of politics and history." Thompson suggests that modern presidents should follow their example. In his words, "The response to this [contemporary] shallowness is to elevate somehow the habit of moral reasoning by, in part at least, reminding ourselves of the political thought of the founding fathers."[2]

No one can be against moral reasoning. However, it must be squarely acknowledged that the era during which Adams, Jefferson, and Madison were president was one of the most difficult and tumultuous in American history. Partisan bitterness reached a fevered pitch in the late 1790s that has rarely been equaled. Hard feelings persisted through Jefferson's administration; only the electoral triumph of the Republicans cooled the partisan crisis. Problems were rekindled by the embargoes and the subsequent War of 1812, when many New Englanders disregarded federal law and seriously pondered secession. While others were more responsible for the sharp tone of the times than these three presidents, their articulations did not prevent the era's politics from being highly divisive. In other words, their well-developed theoretical visions did not lead to a consensus public philosophy. Whether coincidental or not, it was the era's presidents who were less well versed in political theory and less aggressive in their theoretical vision—George Washington and James Monroe—who were the less divisive figures.

Thompson does not claim that a public philosophy will be greeted with universal acclaim, of course. Yet it is a significant error of omission on his part not to acknowledge the highly controversial nature of any vision which is worthy of being called a public philosophy. Though a president must have commitments and principles—and political theory is a promising venue to find them—it may be useful to keep these commitments and principles somewhat vague rather than precisely articulated. We want presidents to have a vision, but for practical reasons that vision must be sufficiently capacious and understandable to appeal to many. Thompson suggests that the hardest part of getting a public philosophy in the White House is intellectual—those who are elected president simply have not thought enough about politics in the right way. While this is a significant obstacle, an even more formidable one may come in trying to articulate a public philosophy to the public.

Though Wilson proclaimed himself to be a Burkean to a Boston audience in 1912, he ultimately did very little to educate the public about his understanding of political theory. As president he rarely mentioned Burke or Bagehot in public, though he did keep mentioning his enthusiasm for them in private. This suggests that Wilson felt that it was easier *not* to articulate the theoretical underpinnings of his decisions in public. Other than a few vague references to Macaulay, one would never have known that FDR possessed a public philosophy beyond the commitments that he was a Christian and a Democrat. If Roosevelt had fully aired his fealty to Macaulay the trimmer, it would likely have done more harm to himself than good. To say you believe fervently in compromise is not the most inspiring of messages. Those suspicious of whether the president had any principles would have exploited this choice of intellectual mentor. Bill Clinton's frequent references to the social contract were vague and conceptually pliable. Audiences did not have to know anything about political theory to digest the phrase. The pliability of the term allowed Clinton to describe almost any policy he thought desirable as contractarian. Perhaps Clinton could have helped himself if he had insisted on articulating his theoretical worldview more consistently in public and in more precise terms. However, there is no guarantee that this would not have backfired by confusing the electorate and dividing his potential allies.

There may be certain times, such as a crisis, when the articulation of a public philosophy is more appropriate. This brings us to James Bryce, who was particularly attentive to how context impacted the relationship between presidents and ideas. Bryce believed that "men of education"—if they could ever get to the presidency—would make better presidents than others because they might transcend the politics of patronage and the satisfaction of interests to emphasize principle. Even more than with Neustadt's "midcentury" presidency, the presidency Bryce knew has long since passed into the history books. Yet whether the president has principles which allow him or her to rise above the views of vested interests and public opinion continues to be a vital question. An orientation toward politics granted by political theory can do that on occasion, as evidenced by the six presidents examined here, even though it does not (and should not) eliminate the other considerations.

Not all who are acquainted with political theory will regularly buck outside pressures. The default position for those committed to democracy is to serve interests rather than to question them. However, Adams was willing to put the national interests above his party's interest. Jefferson challenged the citizens of Danbury, Connecticut, who he felt wanted to problematically mix religion with politics. Madison could have acted vindictively toward New England's discontents during the War of 1812, but he did not. Wilson attempted to dissuade other leaders from taking a punitive approach to the vanquished powers of the Great War so that a global security apparatus could be effectively implemented. FDR's commitment to moderation allowed him to see and oppose Nazi zealotry earlier than most Americans. Clinton stood firm in "preserving the existing social contract." At least some of these examples demonstrate that we might be better off with presidents who are broadly acquainted with political theory, even if the caveat that Bryce does not consider must be raised: "men of learning" can do profound mischief too, depending on the particular ideas to which they are devoted.

No president will always rise above serving his party or the interests typically arrayed with it to act on principle. But a president with a background in political theory is more likely to have the intellectual tools and the confidence to occasionally do so in a way that resists the political winds. As judged by these presidents, political theory can occasionally facilitate resisting popular but problematic suggestions in favor of less popular but better ones. Though any president can be principled, there may be something to Bryce's assertion that a president with a commitment to political theory has a greater ability to help place him- or herself in a particular context and to choose wisely given that context. Benjamin Barber suggests that it is the intellectual's duty to speak truth to power.[3] It may be the duty of a president informed by political theory to use power to serve the truth.

On Theory and the Presidency

Every president who takes political philosophy seriously does so in his or her own unique way. Any two people who read the same text will remember and interpret it differently. Any two people interested in political theory will admire different thinkers and commit themselves to different ideas. Even if we were to posit the unrealistic premise that these things could be held constant, translating theory to practice would produce divergences among two presidents committed to the same things. Each individual would make different choices about the policies which would best implement a theoretical idea in practice. Each would make different judgments. Since only one person is president at a time, any two presidents will find themselves in contexts which differ, triggering different responses even from individuals who would think exactly the same things. Each presidency comes with a different composition of Congress and a different array of public opinion, which may force their own unique set of compromises.

All of these variables should make us very cautious about drawing any firm conclusion about what theoretically oriented individuals bring to the office. The temptation to think of these individuals as unrealistic and naive because they found their approach to politics in books or as particularly intelligent because political theory is dense and difficult and anyone who studies it must be smart are both convenient traps. These are stereotypes traded during campaigns which have very little to do with actual performance in office. None of the individuals featured in this book is well explained by such clichés. Journalists have an obligation to look deeper than these stereotypes during the campaign, to seriously plumb each candidate's ideas. After the campaign, social scientists have the chance and even the obligation to take an even deeper look, to analyze the actual real-world effects of a president's ideas, including a penchant for political theory if it exists.

Thus it is a disappointment when the normally careful Dean Keith Simonton argues in *Why Presidents Succeed* that "a long presence in an academic institution, whether as a graduate student or as a teacher, can inculcate an excessive ivory-tower idealism and inflexibility. The highly abstract and impractical theories of the graduate seminar can be a handicap."[4] This draws too broad a conclusion from too few examples. This pronouncement is a departure from Simonton's goal of making empirical determinations about what helps a president succeed. He is on much firmer ground when he relates the empirical finding that "intellectual brilliance" and writing a book before becoming president are "positively correlated" with presidential greatness.[5] Just like presidents themselves, political theory in the hands of a president is capable of doing both much good or massive harm. It depends on what that theory is and whether it fits the situation it is used in. The best we can say for political theory in the aggregate so far is that it probably has done more good than harm in the hands of presidents.

Examining various presidents through the lens of their understanding of political theory grants insight into what the individuals hoped to accomplish. It allows us to enter more deeply into a president's mind-set, and to explore more rigorously his own understanding about what he was doing. This does not exempt any of these figures from criticism. It does not even preclude the possibility that political theory was used to rationalize what a president was predisposed to do anyway. It is stunning that of the many thousands of pages written about each of the modern presidents, such a tiny fraction is devoted to their political thought. This is not how political scientists and historians treat the early presidents. The political thought of Jefferson and Madison have received a great deal of attention. Adams inspires fewer scholars, but still there are fine monographs dedicated to his political thought. Why no one has written seriously of how Wilson's devotion to Burke and Bagehot affected his presidency, or how FDR's preference for Macaulay informed his decisions, or of Bill Clinton's interest in social-contract theory is an unfortunate mystery.

Perhaps the key to solving that mystery lies in the ever-increasing tendency of scholars to specialize. Clinton Rossiter once noted that those at the Constitutional Convention "embodied the nexus between philosophical thought and action which nearly all modern scholars and politicians lack—the scholars because they are too busy thinking to act and the politicians because they are too busy acting to think."[6] There is a great deal of wisdom in this observation. Adams, Jefferson, and Madison lived at a time when it was not unthinkable that a dedicated reader could digest a substantial percentage of the entire corpus of political philosophy. In fact, Adams and Madison did just that. Their example shows that in their era, politicians—even ones in the highest elective offices—could find the time to read a great deal of material outside of what they had to do for their jobs. Our world is partly of their design, but it is a world in which it is unlikely that a president will have done what they did.

Given this reality, it becomes important to distill lessons about the interaction of political theory and political practice in the hands of the president of the United States. Here are the most important matters for anyone aspiring to the office or in the office to realize about this connection:

Guidelines on Theory and the Presidency

1. Theories can help you to understand the job and what you want to accomplish in it.

2. Every president possesses theories about politics and how to govern, whether their origin is in political theory or not. Be cognizant of your theoretical commitments.

3. If you employ ideas from political theory, you will have to interpret them and do the hard work of fitting these ideas to practice. This makes you, and only you, responsible for what you do with the theories.

4. Most people do not know political theory. It is a challenge to articulate a theory to the public. Do not let this keep you from trying. In doing so you will likely face criticism for being an "out-of-touch intellectual." Face that argument head on because it is a very weak one. This anti-intellectual prejudice can be set at zero by demonstrating the practical benefits of an idea.

5. No one expects the president to be a philosopher, and you should not aspire to be one.

6. Context will limit your ability to pursue your theoretical ideas in practice. You must make clear to others that while you have informed commitments, you work in a separated system and are under many other constraints.

7. You should be aware of whether some of your theoretical commitments hinder the pursuit of others. Engage in continual, self-conscious assessments of political context to determine which commitments to emphasize at any given time.

8. Always be aware of the human impact of your theoretical commitments.

9. Theories can provide direction and grant confidence that you are doing the right thing. However, it is problematic for this confidence to be too pronounced. An acquaintance with political theory should lead one to ponder *more* options rather than fewer, and it should lead to a good deal of circumspection.

10. Choose carefully the political theorists you bring to the White House. Those who are most eager about their ideas will almost inevitably be disappointed by the experience, and they will write about it.

Political theory has become its own profession. In universities and colleges there are thousands of published authors turning out hundreds of books and articles every year which may be considered political theory. No politician could possibly keep up with all of this. Few political scientists can. Presidency scholars tend not to read political theory, having more than enough to do to keep up with developments in their subfield. Few political theorists seriously consider the modern presidency as fertile ground for research. All this is quite understandable and logical. It does mean, however, that social science has inadequately treated the connections between these well-recognized areas of study. This would not be a tragedy, except for the fact that our civic life is at stake. If citizens know more about each candidate's theoretical approach to politics they can make better electoral decisions. The more we know about each president's theoretical enthusiasms, the better we can understand the actions they have taken.

Robert Reich stresses that in choosing members of one's staff, a politician should seek to appoint people unlike himself.[7] Doing so encourages robust discussions and enhances the possibility of remedying the shortcomings of the politician. This observation may be applied to the subject at hand. Hiring staffers who have read political theory or consulting with well-regarded political theorists might be most beneficial to a president who has no acquaintance with it. By extension, reading extensively in political theory is likely be most helpful to the presidential candidates who are least inclined to do it. These individuals are less likely to have thought about politics in theoretical or abstract terms. Reading political theory may prompt considerations that otherwise would not have occurred to them.

So what should a president or a presidential candidate have read in political theory and to what end? A hundred different political theorists would come up with a hundred different lists. But here is a very short reading list, and what I would hope a reader would gain from these books. Despite believing that Daniel Boorstin's thesis fails, I would suggest reading either his *Genius of American Politics* or Edmund Burke's *Reflections on the Revolution in France*. These books effectively make the point that theoretical enthusiasms can become dangerous obsessions. But the reader must apply these authors' own warnings against their theories: we must not be so infused with atheoretical confidence that we set at nought all other writings in political theory.[8] Because of its central place in American intellectual history, John Locke's *Second Treatise on Civil Government* is mandatory reading. Just as Jefferson's words continue to inspire, so should Locke's. Locke suggests that our most critical commitments should be to universal human rights and to freedom. Not bad advice. Alexis de Tocqueville's *Democracy in America* would be valuable if, for no other reason, than it shows how the application of intelligence to the social world can provide significant insight. His primary idea, that democracy cannot work effectively without the social check of communal values, is always relevant.

I could add many more titles. Aristotle's writings emphasize the value of moderation in politics and in life. Machiavelli's works must be approached with caution given his cavalier attitude about such things as political murders, but his *Discourses* properly suggest that a republic is a stronger and more vital form of government than others because the populace is invested in the regime. Communitarian authors like Michael Sandel and Benjamin Barber can reacquaint us with what we are missing when our public sphere emphasizes individual rights and freedom above other values. Abraham Lincoln's writings offer significant insight about the role of government and the president's place in the United States. Let me single out his "Young Men's Lyceum Address" as presenting an important argument about the rule of law: if citizens in a republic do not respect the law, the regime is in trouble, because there are always ambitious and conniving individuals willing to destroy it for their own advantage. Alongside this early Lincoln speech, place Martin Luther King Jr.'s "Letter from a Birmingham Jail," wherein King justifies his own arrest. King emphasizes that he has broken the law "lovingly," and that where injustice is sanctioned by the law, one needs to take action. These authors present eloquent, well-reasoned arguments that are often at odds. And that is part of the point. Political theory does not provide easy answers to the questions of the day; it invites robust discussion and inquiry about the proper course to take. Once one gets into these arguments and takes their reasoning seriously, one has a better appreciation of the tensions within politics, and probably a better grasp on how to make good decisions. And needless to say, this basic reading list is not just for presidential aspirants—it is for citizens too.

If every American presidential candidate were to be asked who his or her favorite political thinker or philosopher is, there would undoubtedly be many different answers. It would probably be best for us if, alongside the candidates who answer Ronald Reagan and Jesus, there would be others who would answer John Locke, or Edmund Burke, or Alexis de Tocqueville, or Mary Wollstonecraft, or John Stuart Mill, or John Rawls, or Michael Walzer, or Cesare Beccaria, or Robert Dahl, or Benjamin Barber. At the very least, with these names and the ideas they represent tossed out as part of our public discourse, our presidential debates would feature a robust clash of ideas. We might even find that the long tradition of political philosophy and the vibrant work being done in this discipline today still have a good deal of value. James Bryce was right after all; the president's ideas *are* important.

$\mathcal{N}otes$

Preface: What We Really Should Know about Barack Obama

Epigraphs. Barack Obama, *The Audacity of Hope,* 53; George F. Will, *Statecraft as Soulcraft: What Government Does,* 18.

1. Ruth Behar, "The Anthropologist's Son," B12–B13.
2. Obama, *Audacity of Hope,* 87.
3. Ibid., 154–59, 176–80.
4. Larry Gordon, "Occidental Recalls 'Barry' Obama," *Los Angeles Times,* January 29, 2007, B1.
5. Obama, *Audacity of Hope,* 30; Barack Obama, "Father's Day 2008" (speech delivered at the Apostolic Church of God in Chicago on June 15, 2008), *Change We Can Believe In,* 240. Obama's narrative about the 1960s and the cultural divisions they spurred are reminiscent of Allan Bloom's *Closing of the American Mind.* Anyone who has read that book, with its commentary on universities, rock music, and a "Dionysian" lifestyle, can hear its echoes in *The Audacity of Hope.* Obama states that the 1960s came to divide Americans along moral lines, based on "how you felt about sex, drugs, rock and roll, the Latin mass or the Western canon" (28), the very things that Bloom focused on in his critique of modern America. Bloom criticized the pervasive but poorly supported commitment to "openness" that was prevailing on college campuses. Obama did not adopt the view that openness was a problem, but he did move in a compatible direction by stressing the importance of values.
6. Obama, *Audacity of Hope,* 9.
7. David Brooks, "Obama, Gospel and Verse," *New York Times,* April 26, 2007.
8. Ibid.; Reinhold Niebuhr, quoted by Brooks in an address at the University of Chicago's Alumni Weekend, Spring 2008, http://magazine.uchicago.edu/0810/features/obama.shtml.
9. Obama, *Audacity of Hope,* 54, 63, 59.
10. Ibid., 32–40, 93, 87.
11. Ibid., 42.

Chapter 1 On Presidents and Ideas

Epigraph. James Bryce, *The American Commonwealth,* 1:68.

1. Ibid., 1:84.
2. Ibid., 1:65.
3. Bryce suggested that Lincoln had inaugurated a new paradigm, where the individuals in the office were not as inconspicuous as the presidents between Jackson and Buchanan.

4. Bryce, *American Commonwealth*, 1:65.

5. I obtained a transcript of the December 13, 1999, debate held in the Des Moines Civic Center at http://www.gwu.edu/~action/primdeb/primdeb1213.html.

6. Complicating matters further, biblical scholars remind us that we cannot be confident that all the words spoken by Jesus in the New Testament were things that Jesus himself actually said. Bush's response was likely disappointing to the questioner because he or she wanted to elicit more information from the candidate. Then again, if the question was a deliberate attempt to expose Bush's anti-intellectual streak, then the questioner may have been delighted with the answer, but in a strategic way: he or she may have thought that Bush's response was weak and he or she may have expected the public (wrongly, as it turns out) to think likewise.

7. Edmund Burke, *Reflections on the Revolution in France*, 29.

8. Sheldon S. Wolin, *Politics and Vision: Continuity and Innovation in Western Political Thought*, 197–200; Niccolo Machiavelli, *The Prince*, trans. Harvey C. Mansfield Jr., 29–30, 34–38, 61–62, 65–68.

9. Warren Harding, quoted in Alexander George, "Adaptation to Stress in Political Decision Making," 187.

10. For example, Hugh B. Urban, *The Secrets of the Kingdom: Religion and Concealment in the Bush Administration*, chap. 4; and Shadia B. Drury, "Leo Strauss and the American Imperial Project."

11. Urban, *Secrets of the Kingdom*, 111.

12. Jacob Weisberg, *The Bush Tragedy*, 204, 164.

13. William Henry Harrison, in *Inaugural Addresses of the Presidents of the United States*, 80, 81.

14. Philip Shriver Klein, *President James Buchanan: A Biography*, 12.

15. John Milton Cooper Jr., *The Warrior and the Priest: Woodrow Wilson and Theodore Roosevelt*, 84.

16. Herbert Storing, ed., *The Complete Antifederalist*, 5:288–95; Richard M. Nixon, *Leaders*, 246.

17. William H. Herndon and Jesse Weik, *Herndon's Lincoln*, xxv.

18. Lincoln, *The Collected Works of Abraham Lincoln*, ed. Roy P. Basler, 2:221–22, 4:426.

19. David J. Siemers, "Principled Pragmatism: Abraham Lincoln's Method of Political Analysis," 805.

20. No political theorist writes in a vacuum. They frequently borrow from or react to others. However, there should also be something distinctive about each work. Karl Marx adopted the idea of owners' "extraction of surplus value" from the classical economists David Ricardo and Adam Smith. The conclusion that Marx drew from that concept was very different from Ricardo's and Smith's. Marx believed that capitalism would have to die as the extraction of surplus value from workers became increasingly efficient and therefore ever more exploitative. To be a political philosopher, there must be something distinctive in one's thinking.

Even political theorists who are culturally sensitive like Edmund Burke make points which are broadly applicable. In Burke's case it is that stable governments are built on the cultural understandings unique to each society. This is his claim which transcends time and political boundaries. Other political theorists offer different claims, but they typically intend them to be widely applicable across time and place, even though their inspiration was inevitably a particular context.

21. Richard E. Neustadt, *Presidential Power and the Modern Presidents: The Politics of Leadership from Roosevelt to Reagan*, 89.

22. Garry Wills, *James Madison*, 2.

23. One problem with this view is that Madison consistently acted with restraint as president. His understanding of lawmaking in a popular government was that

it should be undertaken by the legislature without interference from the executive. Thus, it is unfair of Wills to suggest that Madison foisted his own views upon the nation. If anything, he should be blamed for being too passive or deferential toward Congress, not for insisting upon the correctness of his own views.

24. Kenneth W. Thompson, *The President and the Public Philosophy,* 207.

25. James Bryce to Wilson, in *The Papers of Woodrow Wilson,* ed. Arthur S. Link, David W. Hirst, and J. E. Little, 25:531.

Chapter 2　John Adams: Defense of the Mixed Constitution

Epigraphs. John Adams to Thomas Jefferson, July 15, 1813, in *The Adams-Jefferson Letters: The Complete Correspondence between Thomas Jefferson and Abigail and John Adams,* ed. Lester J. Cappon, 357; John Adams to Charles Holt, September 4, 1820, in *The Works of John Adams, Second President of the United States,* ed. Charles Francis Adams, 10:391.

1. C. Bradley Thompson, "John Adams and the Science of Politics," 238.

2. There are a number of individuals who served in political offices who wrote works recognized as political theory—Cicero and Machiavelli, for instance. Some, like John Stuart Mill and Alexis de Tocqueville, only gained political office after becoming renowned for their political writing. Unlike Adams, none of these theorists became his nation's top political official.

3. Charles Francis Adams, in *Works of John Adams,* 277.

4. Adams to Jefferson, July 16, 1814, in *Adams-Jefferson Letters,* ed. Cappon, 438.

5. Daniel Leonard, in *The Papers of John Adams,* ed. Robert J. Taylor, 2:219.

6. Madison, in Ralph Ketcham, *James Madison: A Biography,* 275. Washington and Madison had apparently preferred either John Jay or Henry Knox as vice president, but both of these men refused to serve in the office, leaving the leading candidates Adams and John Hancock, both of whom Madison objected to.

7. Joseph Ellis, *Passionate Sage: The Character and Legacy of John Adams,* 88.

8. Adams, *The Earliest Diary of John Adams,* ed. L. H. Butterfield, 71.

9. Ibid., 72–73.

10. We know some of the substance of one of these lists, compiled by Royall Taylor, which included Bernard Mandeville's *Fable of the Bees,* and the works of Niccolo Machiavelli, among others. The editors of *The Earliest Diary of John Adams* indicate that "Adams took [this list] quite seriously" (Butterfield, ed., *Earliest Diary of John Adams,* 22).

11. Adams, *Papers of John Adams,* ed. Taylor, 1:313.

12. Adams's library exists almost entirely intact in the Boston Public Library. He also collected books on literature, religion, and human psychology, but the subjects which he aimed for a comprehensive collection in were law and government. Jefferson's first library (sold to the nation to replace the library destroyed in the War of 1812) contained twice the number of books Adams had collected. Jefferson immediately set about collecting books again after the sale of his library, even though he admitted to Adams that he no longer read much.

13. Adams, *Earliest Diary of John Adams,* ed. Butterfield, 38.

14. Adams to the students of New Jersey College, July 1798, in *Works of John Adams,* ed. C. F. Adams, 9:206, my emphasis.

15. C. Bradley Thompson, *John Adams and the Spirit of Liberty,* 113–14.

16. Adams to Jefferson, December 25, 1813, in *Adams-Jefferson Letters,* ed. Cappon, 412.

17. Thompson, "John Adams," 238–42. Not every political theorist who used history did so honestly or well. Adams believed that David Hume, for instance, either deliberately distorted history to suit his own purposes or mistakenly drew lessons from a faulty understanding of history.

18. Niccolo Machiavelli, *The Discourses,* 97, 98.

19. Adams to Francis Vanderkemp, August 9, 1813, Adams Family Papers, Microfilm Reel 95, Massachusetts Historical Society.

20. Viscount Bolingbroke (quoting Dionysius Halicarnassus), quoted in Zoltan Haraszti, *John Adams and the Prophets of Progress*, 58.

21. Ibid., 226.

22. Adams to Jefferson, July 16, 1814, in *Adams-Jefferson Letters*, ed. Cappon, 438.

23. Adams, *Diary and Autobiography of John Adams*, ed. Lyman H. Butterfield, 2:56.

24. Adams to Jefferson, July 9, 1813, in *Adams-Jefferson Letters*, ed. Cappon, 351.

25. Adams, *Works of John Adams*, ed. C. F. Adams, 9:573.

26. Adams, *Papers of John Adams*, ed. Taylor, 10:571.

27. John Patrick Diggins, *John Adams*, 57; James Grant, *John Adams: Party of One*, 331.

28. Adams, *Works of John Adams*, ed. C. F. Adams, 4:284.

29. Thompson, "John Adams," 250.

30. Adams felt that too many people treated Locke as if he had all the answers. They probably did not know that Locke had written a constitution for the early Carolina colony that strongly favored aristocratic interests, and that his concept of the separation of powers was incomplete.

31. Adams, quoted in Thompson, "John Adams," 245–46.

32. Adams, *Papers of John Adams*, ed. Taylor, 1:83.

33. Adams, *Works of John Adams*, ed. C. F. Adams, 4:290.

34. Adams, quoted in Haraszti, *Adams and the Prophets of Progress*, 201.

35. Adams, *Works of John Adams*, ed. C. F. Adams, 4:448–63.

36. Adams was bewildered by the popularity of unicameral systems. Complexity was not greeted with suspicion in other matters, so why should it be so suspected when it came to government? Adams observed that no one wanted a house with just one room instead of three because it was simpler. Nor did they seek to buy a clock with only one part just because it was less complex than a clock with several moving parts (Haraszti, *Adams and the Prophets of Progress*, 214).

37. Adams to Jefferson, June 25, 1813, in *Adams-Jefferson Letters*, ed. Cappon, 334.

38. Writers influenced by Christianity felt that piety made for a good regime. Those who admired Rome touted a kind of selfless civic virtue. George Washington was considered a model of this selfless behavior. Adams thought that these self-denying ideas were rubbish. People did not act altruistically. Even when it appeared that they sacrificed, they did so to gain something, like a good reputation. Washington had gained immeasurably from the belief that he sacrificed for his country. He became a human icon, beyond criticism even while alive. If that wasn't beneficial to his political prospects, what was?

39. Thompson, *John Adams*, 151–56.

40. Adams, *The Political Writings of John Adams*, ed. George A. Peek Jr., xiv.

41. Haraszti, *Adams and the Prophets of Progress*, 50.

42. Alfred Iacuzzi, *John Adams, Scholar*, 49–50. If the highest offices bore august titles, they would be more desirable and the nation's best and brightest would work to serve the public to attain them. Most thought Adams vain for suggesting in 1789 that the president and vice president be addressed by some title, like "His Majesty." A Senate committee whose work Adams approved of suggested that the president be referred to as "His Highness the President of the United States and Protector of the Rights of the Same" (David McCullough, *John Adams*, 405). Adams's motive in endorsing titles was not as selfish as many thought. While he was admittedly vain, Adams felt that vanity was a universal attribute. He would have liked to be addressed by a title like "His Highness," and others would too, meaning they would strive for the nation's highest elective offices and serve the public in them. This suggestion was a public relations disaster which damaged Adams's reputation permanently.

43. Haraszti, *Adams and the Prophets of Progress,* 50.

44. Iacuzzi, *John Adams, Scholar,* 139. Also see Clinton Rossiter, "The Legacy of John Adams," 535.

45. Locke loomed large in Adams's thinking not just for his political prescriptions. In his writings on epistemology and toleration Locke suggested that humans should turn their attention away from what they cannot comprehend—like the nature of God—and toward what they can comprehend: the proper way to order human society. He stressed that people learned only from experience. Adams first read Locke in college, and his experiential epistemology and concern with the political and social rather than spiritual greatly influenced the young Adams.

46. Randall B. Ripley, "Adams, Burke, and Eighteenth-Century Conservatism."

47. While the contributions of Locke and Sidney should be obvious—the separation of powers, representative government, consent of the governed, the rule of law, and guarantees of rights and liberty from government—at first blush it seems odd that Adams would suggest that his work was inspired by Rousseau and de Mably, two thinkers he believed were severely misguided. But Adams approached political theory with enough open-mindedness to see value in certain of their ideas. Rousseau was valuable because he rejected the canon and feudal law that had been part of what Parliament had tried to impose on the American colonies. The Abbe de Mably was a protocommunist monk who thought that private property was the result of the Fall of man (David Miller, ed., *Blackwell Encyclopedia of Political Thought,* 86). Adams thought de Mably's prescriptions on property hopelessly unrealistic and counterproductive, but the Massachusetts Constitution's religious test to hold office, which Adams wrote into his proposed constitution, was something de Mably had advocated. The Massachusetts constitutional convention, however, excised his suggestion that no person "who is not of the Christian religion" should be eligible to hold office in the State Senate or House of Representatives (*The Political Writings of John Adams,* ed. George W. Carey, 520, 525). Also see p. 501, where Adams proposes supporting churches with tax money and compulsory worship "at stated times and seasons." This provision was also eliminated from the document.

48. The presidency's weakness was a source of difficulty to Adams, particularly in the appointments process. At several junctures, he wished to appoint moderate Republicans to provide balance to diplomatic delegations. For example, he floated the idea of naming James Madison to a three-person delegation to be sent to France. The suggestion was disapproved of by Federalists, however (Ralph Adams Brown, *The Presidency of John Adams,* 29).

49. Stanley Elkins and Eric McKitrick, *The Age of Federalism,* 529; Ellis, *Passionate Sage,* 28.

50. On the diplomatic correspondence he made public, Adams had blocked out the names of the French agents who had approached the Americans asking for a bribe, substituting the letters X, Y, and Z for their names, hence the name "XYZ Affair."

51. Elkins and McKitrick, *Age of Federalism,* 537.

52. Diggins, *John Adams,* 173, 176.

53. Brown, *Presidency of John Adams,* 55–56, 94.

54. Ibid., 121.

55. Elkins and McKitrick, *Age of Federalism,* 341–48.

56. Brown, *Presidency of John Adams,* 16.

57. Richard D. Brown, "The Disenchantment of a Radical Whig: John Adams Reckons with Free Speech," 179.

58. Brown, *Presidency of John Adams,* 123; Brown, "Disenchantment," 172.

59. The lame-duck House of Representatives had to choose between Thomas Jefferson and Aaron Burr, who had wound up with the same number of electoral votes. All the Republican electors had known they were voting for a Jefferson presidency

and a Burr vice presidency, but there was no provision for indicating this on their ballots, a loophole in the Electoral College which was remedied with the ratification of the Twelfth Amendment. Whether Jefferson or Burr was selected by the House, a democratic Republican would be president.

60. Adams to Benjamin Rush, December 5, 1811, quoted in Cappon, *Adams-Jefferson Letters*, ed. Cappon, 283–84.

61. The Senate should have been an exclusive repository for the interests and the expertise of the upper class. The president was supposed to be a man admired for his independent judgment, not the leader of a faction. Adams's plan to ensure that aristocratic individuals would populate the Senate and the Senate only was not fully developed. In the mid-1770s he had proposed that states should use their lower chambers to select members of their upper chambers (Thompson, "John Adams," 254). In other words, members of the House would select the Senators. Adams believed at the time that this would segregate those dedicated to democracy from those dedicated to aristocracy. However, this seems to assume that a democratic faction would not want to maximize its influence by placing democratic-identifiers in the Senate. Without stating it, Adams thus seemed to rely on some other-regarding norm to produce what was desirable from this tiered election. This seems to be at odds with his own view of human nature. Adams was not helped by the fact that there was no formal aristocracy in the United States which could fight for its own institution of government, as the aristocracy had done in England. Adams thought that the development of a formal aristocracy was an inevitability, however, so he may have believed that this would happen in time.

62. Adams sent Jefferson a kind note three weeks into his presidency, saying, "I See nothing to obscure your prospect of a quiet and prosperous Administration, which I heartily wish you" (*Adams-Jefferson Letters,* ed. Cappon, 264). Though the Adams-Jefferson correspondence was inactive for more than ten years after the sending of this note, there is every reason to believe that Adams was being genuine in his profession of love for Jefferson. Adams disagreed profoundly with Jefferson about government, but that was neither here nor there to Adams—he disagreed with nearly everyone.

63. The writers best known for this sentiment are John Locke and Cesare Beccaria, and Adams admired both. Beccaria's views on proportionality set down in *On Crimes and Punishments* were an important precursor to the thinking of the utilitarians, who posited that if catching criminals were made more certain, then the punishment doled out for a crime needed simply to be more painful than the crime itself would be pleasurable.

64. Brown, *Presidency of John Adams,* 129.

65. Adams, *Papers of John Adams,* ed. Taylor, 3:216. In preparation for the fiftieth anniversary of American independence on July 4, 1826, town leaders in Quincy, Massachusetts, called on Adams and asked him to provide a message to his fellow Americans for the auspicious occasion. Adams replied, "I will give you, 'Independence Forever!'" The delegation asked Adams if he wished to elaborate. "Not a word," was the second president's response (McCullough, *John Adams,* 645). Unlike Washington, Adams did not issue a formal farewell address, and unlike Madison, he did not write any "advice to my country" to be read upon his death. This pithy two-word statement is Adams's equivalent and his legacy to the American people. For once, Adams was more succinct than his fellow founders.

66. Ralph Lerner, *The Thinking Revolutionary: Principle and Practice in the New Republic,* 36.

67. Richard Alan Ryerson, ed., *John Adams and the Founding of the Republic,* 23.

68. Adams to Jefferson, July 9, 1813, in *Adams-Jefferson Letters,* ed. Cappon, 351–52.

69. Adams to Abigail Adams, December 12, 1796, Adams Family Papers, Massachusetts Historical Society website, http://www.masshist.org/digitaladams/aea/cfm/doc.cfm?id=L17961212ja (accessed March 6, 2009).

70. Benjamin Rush, *The Autobiography of Benjamin Rush: His "Travels through Life" Together with His Commonplace Book for 1789–1813,* ed. George W. Corner, 143.

71. C. Bradley Thompson discusses other blind spots in his fine book on Adams's political thought, *John Adams and the Spirit of Liberty.* Adams was committed to freedom and commerce, but his knowledge of political economy was weak. He never quite hashed out a fully articulated and theoretically backed position on free trade or protectionism like many of his colleagues did. Nor did he meticulously examine or offer well-formed views on how to interpret the Constitution (Thompson, *John Adams,* 276). These were all live issues in the 1790s, and Adams did not offer a vision to the nation concerning them.

72. See Diggins, *John Adams,* 2–10; Peek, ed., *Political Writings of John Adams,* v; Haraszti, *Adams and the Prophets of Progress,* 48; Rossiter, "Legacy of John Adams," 533; and Thompson, "John Adams," 258.

73. Rossiter, "Legacy of John Adams," 548.

Chapter 3 Thomas Jefferson: Notes from a Prophet of Progress

Epigraphs. Thomas Jefferson to Jean Baptiste Say, February 1, 1804, in *The Writings of Thomas Jefferson,* ed. Andrew A. Lipscomb and Albert Ellery Bergh, 11:3; Thomas Jefferson, in James D. Richardson, ed., *Messages and Papers of the Presidents, 1789–1907,* 1:380.

1. Jefferson, *Writings of Thomas Jefferson,* ed. Lipscomb and Bergh, 11:223.

2. Ibid., 7:300.

3. Jefferson to Adams, in *Adams-Jefferson Letters,* ed. Cappon, 505.

4. Jefferson was far from lazy, of course. He spent the bulk of his literary time engaged in his correspondence. In late 1820 he totaled up the letters he had received that year and found that they numbered 1,267. Jefferson did his best to answer all serious inquiries, leaving him very little time for study. He frequently acknowledged the burdensome nature of his correspondence. Adams, by contrast, was never as approachable or seemingly as friendly as Jefferson, and he did not receive anywhere near the number of letters Jefferson did. When Jefferson reported to Adams that he had received 1,267 letters in 1820, Adams responded, "I very much doubt whether I received in the same year one twelfth" of that number (*Adams-Jefferson Letters,* ed. Cappon, 581–82).

5. Carl Becker, *The Declaration of Independence: A Study in the History of Political Ideas,* 27, 79; Lance Banning, *The Jeffersonian Persuasion: Evolution of a Party Ideology,* 62–64, 154–55, 273–91; Joyce Appleby, *Liberalism and Republicanism in the Historical Imagination,* 291–315; Garry Wills, *Inventing America: Jefferson's Declaration of Independence,* 168–204.

6. Jefferson, second inaugural address, in Richardson, ed., *Messages and Papers of the Presidents,* 1:380.

7. In an October 28, 1813, letter to Adams on aristocracy Jefferson maintained that "science ha[s] liberated the ideas of those who read and reflect" (*Adams-Jefferson Letters,* ed. Cappon, 391). Its "data" would destroy the idea that aristocracy was better than democracy. And when the proper "data" would be distributed among Indian tribes, Jefferson was hopeful that they would choose agriculture over a nomadic existence.

8. See Conor Cruise O'Brien, *The Long Affair: Thomas Jefferson and the French Revolution,* 270–90. O'Brien writes about Jefferson's views of African Americans, as do most authors who comment on Jefferson's racism. Nevertheless, there is a pattern of Jefferson's thought that crosses categories. He was very willing to believe stereotypes of African Americans, Indians, women, and others whom he arguably did not know well. Jefferson frequently praised the Indians, their habits, and their customs, and he was motivated by humanitarian concerns in encouraging farming among them. However, as Michael Walzer argues in *Spheres of Justice: A Defense of Pluralism and*

Equality, "this is the crucial sign of tyranny: a continual grabbing of things that don't come naturally, an unrelenting struggle to rule outside one's own company" (315). Jefferson's Indian policy certainly was not implemented without a struggle.

9. Jefferson, *Writings of Thomas Jefferson*, ed. Lipscomb and Bergh, 6:312, 14:319.

10. Jefferson, *Papers of Thomas Jefferson*, ed. Julian P. Boyd, Charles T. Cullen, John Catanzariti, and Barbara B. Oberg, 14:561. The best example of an Enlightenment project which broke the world down into its constituent parts is Diderot's *Encyclopedie*.

11. Adams, in John P. Kaminski, *The Quotable Jefferson*, 464.

12. Writing to Adams in 1820, Jefferson declared, "When I meet with a proposition beyond finite comprehension, I abandon it as I do a weight which human strength cannot lift" (*Adams-Jefferson Letters*, ed. Cappon, 562). All observations and all conclusions had to be tangible to be worth his time. This does not preclude delving into political philosophy, but it seems to be in accord with Jefferson's belief that most traditional political theory was useless.

13. Jefferson to Adams, July 5, 1814, in *Adams-Jefferson Letters*, ed. Cappon, 432.

14. Jefferson to Isaac H. Tiffany, August 26, 1816, *Writings of Thomas Jefferson*, ed. Lipscomb and Bergh, 15:65, 66. While Jefferson was ambivalent about Aristotle, his antipathy for Plato was clear. To William Short he wrote that Plato puts "such quibbles on words, and sophisms a schoolboy would be ashamed of." No other writer, he thought, "has bewildered the world with more *ignis fatui* [false, deceptive goals or hopes]" than Plato in ethics, politics, and physics (August 4, 1820, ibid., 15:258).

15. Jefferson not only translated de Tracy's book from the original French, he also oversaw its publication and included it in the curriculum at the University of Virginia (*Writings of Thomas Jefferson*, ed. Lipscomb and Bergh, 12:405–7, 12:413, 14:419). Also see Appleby, *Liberalism and Republicanism*, 291–96, 304–8. Jefferson also frequently recommended Baxter's revision of David Hume's *History of England*, which corrected the original's aristocratic and Tory slant with what Jefferson believed were valid republican interpretations of the past.

16. Gilbert Chinard, ed., *The Commonplace Book of Thomas Jefferson*, 5.

17. Jefferson to Robert Skipwith, August 3, 1771, in *Papers of Thomas Jefferson*, ed. Boyd et al., 1:77. The young state legislator recommended Montesquieu's *Spirit of the Laws* (evidence that at twenty-eight years of age he either had not read the book closely enough to find it objectionable yet, or had yet to fully develop his own core political beliefs) and *Greatness of the Romans and Their Decline*. He also recommended Locke's *Two Treatises of Government*, Sidney's political writings, Dugald Stewart's *Political Economy*, Marmontel's *Belisarius*, and Petty's *Political Arithmetic*. There are some other titles of political nonfiction under the headings "Law" and "History, Modern," but the sparseness of offerings in political philosophy is no fluke (1:78–81).

18. Jefferson to Henry Lee, May 8, 1825, *Writings of Thomas Jefferson*, ed. Lipscomb and Bergh, 16:118–19.

19. Daniel J. Boorstin, *The Lost World of Thomas Jefferson*, 171.

20. Jefferson to Elbridge Gerry, January 26, 1799, in *Papers of Thomas Jefferson*, ed. Boyd et al., 30:646–47.

21. This is a theme first emphasized by Aristotle. Though Jefferson may have known this about Aristotle, he typically referenced Scottish Enlightenment figures rather than Aristotle to provide backing for this understanding of human nature and his corresponding rejection of the power of "state of nature" arguments.

22. Jefferson to Thomas Law, June 13, 1814, in *Writings of Thomas Jefferson*, ed. Lipscomb and Bergh, 14:143.

23. Jefferson to Peter Carr, August 10, 1787, ibid., 6:256–57.

24. Jefferson to Joseph Milligan, April 6, 1816, ibid., 14:460.

25. Chinard, ed., *Commonplace Book*, 192–93.

26. Ibid., 212–14.

27. Merrill D. Peterson, *Thomas Jefferson and the New Nation*, 58–60.

28. Banning, *Jeffersonian Persuasion*, 55–64, 273–77.

29. Jefferson to Joseph C. Cabell, February 2, 1816, in *Writings of Thomas Jefferson*, ed. Lipscomb and Bergh, 14:421.

30. Some have speculated that Jefferson found his inspiration in New England town governments or in Indian tribal councils (e.g., Richard K. Matthews, *The Radical Politics of Thomas Jefferson: A Revisionist View*, 82–83). The ward would consist of an area just large enough for one constable and one elementary school. Local problems would be treated by it in the first instance, and each ward would elect a representative to serve in county government. This idea lives on in the townships of the Old Northwest, now the Midwest, which were organized according to Jefferson's plan, and were typically platted out in six-mile by six-mile squares.

31. In 1776 Jefferson had proposed a solution to this problem: the property requirement for voters would be set at ownership of fifty acres of land, and the state would distribute the requisite acreage to any white male who owned less than that amount.

32. *Writings of Thomas Jefferson*, ed. Lipscomb and Bergh, 2:160–78.

33. Jefferson to James Madison, November 18, 1788, in *Papers of Thomas Jefferson*, ed. Boyd et al., 14:188.

34. Jefferson to Monsieur D'Ivernois, February 6, 1795, in *Writings of Thomas Jefferson*, ed. Lipscomb and Bergh, 9:299–300.

35. Jefferson to James Madison, September 6, 1789, ibid., 15:333. Herbert Sloan's essay titled "The Earth Belongs in Usufruct to the Living" emphasizes that the word "usufruct" implies a trust. In other words, Jefferson is claiming that any ownership is temporary, like the owner's life, and that the owner therefore has an obligation to pass that property on to future generations.

36. Joseph J. Ellis, *American Sphinx: The Character of Thomas Jefferson*, 113. The idea that the earth was designed to be useful to humans is found in the early books of the Bible. In Genesis, God grants the earth to humans to use and commands them to "be fruitful and multiply." In the hands of John Locke, this command meant that property rightfully belonged to the person who labored in its creation. Jefferson applied this "labor theory of value" collectively. The earth "belongs to the living" generation, because it is the living generation's charge to make it useful to them through their labor. People who are dead or yet to be born cannot experience happiness, and thus it is only the living who count politically. But these influences on Jefferson were oblique; Condorcet's seems to have been direct.

37. Jefferson to Abigail Adams, February 22, 1787, in *Adams-Jefferson Letters*, ed. Cappon, 173.

38. Jefferson to John Adams, September 4, 1823, ibid., 596.

39. Jefferson to President Washington, memo, April 28, 1793, in *Papers of Thomas Jefferson*, ed. Boyd et al., 25:613.

40. Joyce Appleby, *Thomas Jefferson*, 111.

41. Becker, *Declaration of Independence*, 79.

42. Wills, *Inventing America*, 157–58; Morton White, *The Philosophy of the American Revolution*, 161–66.

43. Jefferson cribbed Locke's epistemological premise (i.e., human beings are not mentally equipped to *know* God, who is incomprehensible; therefore, what we think about him is largely a matter of speculation) and his arguments against religious coercion (e.g., the use of force is an entirely ineffectual way of trying to get someone to believe something). Jefferson was, however, willing to extend religious toleration more broadly than Locke, but there is no question that he employed the latter's arguments to make his case.

44. Beccaria argued that government had no right to extend its authority beyond what was needed to protect its members. Therefore, crimes could be punished only

proportionally—to the extent that they harmed members of society. This work struck Jefferson as both humane and scientific, and he worked to make its suggestions a reality in Virginia (Wills, *Inventing America*, 152).

45. Jefferson, second inaugural speech, in Richardson, ed., *Messages and Papers of the Presidents*, 379.

46. Banning, *Jeffersonian Persuasion*, 273.

47. Merrill Peterson estimates that more than 2,000 sailors were pressed into the British service in Jefferson's second term (*Jefferson and the New Nation*, 825–27).

48. Ketcham, *James Madison*, 443.

49. Jefferson to Thomas Law, June 13, 1814, in *Writings of Thomas Jefferson*, ed. Lipscomb and Bergh, 14:143.

50. Jefferson to the Baptists of Danbury, CT, January 1, 1802, in *Thomas Jefferson: Writings*, ed. Merrill D. Peterson, 510.

51. Ibid.

52. Diggins, *John Adams*, 11–15; Appleby, *Thomas Jefferson*, 1–5.

53. John Locke, *The Second Treatise on Civil Government*, 27 (paragraph 43).

54. Dumas Malone, *Jefferson and His Time: Jefferson the Virginian*, xii.

55. Siemers, "Principled Pragmatism: Abraham Lincoln's Method of Political Analysis."

56. Adams to Jefferson, in *Adams-Jefferson Letters*, ed. Cappon, 359. In the first two years of their correspondence, Adams sent Jefferson a total of thirty-seven letters. Jefferson sent seven back, including one addressed to Abigail Adams.

57. Jefferson did elaborate on the subject of aristocracy in his letter of October 28, 1813, but he went to pains to minimize the difference between his and Adams's thinking. In this letter Jefferson suggested that he believed in a natural aristocracy of talent, while Adams wished to populate government with those of a "pseudo-aristocracy" of wealth and heredity. He noted that this difference of opinion had not prevented them from "act[ing] in perfect harmony thro' a long and perilous contest for our liberty and independence" and that "it matters little to our country which, after devoting to it long lives of disinterested labor, we have delivered over to our successors in life, who will be able to take care of it, and of themselves" (*Adams-Jefferson Letters*, ed. Cappon, 391, 392). In other venues, Jefferson made clear that he thought the Federalists, Adams included, were threatening republican government by their actions. He also felt that it was very important that his successors were Jeffersonians rather than those Federalists who shared Adams's values. He could have broached these ideas to Adams, but he chose not to, declaring instead, "We are both too old to change opinions which are the result of a long life of inquiry and reflection" (391).

58. Jefferson's original draft of the Declaration of Independence did not proclaim the idea that all men are created equal to be "self-evident," but rather "sacred and inviolable." Whether Jefferson himself edited his copy or this was inserted by others is unclear. For a general discussion of the consequences of the difference between the two versions, see Morton White's *Philosophy of the American Revolution*.

59. Jefferson to Adams, June 15, 1813, in *Adams-Jefferson Letters*, ed. Cappon, 332.

Chapter 4 James Madison: Political Theory Must Be Made to Counteract Political Theory

Epigraphs. James Madison, in Alexander Hamilton, John Jay, and James Madison, *The Federalist*, ed. Jacob E. Cooke, 61–62 (this essay was printed in several New York papers over a three-day period: the *Daily Advertiser,* the *New-York Packet,* and the *Independent Journal*); Madison, *The Writings of James Madison*, ed. Gaillard Hunt, 6:94.

1. Madison, in *Papers of Thomas Jefferson*, ed. Boyd et al., 11:402.

2. In *The Complete Madison: His Basic Writings*, editor Saul K. Padover declared, "It is my conviction that not only should Madison's place as an original political philosopher

be re-established but also that the time has come when his ideas should be made available and known to a larger public" (1). In subsequent decades historians and scholars of political thought have taken Padover's suggestion to heart. There are now scores of books and articles devoted to Madison's political thought. Today the features and consequences of his political thought are these scholars' primary concerns, not whether Madison's political thought is worthy of notice, which seems firmly established.

3. Robert A. Dahl, *A Preface to Democratic Theory,* 5.

4. Douglass Adair, "'That Politics May Be Reduced to a Science': David Hume, James Madison, and the Tenth *Federalist.*"

5. William Lee Miller, *The Business of May Next: James Madison and the Founding,* 5.

6. Elkins and McKitrick, *Age of Federalism,* 80.

7. Madison remembered that he had performed an "indiscreet experiment" in college, trying to get by on "the minimum of sleep & the maximum of application, which [his] constitution would bear." For Madison, this meant sleeping just four or five hours a night—a foolish choice, he understood in retrospect, because he found that it adversely affected his health and thus proved counterproductive even to his studies (Madison, "James Madison's Autobiography," ed. Douglass Adair, 197). Madison was so studious he made himself sick.

8. Madison, *The Papers of James Madison,* ed. William T. Hutchinson et al., 6:62–65.

9. Ketcham, *James Madison,* 85.

10. Douglass Adair, *Fame and the Founding Fathers: Essays,* 134.

11. Madison must have thought that Aristotle could not have been authoritative on the subject, as he never knew a popular government anywhere but in a Greek city-state. His own inexperience blinded him to the possibility of an extended republic. Montesquieu contemplated the possibility of a federation of republics. Even though Montesquieu stressed that republics had to remain small in size, Madison may have felt that Montesquieu's thinking was not necessarily at odds with the Constitution.

12. Madison, *The Federalist,* ed. Cooke, 84.

13. Ibid., 128, 114.

14. Ibid., 349.

15. Ibid., 88.

16. In *The Federalist* Madison acknowledged that the new government was unique and untried (88–89, 257). No previous political philosopher had envisioned anything quite like it. The innovation with the least intellectual backing was the splitting of sovereignty between levels of government. Revered thinkers from classical times through the Enlightenment had argued that sovereignty could not be split between governing units, that good governments balanced the interests of the common citizenry with those of the upper class, and that popular governments had to remain small in size.

17. Madison, *Writings of James Madison,* ed. Hunt, 6:94.

18. Ketcham, *James Madison,* 473.

19. Marvin Myers, ed., *The Mind of the Founder: Sources of the Political Thought of James Madison,* xxii–xxiii.

20. Madison, *The Federalist,* ed. Cooke, 59.

21. Michael P. Zuckert, "The Political Science of James Madison," 155.

22. Legislative supremacy was also a potential danger. Montesquieu in particular stressed that "if the executive power does not have the right to check enterprises of the legislative body, the latter will be despotic, for it will wipe out all other powers" (*The Spirit of the Laws,* 157). To remedy this problem Montesquieu suggested splitting the legislative branch in two and giving the executive veto power over legislation. The executive could, in turn, be impeached by the larger chamber and removed from office by the smaller chamber for serious misconduct. Each branch of the legislature held a check over the other. This was not the traditional Lockean separation of powers, this was "separated institutions sharing powers."

These suggestions were incorporated into the Constitution and Madison supported them. Federalist No. 51 noted that the Constitution maintains the separation of powers by "contriving the interior structure of the government as that its several constituent parts may, by their mutual relations, be the means of keeping each other in their proper places" (*The Federalist,* ed. Cooke, 347–48). Madison was committed to legislative supremacy, with the understanding that there had to be both internal and external checks on the legislative branch.

23. Madison, *The Federalist,* ed. Cooke, 350.

24. Gary Rosen, *American Compact: James Madison and the Problem of Founding,* 7–8, 10.

25. Bernard Bailyn, *The Ideological Origins of the American Revolution,* 178.

26. As the ratification process progressed, Madison recognized the need to bring well-meaning Antifederalists into the constitutional fold in an orderly and nondisruptive way. When the New York Antifederalists proposed a second convention to revise the Constitution along with their ratification, Madison viewed the possibility with alarm. A second convention could reverse everything that had been gained in the first one. To address Antifederalist fears that the national government would become a tyranny, Madison agreed to codify the personal rights which all citizens held (the First through the Eighth Amendments) and the fact that the national government was a government of enumerated powers only (the Ninth and Tenth Amendments). Madison's wariness of bills of rights had not gone away. Rather, the necessity of making the Constitution consensually legitimate was ultimately more important to him than heeding his scruples about mere "parchment barriers" (see Siemers, *Ratifying the Republic,* especially chaps. 4 and 5).

27. Garrett Ward Sheldon, *The Political Philosophy of James Madison.*

28. Like Jefferson, Madison deemphasized the state of nature's literal existence. People live socially, and that does not change, regardless of what state of repair their government is in. Hobbes and Locke had both used the concept to submerge differences between people. Beginning with a more socially grounded viewpoint did not look past the reality of social and economic differences. It also accepted government as a practical necessity. In this way Madison's thinking was more reminiscent of Aristotle's than of Hobbes's or Locke's.

This claim would be disputed by Richard K. Matthews. His *If Men Were Angels: James Madison and the Heartless Empire of Reason* calls Madison's plan for government a "heartless empire of reason" inspired as much by Hobbes, Machiavelli, Malthus, and Calvin as by Locke and Montesquieu. Matthews argues that Madison deeply distrusted people and wanted to lift from them the ability to govern by setting in place his own mechanistic government. The argument that Madison's regime has produced an uninspiring, antidemocratic style of government must be taken seriously, but Madison was far from being as pessimistic about human nature as Matthews portrays.

In his updated preface to his biography of Madison, Ralph Ketcham notes that the most significant change he would make to the book is in emphasizing a civic republican or Aristotelian strand in Madison's thinking. He credits J. G. A. Pocock, Joyce Appleby, Lance Banning, Drew McCoy, Isaac Kramnick, and John Murrin with rediscovering the influence this premodern view had on the American founders. Gary Rosen also stresses the connection between Aristotle and Madison. In *American Compact,* Rosen discusses the importance of prudence and experience (*phronesis*) in the views of both men. This concept was particularly important to both thinkers in efforts to found governments (pp. 88–99, 138).

29. Madison, *Writings of James Madison,* ed. Hunt, 6:101–3.

30. Drew R. McCoy, *The Last of the Fathers: James Madison and the Republican Legacy,* 194.

31. In "A Letter concerning Toleration," Locke outlined how different Protestant sects should not persecute each other or use politics to enforce their views of scripture.

He did not argue for the toleration of non-Christian views, Catholicism, or atheism. Madison would tolerate them all.

32. Arthur Nussbaum, *A Concise History of the Law of Nations,* 110–12.

33. Ibid., 169–70.

34. Bailyn, *Ideological Origins,* 178, 27.

35. Madison, *Writings of James Madison,* ed. Hunt, 6:88–91; Robert W. Tucker and David C. Hendrickson, *Empire of Liberty: The Statecraft of Thomas Jefferson,* 266n48.

36. Drew R. McCoy, *The Elusive Republic: Political Economy in Jeffersonian America,* 19–20, 36–40.

37. Miller, *Business of May Next,* 13.

38. Ralph Ketcham, *Presidents Above Party: The First American Presidency, 1789–1829,* 60.

39. Since Britain's fleet was able to control the seas to a much greater extent than France's, there would be a far different result if it agreed to these terms than if France did. If France agreed to respect American shipping and the British refused, American ships would still be harassed and there would be relatively little international trade. If Britain agreed to these terms and France refused, then American ships would be fairly free to ply the Atlantic. That latter result depended on the British trusting the Americans, which they did not. The American policy had allowed Madison to be "suckered" by the French, to quote Garry Wills (*James Madison,* chap. 6).

40. Jack N. Rakove, *James Madison and the Creation of the American Republic,* 151.

41. The quote is from Article II, Section 3 of the Constitution. Madison's "Annual Messages," never delivered in person, clearly pay homage to the boundary between the legislative and executive branches. In these messages Madison often uses the Constitution's word "recommend." At times his recommendations are so weak and disembodied that one almost wonders if Madison was really committed to his own suggestions. Consider these two examples:

> It will rest with the consideration of Congress also whether a provident as well as fair encouragement would not be given to our navigation by such regulations as would place it on a level competition with foreign vessels . . . (*Writings of James Madison,* ed. Hunt, 8:126)

> I can not presume it to be unreasonable to invite your attention to the advantages of superadding to the means of education provided by the several States a seminary of learning instituted by the National Legislature within the limits of their exclusive jurisdiction . . . (*Writings of James Madison,* ed. Hunt, 8:127)

42. In *Fame and the Founding Fathers,* Adair points out that this difficulty continued during the War of 1812. "Throughout the conflict, he was hampered in executive leadership by his theory that Congress should take the initiative in determining policy" (139).

43. Rakove, *James Madison,* 149.

44. Wills, *James Madison,* 78.

45. Madison, message to the U.S. Senate and House of Representatives, June 1, 1812, in Richardson, ed., *Messages and Papers of the Presidents,* 1:505.

46. Adams, quoted in Ketcham, *James Madison,* 565.

47. Madison, in *Inaugural Addresses,* 27.

48. Of Jefferson's and Madison's actions in 1808 and 1809, Ketcham explains, "Their difficulties arose from the unprecedented fury of the European war, the weakness of their country, and the limitations they imposed on themselves in fidelity to their republican principles" (*James Madison,* 470).

49. Madison, in Richardson, ed., *Messages and Papers of the Presidents,* 1:553.

50. Ketcham, *James Madison*, 532.

51. Madison, in Richardson, ed., *Messages and Papers of the Presidents*, 1:490.

52. Adams to Jefferson, February 2, 1817, *Adams-Jefferson Letters*, ed. Cappon, 508.

53. Ketcham, *James Madison*, 471.

54. Madison, *Writings of James Madison*, ed. Hunt, 8:400–401.

Chapter 5   Woodrow Wilson: Keeping the World Safe from Philosophy

Epigraphs. Woodrow Wilson, *Papers of Woodrow Wilson*, ed. Link et al., 5:58, 19:39.

1. Ibid., 2:499–500.

2. A. J. Wann, "The Development of Woodrow Wilson's Theory of the Presidency: Continuity and Change," 46.

3. Wilson, *Papers of Woodrow Wilson*, ed. Link et al., 2:499–500.

4. Ibid., 6:463.

5. Ibid., 5:57–58, 12:240, 14:190.

6. Ibid., 2:503.

7. Colonel George Henry first proposed that Woodrow Wilson should be taken seriously as a possible presidential candidate in a speech to the Lotos Club in February 1906 (*Papers of Woodrow Wilson*, ed. Link et al., 16:299–301). His speech was printed as an article in *Harper's Weekly* March 10, 1906. Around the same time, Wilson was seriously considered by some in New Jersey as a possible choice for the state legislature to send to the U.S. Senate. Wilson made clear that he would not be considered as a candidate for Senate because he would have had to leave the presidency of Princeton University (ibid., 16:549–50). These boomlets prepared the way for Democrats to consider him a possible gubernatorial candidate in late 1909.

8. Cooper, *The Warrior and the Priest*, 20.

9. Arthur S. Link, "Portrait of the President," 4–5.

10. Wilson, *Papers of Woodrow Wilson*, ed. Link et al., 1:492.

11. As does anyone's, Wilson's thinking did evolve, but the last fundamental adjustment in his political thought seems to have occurred during his time in graduate school, where he embraced Burke more ardently than he had before. The editors of *The Papers of Woodrow Wilson* note that at this time Wilson exchanged Bagehot for Burke as his "master."

12. *Papers of Woodrow Wilson*, ed. Link et al., 2:152–53.

13. Ibid., 1:515.

14. John M. Mulder, *Woodrow Wilson: The Years of Preparation*, 103.

15. Wilson to Ellen Axson, in *Papers of Woodrow Wilson*, ed. Link et al., 2:228–30, 641.

16. Wilson, *Papers of Woodrow Wilson*, ed. Link et al., 8:220.

17. Ibid., 14:324, 19:39.

18. Ibid., 18:594. Wilson also acknowledged the influence of Aristotle in this regard. In his standard lecture on Edmund Burke, Wilson quoted Burke referencing Aristotle. Burke wrote that the issues government deals with are moral questions, which cannot be reduced to rules of logic. Burke's authority on the subject was "Aristotle, the great master of reasoning, [who] cautions us, and with great weight and propriety, against . . . delusive geometrical accuracy in moral arguments, as the most fallacious of all sophistry" (8:334).

19. Franklin William Hooper to Wilson, in *Papers of Woodrow Wilson*, ed. Link et al., 9:334–35.

20. Wilson not only admired the ideas of these figures, he admired their style. To be a "great leader of political thought," one must be persuasive. The better a thinker's style, the more persuasive. Wilson self-consciously honed his own oratory and writing to be like theirs, particularly like Burke's. Philosophically deep lectures might have been more innovative and stimulating, but they would not impress the average

listener so much as a good story about the life of a great leader of political thought.

21. Henry W. Bragdon, *Woodrow Wilson: The Academic Years,* 87; Wilson, *Papers of Woodrow Wilson,* ed. Link et al., 1:158. Wilson explained his decision to quit the practice of law thus: "Whoever thinks, as I thought, that he can practise law successfully and study history and politics at the same time is woefully mistaken." Through the remainder of his life, Wilson was heartened that both Edmund Burke and Walter Bagehot had also found the practice of law intolerable (Bragdon, 99).

22. While political theory helped Wilson to find his niche in academia, his experience in graduate school was somewhat unsatisfying. Much of what he read was broad and theoretical, but the German model of university education that had recently been adopted at Johns Hopkins dictated that each student select a well-defined research project on which to write a dissertation. Each Ph.D. student was to paint a single tile in the mosaic of human knowledge. This approach seemed confining to Wilson for the same reason that he found the study of law confining: it prevented him from being a generalist. He wanted "to contribute to our literature what no American has ever contributed, studies in the philosophy of our institutions," by elucidating "the practical and suggestive, philosophy which is at the core of our governmental methods" (Wilson, *Papers of Woodrow Wilson,* ed. Link et al., 2:502). In short, he was too ambitious to paint a single tile in the mosaic of human knowledge. Wilson wanted to comment on the mosaic itself, as had most of the authors he read in graduate school. Not wanting to be pigeonholed, Wilson left Johns Hopkins without his Ph.D., not intending ever to get one. Only the success of *Congressional Government* allowed him to get the Ph.D. He was granted a doctorate through a waiver which allowed the book to qualify as his dissertation.

23. Wilson, *Papers of Woodrow Wilson,* ed. Link et al., 6:337, 338.

24. Ibid., 24:365.

25. See Walter Bagehot, *Physics and Politics,* 53–54. The organism metaphor was employed in different ways by Georg Wilhelm Friedrich Hegel, Johann Bluntschli, and a slew of German and American academics who learned from them. One of the German-trained Americans who adopted the idea was Wilson's teacher at Johns Hopkins, Herbert Baxter Adams. It was also a favored metaphor of the American social Darwinist Herbert Spencer. Since the metaphor's use was so widespread, it is impossible to precisely pin down the intellectual origins of Wilson's organicism, but his use of the metaphor was in reference to the ideas of Burke and Bagehot and not the German thinkers, for whom he expressed contempt.

26. Woodrow Wilson, *The State: Elements of Historical and Practical Politics,* 576.

27. Wilson, *Papers of Woodrow Wilson,* ed. Link et al., 18:104–5, 8:341.

28. Wilson, quoted in Niels Aage Thorsen, *The Political Thought of Woodrow Wilson, 1875–1910,* 105. This view required Wilson to harbor distinct views about the American Revolution and the Constitution. Since revolutionary change was unsustainable, the American Revolution really was not a revolution at all, but a confirmation of the rights of Englishmen. It built on the long British tradition of rights, first confirmed by the Magna Charta of 1215 and much later by the English Bill of Rights of 1689. The Americans were simply asserting that they belonged to this tradition. They fought to preserve and confirm their ancient prerogatives, not to assume new ones.

Likewise the Constitution was not a departure from tradition but a confirmation of an already existing one. The Constitution conformed to America's values and embodied its spirit. It was not an unimportant document, but most scholars of the Constitution had their causal arrows wrong. The Constitution was a product and embodiment of American values; it did not produce them. If you wanted to understand America, the first place to look was not the Constitution but the hearts of the American people, a sentiment that Wilson shared with Tocqueville, built on Burke's premise.

29. Burke, *Reflections,* 19; Wilson, *The State,* 639.

30. Wilson, *Papers of Woodrow Wilson,* ed. Link et al., 2:159–275.

31. Tocqueville's introduction to *Democracy in America* begins with a description of France's political history:

> In running over the pages of our history for seven hundred years, we shall scarcely find a single great event which has not promoted equality of condition. . . . If, beginning with the eleventh century, we examine what has happened in France from one half-century to another, we shall not fail to perceive, at the end of each of these periods . . . the noble has gone down on the social ladder, and the commoner has gone up; the one descends as the other rises. Every half-century brings them nearer to each other, and they will soon meet.
>
> Nor is this peculiar to France. Whithersoever we turn our eyes, we perceive the same revolution going on throughout the Christian world. (28–29)

32. By today's standards Wilson's commitment to democracy is inadequate because he was a latecomer to the women's suffrage movement and he was frighteningly comfortable with the United States' practice of racial apartheid.

33. Wilson, *Papers of Woodrow Wilson,* ed. Link et al., 9:375.

34. Ibid., 27:270.

35. Ibid., 7:280.

36. Wilson, *The State,* 13.

37. Wilson, *Papers of Woodrow Wilson,* ed. Link et al., 18:51.

38. Ibid., 5:55.

39. Bragdon, *Woodrow Wilson,* 106.

40. Richard P. Longaker, "Woodrow Wilson and the Presidency," 68.

41. Robert E. Osgood, "Woodrow Wilson, Collective Security, and the Lessons of History," 194.

42. Robert Alexander Kraig, *Woodrow Wilson and the Lost World of the Oratorical Statesman,* 130.

43. Before 1911 Wilson emphasized that regulation would put the nation on a road to socialism. This was a plausible Burkean position. He feared that the United States, without a tradition of regulation, would fundamentally change its character by embracing regulation. And he felt, quite naturally as a Burkean, that socialism was a most dreadful rationalist philosophy. Nevertheless, even before 1910 Wilson did leave room for the presence of some regulation. In his March 1908 speech to the Commercial Club of Chicago, he suggested that regulations on businesses were an ill-conceived curtailment of freedom, but that regulating transactions would be valid (*Papers of Woodrow Wilson,* ed. Link et al., 18:35–51).

44. In *The Warrior and the Priest,* John Milton Cooper Jr. strikes a different tone, explaining, "Wilson was not a long-standing conservative who gradually converted to progressivism. Rather, he was a detached observer who, when he was nearly fifty, made his first foray into political engagement on behalf of conservative views. He dropped these views with almost unseemly haste during a single year and then set out boldly on the opposite tack" (121–22). Wilson's conversion experience was undoubtedly the product of increased engagement and the learning that went along with it. However, it is important to add that Wilson did not understand these changes to be a repudiation of his political thought, but the logical refinement of them.

45. Ibid., 141.

46. Wilson, quoted in James Kerney, *The Political Education of Woodrow Wilson,* 365; *Papers of Woodrow Wilson,* ed. Link et al., 31:402–3.

47. Harley Notter, *The Origins of the Foreign Policy of Woodrow Wilson,* v; Daniel D. Stid, *The President as Statesman: Woodrow Wilson and the Constitution,* 2.

48. Kendrick A. Clements, *The Presidency of Woodrow Wilson,* 43.

49. William Diamond, *The Economic Thought of Woodrow Wilson,* 192.

50. Clements, *Presidency of Woodrow Wilson,* 99.

51. Wilson, *Papers of Woodrow Wilson,* ed. Link et al., 29:474.

52. Ibid., 29:516, 517, 520.

53. Wilson may have learned from his experiences. Pressure built to intervene in Mexico again in 1919, but he steadfastly refused to send troops. It did not help the cause of those who favored intervention that they had an interest in profiting from Mexico's oil.

54. Clements, *Presidency of Woodrow Wilson,* 106.

55. Wilson, speech to a joint session of Congress, April 2, 1917, 65th Cong., 1st sess., Senate Doc. No. 5, Serial No. 7264, Washington, D.C.; Thomas J. Knock, *To End All Wars: Woodrow Wilson and the Quest for a New World Order,* 41.

56. Wilson, *Woodrow Wilson: Essential Writings and Speeches of the Scholar-President,* ed. Mario R. DiNunzio, 396.

57. Ibid., 396–97.

58. Wilson, *Papers of Woodrow Wilson,* ed. Link et al., 27:269–70.

59. Kraig, *Woodrow Wilson,* 131, 9.

60. Stid, *President as Statesman,* 92.

61. Clements, *Presidency of Woodrow Wilson,* 14. This behavior was scandalous to many because of the nation's traditional separation of powers and a long-standing wariness of political parties. As a result, Wilson had to justify his party-coordinating actions. His reasoning is reminiscent of Burke's; Burke noted that when bad men combine, the good must also join together to oppose them. To a longtime friend who protested his partisan tactics, Wilson wrote the memorable response "I cannot fight rottenness with rosewater" (Wilson to Nancy Toy, January 31, 1915, in E. David Cronon, ed., *The Political Thought of Woodrow Wilson,* 100).

62. Wilson's physician, Cary T. Grayson, writing of Wilson before his stroke, observed that he "frequently referr[ed] to or read . . . some passage from Burke or Bagehot" (*Woodrow Wilson: An Intimate Memoir,* 11). After a visit to Wilson in April 1922, Ray Stannard Baker "found him much more lively in spirit, with his old liveliness of mind. We got on the subject of Edmund Burke of whom he is a great admirer & he was positively brilliant in his comments on Burke's service. He spoke of him as knowing, profoundly, 'the wisdom of concession'" (*Papers of Woodrow Wilson,* ed. Link et al., 67:585). One of the last things that Wilson wrote—just two weeks before his death—was a brief set of notes for an acceptance speech for the Democratic nomination and a third inaugural. Wilson's grasp on reality was weak, and any mention of his unlikely prospects in the newspapers returned him to thinking that he was what the nation needed. Among these notes is a reference to Burke (ibid., 68:541).

63. Wilson, *Papers of Woodrow Wilson,* ed. Link et al., 62:637–38.

64. Clements, *Presidency of Woodrow Wilson,* 113; Arthur S. Link, *Wilson,* 32. Also see Cooper, *The Warrior and the Priest,* 121–22.

65. Cooper, *The Warrior and the Priest,* 208. In the three-way race of 1912 the accusations of those like Roosevelt did not gain sufficient traction to prevent Wilson's election. By 1916 Wilson was a known commodity, blunting the effectiveness of charges which played on fears of the unknown intellectual.

66. Cooper, *The Warrior and the Priest,* 121–22.

Chapter 6 Franklin Delano Roosevelt: A First-Class Trimmer

Epigraphs. Franklin Delano Roosevelt, *The Public Addresses and Papers of Franklin D. Roosevelt,* ed. Samuel I. Rosenman, 5:390, 7:445.

1. James MacGregor Burns, *Roosevelt: The Lion and the Fox,* 13–21; Geoffrey C. Ward, *Before the Trumpet: Young Franklin Roosevelt, 1882–1905,* 215–42.

2. Bernard Asbell, *The F.D.R. Memoirs: As Written by Bernard Asbell,* appendix 1; Rexford G. Tugwell, *The Brains Trust,* 310.

3. Patrick J. Maney, *The Roosevelt Presence: The Life and Legacy of FDR,* 201. Several authors have suggested that the elderly Holmes might have been speaking of Teddy Roosevelt rather than Franklin Roosevelt (if and) when he made this comment. Even if that is true, the point remains: scholars have evaluated Roosevelt's presidency as a product of his temperament more than his intellect.

4. Kenneth S. Davis, "FDR as a Biographer's Problem," 100–108.

5. Rexford G. Tugwell, *Roosevelt's Revolution: The First Year, a Personal Perspective,* xiv; Tugwell, *Brains Trust,* 521; Raymond Moley, *After Seven Years,* 391–92.

6. Roosevelt, *Addresses and Papers of FDR,* ed. Rosenman, 5:390. If Macaulay's view sounds a lot like Burke's, it is not a coincidence. Recall that Burke had written in his *Reflections on the Revolution in France* that "a state without the means of some change is without the means of its conservation" (19). Macaulay had been influenced by Burke's idea that one needs to reform to preserve. However, while Burke's conservatism stressed the value of indigenous cultural norms and institutions, Macaulay's conservatism was directed much more squarely at finding a middle ground that was between two polarized ideologies.

7. Ibid., 7:445.

8. Ibid., 13:436.

9. In *Franklin D. Roosevelt: His Life and Times, an Encyclopedic View,* ed. Otis L. Graham Jr. and Meghan Robinson Wander, Kenneth S. Davis's entry titled "Reading" maintains that after 1928 "detective stories seem to have constituted the whole of his book reading save for that required by his job" (346). While he did read books as a youth and a young man, "he gave no sign, then or later, in his public speeches or published writings, that he ever read so much as a page of Marx, Freud, Spengler, Ortega y Gasset, Lenin, Dewey, Bergson, Whitehead, Veblen, Russell, Parrington, Beard, the Webbs, Keynes, Henry Adams (though his wife had given him the *Education* for Christmas in 1919)—all of whom had a major impact upon the intellectual life of America in those years" (346).

10. George McJimsey, *The Presidency of Franklin Delano Roosevelt,* 124.

11. Davis, "FDR as a Biographer's Problem," 107.

12. Roosevelt, quoted in Arthur M. Schlesinger Jr., *The Age of Roosevelt: The Coming of the New Deal,* 585–86.

13. Ward, *Before the Trumpet,* 215.

14. Burns, *Roosevelt: Lion and Fox,* 20; Kenneth S. Davis, "Education," in Otis L. Graham Jr. and Meghan Robinson Wander, eds., *Franklin D. Roosevelt: His Life and Times,* 110.

15. Tugwell, *Brains Trust,* 36–38. In his third fireside chat, FDR said, "I have no sympathy with the professional economists who insist that things must run their course and that human agencies can have no influence on economic ills. One reason is that I happen to know that professional economists have changed their definition of economic laws every five or ten years for a very long time" (*Addresses and Papers of FDR,* ed. Rosenman, 2:302).

16. Tugwell, *Brains Trust,* 286.

17. Roosevelt, *Addresses and Papers of FDR,* ed. Rosenman, 1:646.

18. Howard Zinn, ed., *New Deal Thought,* xxviii; Tugwell, *Brains Trust,* 488.

19. Roosevelt, *Addresses and Papers of FDR,* ed. Rosenman, 11:350.

20. Bruce Bliven, "Franklin D. Roosevelt: Patron of Politics," 62–64. This concern is what may have prompted FDR to rely less on the Brains Trust late in the 1932 campaign and to break up this group after taking office and distribute them among different government agencies. Despite having done this, FDR was still chided by many for his "ivory tower" advisers.

21. Roosevelt, *Addresses and Papers of FDR,* ed. Rosenman, 1:659. This sentence was also self-referential, harking back to the "Forgotten Man" address of April 7, 1932, in which Roosevelt said that we need a plan that puts "faith once more in the forgotten man at the bottom of the pyramid" (1:625). "The forgotten man" was a phrase employed by the social Darwinist William Graham Sumner during the Gilded Age. As Raymond Moley remembered it, he inserted the phrase into FDR's speech, giving it a meaning totally foreign to Sumner (*After Seven Years,* 11). Needless to say, FDR used the phrase without attribution.

22. Roosevelt, *Addresses and Papers of FDR,* ed. Rosenman, 1:646, 643. There is good evidence that the Harvard economics professors whose work FDR remained so uninterested in and which he dismissed as doctrinaire later in life actually favored government regulation of the economy (see Daniel R. Fusfeld's *The Economic Thought of Franklin D. Roosevelt and the Origins of the New Deal*). Perhaps if he had been an enthusiastic student rather than an indifferent one he would have realized this.

23. Roosevelt, *Addresses and Papers of FDR,* ed. Rosenman, 1:632, 773–74.

24. Ibid., 5:384, 13:323.

25. Ibid., 4:339.

26. Ibid., 6:361.

27. Ibid., 4:101.

28. Thomas Babington Macaulay, *Miscellanies,* 445–46.

29. Burke, *Reflections,* 19.

30. Roosevelt, *Addresses and Papers of FDR,* ed. Rosenman, 3:317–18, 195.

31. Miller, ed., *Blackwell Encyclopedia of Political Thought,* 303.

32. Asbell, *F.D.R. Memoirs,* 428–32.

33. Roosevelt, *Addresses and Papers of FDR,* ed. Rosenman, 9:440.

34. Ibid., 9:32.

35. Roosevelt to Theodore Dreiser, excerpt printed in Jordan A. Schwartz, *The New Dealers: Power Politics in the Age of Roosevelt,* vii.

36. Roosevelt, *Addresses and Papers of FDR,* ed. Rosenman, 6:329–31.

37. Theodore Roosevelt to Sir George Otto Trevelyan, September 10, 1909, excerpt printed in Albert Bushnell Hart and Herbert Ronald Ferleger, eds., *The Theodore Roosevelt Cyclopedia,* 313. TR was not shy about offering Macaulayesque advice. For instance, he wrote his son Kermit, "All my life in politics, I have striven to make the necessary working compromise between the ideal and the practical. If a man does not have an ideal and try to live up to it, then he becomes a mean, base and sordid creature, no matter how successful. If, on the other hand, he does not work practically, with the knowledge that he is in the world of actual men and must get results, he becomes a worthless head-in-the-air creature" (ibid., 239–40)

38. Tugwell, *Brains Trust,* 408–9; Tugwell, *Roosevelt's Revolution,* 10–11.

39. Roosevelt, *Addresses and Papers of FDR,* ed. Rosenman, 1:650, 9:596.

40. Burns, *Roosevelt: Lion and Fox,* 60–61.

41. Roosevelt, *Addresses and Papers of FDR,* ed. Rosenman, 1:750.

42. Ibid., 1:752. FDR missed the first six weeks of the class he had with Turner because he was on a Caribbean cruise. Tugwell speculates that he learned Turner secondhand, through "Uncle Ted" (*The Democratic Roosevelt: A Biography of Franklin D. Roosevelt,* 55–56).

43. Moley, *After Seven Years,* 48.

44. Tugwell seems to have convinced Roosevelt of his "oversavings theory" of the Great Depression. Not an idea original to him, Tugwell believed that the depression resulted from the growing efficiency of capitalist production. In the nineteenth century, all the nation's labor was needed to produce what was needed for consumption. By the 1920s, what the nation needed could be produced by many fewer workers than

there actually were. The owners of industries employed fewer people, and thus paid out less in wages, reaping greater profits.

In the agricultural sector, an oversupply of commodities resulted. This drove prices down, so even if farmers sold their crops they did not have the capital to buy goods. This imbalance caught up to industry in 1929. The problem during the Great Depression was not an overall lack of capital or of goods—it was the lack of purchasing power by consumers. Taking agricultural land out of production served to bolster commodity prices and increase agricultural purchasing power. Public works projects also put cash in the pockets of those who would spend it.

This vision was built around the idea from classical economics that capitalism is prone to ever-greater efficiencies and Marx's understanding that this results in the problematic concentration of capital by owners of industry. Tugwell was a devotee of neither the classical economists like Smith and Ricardo nor Marx, but his economic views were deeply informed by both.

45. Tugwell, *Roosevelt's Revolution*, 43, 293.

46. Roosevelt, *Addresses and Papers of FDR*, ed. Rosenman, 3:125.

47. McJimsey, *Presidency of Franklin Delano Roosevelt*, 7–8, 20–21, 69–72, 230–38.

48. Edwin E. Witte, *The Development of the Social Security Act*, 18. Witte reports, "I learned nothing about his wishes and preferences beyond the general policies outlined in the [June 8, 1934] message" (19).

49. During 1932, FDR did tip his cap to isolationist forces in the Democratic Party a bit after a New Year's Day address by William Randolph Hearst. Roosevelt, who had long spoken in favor of the League of Nations, went on record saying that he did not favor immediate U.S. participation in a global organization.

50. Roosevelt is sometimes blamed for not recognizing the threat Soviet Communism posed to its neighbors and the free world. Unfortunately the president died at a very inopportune time, when the postwar future of Europe was very much in doubt. Roosevelt's death itself may have contributed to Joseph Stalin's taking a hard line on a Communist sphere of influence.

51. Samuel I. Rosenman, *Working with Roosevelt*, 55.

52. Additionally, Roosevelt bowed to pressure for Japanese-Americans to be interred in camps, a flagrant violation of due process and equal protection.

Chapter 7 Bill Clinton: Flirtation with the Social Contract

Epigraphs. "Speech by President to Farmers and Students in Seattle," December 1, 1999; "Speech by President Opening at SS Conference," December 8, 1998, both accessed at the Clinton Foundation archive of presidential documents, http://www.clintonfoundation.org/legacy. I reference every document retrieved from the Clinton Foundation website using the exact title provided on the website. In the two years since I have accessed this material, the host site has moved from the Clinton Foundation Legacy address to the William J. Clinton Presidential Center Online Library Archives http://archives.clintonpresidentialcenter.org/.

1. Clinton, quoted in George C. Edwards III, "Frustration and Folly: Bill Clinton and the Public Presidency," 168; Michael Waldman, *POTUS Speaks: Finding the Words that Defined the Clinton Presidency*, 198.

2. Joe Klein, *The Natural: The Misunderstood Presidency of Bill Clinton*, 19; David J. Siemers, "Bill Clinton's Contractarian Worldview: The Intellectual Origins and Public Face of the Clinton Presidency," 65–86.

3. Of the public addresses posted to the Clinton Foundation's website, fourteen contain this same reference. Most of the references occur after it became clear that Clinton's health-care proposal would fail, with eight references to the same passage made between June 16 and November 10, 1994.

4. The part of the chapter that Clinton references reads as follows in Harvey C. Mansfield Jr.'s translation of *The Prince:*

> It should be considered that nothing is more difficult to handle, more doubtful of success, nor more dangerous to manage, than to put oneself at the head of introducing new orders. For the introducer has all those who benefit from the old orders as enemies, and he has lukewarm defenders in all those who might benefit from the new orders. This lukewarmness arises partly from fear of adversaries who have the laws on their side and partly from the incredulity of men, who do not truly believe in new things unless they come to have a firm experience of them. Consequently, whenever those who are enemies have opportunity to attack, they do so with partisan zeal, and the others defend lukewarmly so that one is in peril along with them. (23–24)

Machiavelli proceeds to say that if those who want change have to "beg" to effect it, "they always come to ill and never accomplish anything," but those who "are able to use force . . . are rarely in peril" (24). One wonders that this did not deter Clinton, as an American president is rarely in a position of using force against domestic foes.

The first instance of Clinton's referencing this passage was in March of 1994, when he related that a nun, Sister Bernice Coreil, had quoted it. Clinton may have reread *The Prince* afterward, because after an interval of two months, he referenced this same passage at least eight times in public addresses over the next five months.

5. The "teacher of evil" phrase is Leo Strauss's (*Thoughts on Machiavelli*, 9–13). Richard Nixon's book *Leaders* references Machiavelli. In discussing Chiang Kai-shek's efforts to maintain control in mainland China, Nixon comments that "Machiavelli would have been right" in advising Chiang to limit the independence of regional warlords (246).

6. This temptation was not lost on Abraham Lincoln. In his earliest recorded speech, the Address to the Young Men's Lyceum of Springfield, Lincoln suggested that those with vaulting ambition would seek to tear down even a working government so that they could build one anew and in so doing achieve political immortality. He argued that Americans should dedicate themselves to following the law as a kind of civil religion which would prevent this from occurring.

7. This view would, of course, discount the substantial array of interests which favored the expansion of free trade, which were allied with Clinton.

8. Bill Clinton, *My Life,* 150, 148.

9. Tevi Troy, *Intellectuals and the American Presidency: Philosophers, Jesters, or Technicians?* 171–72.

10. Clinton, *My Life,* 70; *The Ratio Studiorum: The Official Plan for Jesuit Education,* 101.

11. Clinton, *My Life,* 109–10, 77, 111, 105.

12. Ibid., 115.

13. Ibid., 141, 171–73, 148.

14. Talbott would turn his research on the memoirs of Nikita Khrushchev into the book *Khrushchev Remembers* and proceed to write for *Time* before serving as Clinton's deputy secretary of state. Frank Aller committed suicide shortly after he returned to the United States, a tragedy that was one of the most painful experiences of Bill Clinton's life.

15. Troy, *Intellectuals and the Presidency,* 173.

16. Troy relates that the invitations to the White House and the attention Clinton showed academics were useful in another way: they created a reservoir of goodwill which was mobilized to help save Clinton's presidency during the Lewinsky scandal.

17. Benjamin R. Barber, *The Truth of Power: Intellectual Affairs in the Clinton White House,* 13.

18. David Maraniss, *First in His Class: A Biography of Bill Clinton,* 138; John F. Harris, *The Survivor: Bill Clinton in the White House,* 18–19.

19. Benjamin R. Barber, *Strong Democracy: Participatory Politics for a New Age,* chap. 1.

20. James Fallows, "The Passionless President: The Trouble with Jimmy Carter's Presidency."

21. Kenneth S. Baer, *Reinventing Democrats: The Politics of Liberalism from Reagan to Clinton,* 199.

22. Bill Clinton and Al Gore, *Putting People First: How We Can All Change America,* 226.

23. "Speech by President at New England Dinner Boston MA," March 14, 1994, Clinton Foundation web archive.

24. Clinton may have remembered political theory casually, by a process that political psychologists call "on-line processing." An individual can actively take in specific information, like a movie plot or a candidate's position on the issues, fitting it into an overall assessment. Later that individual can easily say whether he liked or disliked a movie or whether he or she would vote for a candidate, but cannot articulate (or, more accurately, cannot remember) exactly why. Clinton had read a good deal of political theory, but in articulating his own political thought spoke in very general terms without referencing the specific ideas of individual thinkers.

25. David Boucher and Paul Kelly, eds., *The Social Contract from Hobbes to Rawls,* 1–3.

26. "Speech by President at Georgetown," June 25, 1999; "Presidential Radio Address on Education Reforms," April 1, 1995, both at Clinton Foundation web archive.

27. "Speech by President at National Medal of Arts Awards," September 29, 1999, Clinton Foundation web archive.

28. "Speech by President to the Democratic Leadership Council," October 27, 1997, Clinton Foundation web archive, my emphasis.

29. Harris, *The Survivor,* 436.

30. "Speech by President at DNC Dinner," October 8, 1997, Clinton Foundation web archive.

31. Bill Clinton, *Preface to the Presidency: Selected Speeches of Bill Clinton, 1974–1992,* ed. Stephen A. Smith, 362.

32. Robert B. Reich, *The Work of Nations: Preparing Ourselves for 21st Century Capitalism.* Clinton employed Reich's quasi-contractarianism to make his political name. Early in his tenure as governor of Arkansas, Clinton exhorted state legislators to raise spending per pupil in the public schools, arguing that the state was obliged to provide a better quality of education to its young citizens. The increase in funding was tied to new obligations on the part of schools and teachers. In exchange for more spending Clinton pledged "better accountability and assessment for students and teachers, a fairer distribution of aid, more efficient organization" and enhanced special programs (*Preface to the Presidency,* ed. Smith, 12). The state would provide more money and expect higher performance in return. Clinton emphasized that citizens could expect to be repaid on their "investment" through a growth in state wealth and the rising prosperity provided by having a more educated populace. Those educated in Arkansas would receive a benefit, but not in the form of a gift; Clinton emphasized that they had an obligation to act responsibly, repaying the public's investment by being productive members of society.

33. Brian Skyrms, *The Evolution of the Social Contract,* xi. For instance, Locke and Hobbes each use the social contract to describe what the proper relationship between citizens and government should be—for all time. Neither author suggests that their preferred arrangements will ever become inappropriate or had ever been inappropriate in the past.

34. Clinton recognized that there had been significant policy alterations since the New Deal—most notably those brought during the Great Society and the backlash

against the New Deal philosophy articulated by Ronald Reagan, but the shared conception of the relationship between the American government and its citizens had not fundamentally changed from the 1930s.

35. "Speech by President to Conference on Progressive Tradition," October 5, 2000, Clinton Foundation web archive. These five periods of transition were the founding, the Civil War and its aftermath, the Progressive Era, the New Deal, and the time during which Clinton was president.

36. Clinton, *My Life*, 77, 78.

37. Stephen Skowronek, *The Politics Presidents Make: Leadership from John Adams to George Bush*, chaps. 1–3; Waldman, *POTUS Speaks*, 151.

38. The periods of surge and degeneration that Quigley outlined in *The Evolution of Civilizations: An Introduction to Historical Analysis* lasted centuries, not decades. It is a testament to Clinton's ability to paper over differences that he could neatly fold both Skowronek's and Quigley's views into his own political thought. Quigley offered 970 A.D. to 1270 A.D. as the first era of expansion in Western civilization, followed by a decline lasting the next 150 years. The next era of expansion was 1420–1650, followed by an 80-year decline. The final era of expansion was defined by industrialization and lasted from 1730 to 1929. Quigley believed that the West was in decline when he wrote his book but that it was fully capable of renewal because of its "future preference" (chap. 10).

39. See Robert F. Durant, "A 'New Covenant' Kept: Core Values, Presidential Communications, and the Paradox of the Clinton Presidency"; and Siemers, "Clinton's Contractarian Worldview."

40. In 1992 President Clinton touted universal health care as part of the New Covenant, and after 1994 he repeatedly emphasized that Medicare and Medicaid were part of an existing social contract. But it is somewhat difficult to understand the citizen-responsibility component of these programs. Market mechanisms like copayments and insurance pools were envisioned as part of universal care which would keep costs down. However, if Clinton was serious about requiring responsibility from citizens in exchange for government benefits, he logically would have had to stress that participants should lead healthful lifestyles. Many construed the push for universal health care as an old-style New Deal policy, which promised a government benefit to all citizens without any substantial effort on their part. Clinton did very little to dispel that impression.

41. Sidney Blumenthal, *The Clinton Wars*, 33. I call Blumenthal's account of the Clinton presidency semiofficial because his book contract with a sympathetic publisher was arranged before he left the White House. Blumenthal relates that his "public service" would be continuing after Clinton left office, an apparent reference to the writing of *The Clinton Wars*. Blumenthal also dutifully repeats Clinton's favorite part of Machiavelli's *Prince* (the one in this chapter's first epigraph) not once, but twice (45, 672), not mentioning that the president himself referenced this quote in the same way.

42. "Speech by President in NAFTA Bill Signing Ceremony," December 8, 1993, Clinton Foundation web archive.

43. "Speech by President to Business Council at Williamsburg," October 13, 1995, Clinton Foundation web archive.

44. "Remarks by President Aboard Air Force One in Brazil," October 13, 1997, Clinton Foundation web archive.

45. "Remarks by President and NATO Leaders in DLC Roundtable," April 25, 1999, Clinton Foundation web archive.

46. "Speech by President to the University of Warwick," December 14, 2000; "Speech by President to the Duma," June 5, 2000, both in Clinton Foundation web archive.

47. "Speech by President at Rego Event," March 16, 1995, Clinton Foundation web archive.

48. "Speech by President, SOTU Address," January 24, 1995, Clinton Foundation web archive.

49. Robert B. Reich, *Locked in the Cabinet*, 17; Baer, *Reinventing Democrats*, 252; David Gergen, *Eyewitness to Power: The Essence of Leadership, Nixon to Clinton*, 328–30; Barber, *Truth of Power*; Dick Morris and Eileen McGann, *Because He Could*, 27–29; Joel D. Aberbach, "The Federal Executive under Clinton," 179; James MacGregor Burns and Georgia Sorenson, *Dead Center: Clinton-Gore Leadership and the Perils of Moderation*; Philip Klinkner, "Democratic Party Ideology in the 1990s," in *The Politics of Ideas: Intellectual Challenges Facing the American Political Parties*.

50. Thomas B. Edsall, "A Man for This Season," 48–53.

51. Ronald Brownstein, "State of the Debate: Clinton: The Untold Story," 33–37.

52. Klein, *The Natural*, 12, 58.

53. Durant, "A 'New Covenant' Kept." Also see David Brady and D. Sunshine Hillygus, "Assessing the Clinton Presidency: The Political Constraints of Legislative Policy"; and Siemers, "Clinton's Contractarian Worldview."

54. Charles O. Jones, *The Presidency in a Separated System*; Neustadt, *Presidential Power*.

Conclusion: Dear Mr. President

Epigraphs. Matthew Wren's *Considerations* and James Harrington's reply are quoted in Charles Blitzer, *An Immortal Commonwealth*, 80–81.

1. Troy, *Intellectuals and the Presidency*.

2. Thompson, *The President and the Public Philosophy*, 208, 74.

3. Barber, *Truth of Power*, 14.

4. Dean Keith Simonton, *Why Presidents Succeed: A Political Psychology of Leadership*, 156.

5. Simonton, *Why Presidents Succeed*, 198–203.

6. Clinton L. Rossiter, quoted by Michael Nelson in his foreword to *The Invention of the United States Senate*, by Daniel Wirls and Stephen Wirls, vii.

7. Reich, *Locked in the Cabinet*, 54–55.

8. This point is possibly better stated—in a more sober, reflective, and less absolutist way—by Michael Oakeshott in the various essays contained in *Rationalism in Politics and Other Essays*.

Bibliography

Aberbach, Joel D. "The Federal Executive under Clinton." In *The Clinton Presidency: First Appraisals,* 163–87. Chatham, NJ: Chatham House, 1996.

Adair, Douglass. *Fame and the Founding Fathers: Essays.* New York: W. W. Norton, 1974.

———. "'That Politics May Be Reduced to a Science': David Hume, James Madison, and the Tenth *Federalist.*" *Huntington Library Quarterly* 20 (August 1957): 343–60.

Adams, Abigail, John Adams, and Thomas Jefferson. *The Adams-Jefferson Letters: The Complete Correspondence between Thomas Jefferson and Abigail and John Adams.* Ed. Lester J. Cappon. Chapel Hill: University of North Carolina Press, 1987.

Adams, John. *Diary and Autobiography of John Adams.* Ed. Lyman H. Butterfield. 4 vols. Cambridge, MA: Harvard University Press, 1961.

———. *The Earliest Diary of John Adams.* Ed. L. H. Butterfield. Cambridge, MA: Belknap Press of Harvard University Press, 1966.

———. *The Papers of John Adams.* Series III, General Correspondence and Other Papers of the Adams Statesmen. Ed. Robert J. Taylor. Cambridge, MA: Belknap Press of Harvard University Press, 1977– .

———. *The Political Writings of John Adams.* Ed. George W. Carey. Washington, D.C.: Regnery, 2000.

———. *The Works of John Adams, Second President of the United States.* Ed. Charles Francis Adams. 10 vols. Boston: Little, Brown, 1850–1856.

Appleby, Joyce. *Liberalism and Republicanism in the Historical Imagination.* Cambridge, MA: Harvard University Press, 1992.

———. *Thomas Jefferson.* New York: Times Books, 2003.

Asbell, Bernard. *The F.D.R. Memoirs: As Written by Bernard Asbell.* Garden City, NY: Doubleday, 1973.

Baer, Kenneth S. *Reinventing Democrats: The Politics of Liberalism from Reagan to Clinton.* Lawrence: University Press of Kansas, 2000.

Bagehot, Walter. *Physics and Politics: or Thoughts on the Application of the Principles of "Natural Selection" and "Inheritance" to Political Society.* New York: D. Appleton, 1916.

Bailyn, Bernard. *The Ideological Origins of the American Revolution.* Cambridge, MA: Harvard University Press, 1967.

Banning, Lance. *The Jeffersonian Persuasion: Evolution of a Party Ideology.* Ithaca, NY: Cornell University Press, 1978.

Barber, Benjamin R. *Strong Democracy: Participatory Politics for a New Age.* Berkeley: University of California Press, 1984.

_____. *The Truth of Power: Intellectual Affairs in the Clinton White House.* New York: W. W. Norton, 2001.

Becker, Carl. *The Declaration of Independence: A Study in the History of Political Ideas.* New York: Harcourt, Brace, 1922.

Behar, Ruth. "The Anthropologist's Son." *The Chronicle of Higher Education* 55 (December 5, 2008): B12–B13.

Blitzer, Charles. *An Immortal Commonwealth.* New Haven, CT: Yale University Press, 1960.

Bliven, Bruce. "Franklin D. Roosevelt: Patron of Politics." *The New Republic* (June 1, 1932): 62–64.

Bloom, Allan. *The Closing of the American Mind.* New York: Simon & Schuster, 1987.

Blumenthal, Sidney. *The Clinton Wars.* New York: Farrar, Straus & Giroux, 2003.

Boorstin, Daniel J. *The Genius of American Politics.* Chicago: University of Chicago Press, 1953.

_____. *The Lost World of Thomas Jefferson.* New York: Henry Holt, 1948.

Boucher, David, and Paul Kelly, eds. *The Social Contract from Hobbes to Rawls.* New York: Routledge, 1994.

Brady, David, and D. Sunshine Hillygus. "Assessing the Clinton Presidency: The Political Constraints of Legislative Policy." In *The Clinton Riddle: Perspectives on the Forty-second President,* 47–78. Little Rock: University of Arkansas Press, 2004.

Bragdon, Henry W. *Woodrow Wilson: The Academic Years.* Cambridge, MA: Belknap Press of Harvard University Press, 1967.

Brown, Ralph Adams. *The Presidency of John Adams.* Lawrence: University Press of Kansas, 1975.

Brown, Richard D. "The Disenchantment of a Radical Whig: John Adams Reckons with Free Speech," In *John Adams and the Founding of the Republic.* Boston: Massachusetts Historical Society, 2001.

Brownstein, Ronald. "State of the Debate: Clinton: The Untold Story." *American Prospect* 13, no. 4 (February 25, 2002): 33–37.

Bryce, James. *The American Commonwealth.* 3rd ed. 2 vols. New York: Macmillan, 1903.

Burke, Edmund. *Reflections on the Revolution in France.* Indianapolis: Hackett, 1987.

Burns, James MacGregor. *Roosevelt: The Lion and the Fox.* New York: Harcourt, Brace, 1956.

Burns, James MacGregor, and Georgia Sorenson. *Dead Center: Clinton-Gore Leadership and the Perils of Moderation.* New York: Simon & Schuster, 1999.

Campbell, Colin, and Bert Rockman, eds. *Clinton Presidency: First Appraisals.* Chatham, NJ: Chatham House, 1996.

Chinard, Gilbert, ed. *The Commonplace Book of Thomas Jefferson.* Baltimore: Johns Hopkins University Press, 1926.

Clements, Kendrick A. *The Presidency of Woodrow Wilson.* Lawrence: University Press of Kansas, 1992.

Clinton, Bill. *My Life.* New York: Alfred A. Knopf, 2004.

———. *Preface to the Presidency: Selected Speeches of Bill Clinton, 1974–1992.* Ed. Stephen A. Smith. Fayetteville: University of Arkansas Press, 1996.

Clinton, Bill, and Al Gore. *Putting People First: How We Can All Change America.* New York: Times Books, 1992.

Clinton Foundation website. http://archives.clintonpresidentialcenter.org/.

Cooper, John Milton, Jr. *The Warrior and the Priest: Woodrow Wilson and Theodore Roosevelt.* Cambridge, MA: Harvard University Press, 1983.

Cronon, E. David. *The Political Thought of Woodrow Wilson.* New York: Bobbs-Merrill, 1965.

Dahl, Robert A. *A Preface to Democratic Theory.* Chicago: University of Chicago Press, 1956.

Danoff, Brian F. "Lincoln, Machiavelli, and American Political Thought." *Presidential Studies Quarterly* 30, no. 2 (June 2000): 290–311.

Davis, Kenneth S. "FDR as a Biographer's Problem." *The American Scholar,* 53, no. 1 (Winter 1983): 100–108.

Diamond, William. *The Economic Thought of Woodrow Wilson.* Baltimore: Johns Hopkins University Press, 1943.

Diggins, John Patrick. *John Adams.* New York: Times Books, 2003.

Drury, Shadia B. "Leo Strauss and the American Imperial Project." *Political Theory* 35, no. 1 (February 2007): 62–67.

Durant, Robert F. "A 'New Covenant' Kept: Core Values, Presidential Communications, and the Paradox of the Clinton Presidency." *Presidential Studies Quarterly* 36, no. 3 (September 2006): 345–72.

Edsall, Thomas B. "A Man for this Season." *American Prospect* 11, no. 8 (February 28, 2000): 48–53.

Edwards, George C., III. "Frustration and Folly: Bill Clinton and the Public Presidency." In *The Clinton Presidency: First Appraisals*, 234–61. Chatham, NJ: Chatham House, 1996.

Elkins, Stanley, and Eric McKitrick. *The Age of Federalism*. Oxford: Oxford University Press, 1993.

Ellis, Joseph J. *American Sphinx: The Character of Thomas Jefferson*. New York: Alfred A. Knopf, 1997.

———. *Passionate Sage: The Character and Legacy of John Adams*. New York: W. W. Norton, 1993.

Fallows, James. "The Passionless President: The Trouble with Jimmy Carter's Presidency." *Atlantic Monthly* 243, no. 5 (May 1979): 33–48, and 243, no. 6 (June 1979): 75–81.

Fusfeld, Daniel R. *The Economic Thought of Franklin D. Roosevelt and the Origins of the New Deal*. New York: Columbia University Press, 1954.

George, Alexander L. "Adaptation to Stress in Political Decision Making." In *Coping and Adaptation*. New York: Basic Books, 1974.

Gergen, David. *Eyewitness to Power: The Essence of Leadership, Nixon to Clinton*. New York: Simon & Schuster, 2000.

Graham, Otis L., Jr., and Meghan Robinson Wander, eds. *Franklin D. Roosevelt: His Life and Times, an Encyclopedic View*. Boston: G. K. Hall, 1985.

Grant, James. *John Adams: Party of One*. New York: Farrar, Straus & Giroux, 2005.

Grayson, Cary T. *Woodrow Wilson: An Intimate Memoir*. New York: Holt, Rinehart & Winston, 1960.

Greenstein, Fred I. *The Presidential Difference: Leadership Style from FDR to Clinton*. New York: Free Press, 2000.

Hamilton, Alexander, John Jay, and James Madison. *The Federalist*. Ed. Jacob E. Cooke. Cleveland: World Publishing, 1961.

Haraszti, Zoltan. *John Adams and the Prophets of Progress*. Cambridge, MA: Harvard University Press, 1952.

Harris, John F. *The Survivor: Bill Clinton in the White House*. New York: Random House, 2005.

Hart, Albert Bushnell, and Herbert Ronald Ferleger, eds. *The Theodore Roosevelt Cyclopedia*. New York: Roosevelt Memorial Association, 1941.

Herndon, William H., and Jesse Weik. *Herndon's Lincoln*. Springfield, IL: Herndon's Lincoln Publishing Co., 1888.

Hobbes, Thomas. *Leviathan*. London: Penguin Books, 1985.

Hoover, Herbert. *American Individualism*. Garden City, NY: Doubleday, Page, 1923.

Iacuzzi, Alfred. *John Adams, Scholar.* New York: S. F. Vanni, 1952.

Inaugural Addresses of the Presidents of the United States. Washington, DC: United States Government Printing Office, 1989.

Jefferson, Thomas. *Papers of Thomas Jefferson.* Ed. Julian P. Boyd, Charles T. Cullen, John Catanzariti, and Barbara B. Oberg. Princeton, NJ: Princeton University Press, 1950– .

——. *Thomas Jefferson: Writings.* Ed. Merrill D. Peterson. New York: Library of America, 1984.

——. *The Writings of Thomas Jefferson.* Ed. Andrew A. Lipscomb and Albert Ellery Bergh. 20 vols. Washington, DC: Thomas Jefferson Memorial Association, 1903–1904.

Jones, Charles O. *The Presidency in a Separated System.* Washington, DC: Brookings Institution, 1994.

Kaminski, John P. *The Quotable Jefferson.* Princeton, NJ: Princeton University Press, 2006.

Kerney, James. *The Political Education of Woodrow Wilson.* New York: Century, 1926.

Ketcham, Ralph. *James Madison: A Biography.* Charlottesville: University Press of Virginia, 1990.

——. *Presidents Above Party: The First American Presidency, 1789–1829.* Chapel Hill: University of North Carolina Press, 1984.

Klein, Joe. *The Natural: The Misunderstood Presidency of Bill Clinton.* New York: Doubleday, 2002.

Klein, Philip Shriver. *President James Buchanan: A Biography.* University Park: Pennsylvania State University Press, 1962.

Klinkner, Philip. "Democratic Party Ideology in the 1990s." In *The Politics of Ideas: Intellectual Challenges Facing the American Political Parties,* 113–32. Albany: State University of New York Press, 2001.

Knock, Thomas J. *To End All Wars: Woodrow Wilson and the Quest for a New World Order.* Oxford: Oxford University Press, 1992.

Kraig, Robert Alexander. *Woodrow Wilson and the Lost World of the Oratorical Statesman.* College Station: Texas A & M University Press, 2004.

Latham, Earl, ed. *The Philosophy and Policies of Woodrow Wilson.* Chicago: University of Chicago Press, 1958.

Lerner, Ralph. *The Thinking Revolutionary: Principle and Practice in the New Republic.* Ithaca, NY: Cornell University Press, 1987.

Lincoln, Abraham. *The Collected Works of Abraham Lincoln.* Ed. Roy P. Basler. 8 vols. New Brunswick: Rutgers University Press, 1953.

Link, Arthur S. "Portrait of the President." In *The Philosophy and Policies of Woodrow Wilson,* ed. Earl Latham, 3–27. Chicago: University of Chicago Press, 1958.

_____. *Wilson*. Princeton, NJ: Princeton University Press, 1947.

Locke, John. *The Second Treatise on Civil Government*. Buffalo: Prometheus Books, 1986.

Longaker, Richard P. "Woodrow Wilson and the Presidency." In *The Philosophy and Policies of Woodrow Wilson,* ed. Earl Latham, 67–81. Chicago: University of Chicago Press, 1958.

Macaulay, Thomas Babington. *Miscellanies*. Boston: Houghton Mifflin, 1900.

Machiavelli, Niccolo. *The Discourses*. London: Penguin Books, 1983.

_____. *The Prince*. Trans. Harvey C. Mansfield Jr. Chicago: University of Chicago Press, 1985.

Madison, James. *The Complete Madison: His Basic Writings*. Ed. Saul K. Padover. New York: Harper, 1953.

_____. "An Examination of the British Doctrine." Online Library of Liberty, http://oll.libertyfund.org/title/1938.119003

_____. "James Madison's Autobiography." Ed. Douglass Adair. *The William & Mary Quarterly* 2, no. 2 (April 1945): 191–209.

_____. *Papers of James Madison: Presidential Series*. Ed. Robert A. Rutland, J. C. A. Stagg, Susan Holbrook Perdue, Martha J. King, and Angela Kreider. 6 vols. Charlottesville: University of Virginia Press, 1984– .

_____. *The Papers of James Madison*. Ed. William T. Hutchinson, William M. E. Rachal, Charles F. Hobson, Thomas A. Mason, J. C. A. Stagg, and David B. Mattern. Chicago and Princeton: University of Chicago Press and Princeton University Press, 1962–1991.

_____. *The Writings of James Madison*. Ed. Gaillard Hunt. 9 vols. New York: G. P. Putnam's Sons, 1900–1910.

Malone, Dumas. *Jefferson and His Time: Jefferson the Virginian*. Boston: Little, Brown, 1948.

Maney, Patrick J. *The Roosevelt Presence: The Life and Legacy of FDR*. New York: Twayne Publishers, 1992.

Maraniss, David. *First in His Class: A Biography of Bill Clinton*. New York: Simon & Schuster, 1995.

Matthews, Richard K. *If Men Were Angels: James Madison and the Heartless Empire of Reason*. Lawrence: University Press of Kansas, 1995.

_____. *The Radical Politics of Thomas Jefferson: A Revisionist View*. Lawrence: University Press of Kansas, 1984.

McCoy, Drew R. *The Elusive Republic: Political Economy in Jeffersonian America*. Chapel Hill: University of North Carolina Press, 1980.

_____. *The Last of the Fathers: James Madison and the Republican Legacy*. Cambridge: Cambridge University Press, 1989.

McCullough, David. *John Adams*. New York: Simon & Schuster, 2001.

McJimsey, George. *The Presidency of Franklin Delano Roosevelt.* Lawrence: University Press of Kansas, 2000.

Miller, David, ed. *The Blackwell Encyclopedia of Political Thought.* Oxford: Blackwell, 1987.

Miller, William Lee. *The Business of May Next: James Madison and the Founding.* Charlottesville: University Press of Virginia, 1992.

Moley, Raymond. *After Seven Years.* New York: Harper, 1939.

Montesquieu, Charles de Secondat, Baron de. *The Spirit of the Laws.* Trans. and ed. Anne Cohler, Basia Miller, and Harold Stone. Cambridge: Cambridge University Press, 1989.

Morris, Dick, and Eileen McGann. *Because He Could.* New York: Regan Books, 2004.

Mulder, John M. *Woodrow Wilson: The Years of Preparation.* Princeton, NJ: Princeton University Press, 1978.

Myers, Marvin, ed. *The Mind of the Founder: Sources of the Political Thought of James Madison.* Indianapolis: Bobbs-Merrill, 1973.

Nelson, Michael. Foreword to *The Invention of the United States Senate,* by Daniel Wirls and Stephen Wirls. Baltimore: Johns Hopkins University Press, 2004.

Neustadt, Richard E. *Presidential Power: The Politics of Leadership.* New York: Wiley, 1960.

———. *Presidential Power and the Modern Presidents: The Politics of Leadership from Roosevelt to Reagan.* New York: Free Press, 1990.

Nixon, Richard M. *Leaders.* New York: Warner Books, 1982.

Notter, Harley. *The Origins of the Foreign Policy of Woodrow Wilson.* New York: Russell & Russell, 1965.

Nussbaum, Arthur. *A Concise History of the Law of Nations.* New York: Macmillan, 1962.

Oakeshott, Michael. *Rationalism in Politics and Other Essays.* Indianapolis: Hackett, 1986.

Obama, Barack. *The Audacity of Hope.* New York: Crown, 2006.

———. *Change We Can Believe In.* New York: Three Rivers, 2008.

———. *Dreams from My Father.* New York: Times Books, 1995.

O'Brien, Conor Cruise. *The Long Affair: Thomas Jefferson and the French Revolution.* Chicago: University of Chicago Press, 1996.

Osgood, Robert E. "Woodrow Wilson, Collective Security, and the Lessons of History." In *The Philosophy and Policies of Woodrow Wilson,* ed. Earl Latham, 187–98. Chicago: University of Chicago Press, 1958.

Peek, George A., Jr. *The Political Writings of John Adams.* Indianapolis: Bobbs-Merrill, 1954.

Peterson, Merrill D. *Thomas Jefferson and the New Nation.* Oxford: Oxford University Press, 1970.

Plato. *The Republic.* Trans. and ed. Allan Bloom. New York: Basic Books, 1968.

Quigley, Carroll. *The Evolution of Civilizations: An Introduction to Historical Analysis.* New York: Macmillan, 1961.

Rakove, Jack N. *James Madison and the Creation of the American Republic.* Glenview, IL: Scott, Foresman/Little, Brown, 1990.

The Ratio Studiorum: The Official Plan for Jesuit Education. Trans. Claude Pavur. St. Louis: Institute of Jesuit Sources, 2005.

Rawls, John. *A Theory of Justice.* Cambridge, MA: Belknap Press of Harvard University Press, 1971.

Reich, Robert B. *Locked in the Cabinet.* New York: Vintage Books, 1998.

———. *The Work of Nations: Preparing Ourselves for 21st Century Capitalism.* New York: Alfred A. Knopf, 1991.

Richardson, James D., ed. *Messages and Papers of the Presidents, 1789–1907.* 11 vols. Washington: Bureau of National Literature and Art, 1908.

Ripley, Randall B. "Adams, Burke, and Eighteenth-Century Conservatism." *Political Science Quarterly* 80 (June 1965): 216–35.

Roosevelt, Franklin Delano. *The Public Addresses and Papers of Franklin D. Roosevelt.* Ed. Samuel I. Rosenman. 13 vols. New York: Random House, 1938–1950.

Rosen, Gary. *American Compact: James Madison and the Problem of Founding.* Lawrence: University Press of Kansas, 1999.

Rosenman, Samuel I. *Working with Roosevelt.* New York: Harper, 1952.

Rossiter, Clinton. "The Legacy of John Adams." *Yale Review,* 46, no. 4 (1957): 528–50.

Rush, Benjamin. *The Autobiography of Benjamin Rush: His "Travels through Life" Together with His Commonplace Book for 1789–1813.* Ed. George W. Corner. Princeton, NJ: Princeton University Press, 1948.

Ryerson, Richard Alan, ed. *John Adams and the Founding of the Republic.* Boston: Massachusetts Historical Society, 2001.

Schlesinger, Arthur M., Jr. *The Age of Roosevelt: The Coming of the New Deal.* Boston: Houghton Mifflin, 1958.

Schlesinger, Arthur M., Jr., and Fred L. Israel, eds. *The History of American Presidential Elections, 1789–1968.* 4 vols. New York: McGraw-Hill, 1971.

Schwartz, Jordan A. *The New Dealers: Power Politics in the Age of Roosevelt.* New York: Alfred A. Knopf, 1993.

Sheldon, Garrett Ward. *The Political Philosophy of James Madison.* Baltimore: Johns Hopkins University Press, 2001.

Siemers, David J. "Bill Clinton's Contractarian Worldview: The Intellectual Origins and Public Face of the Clinton Presidency." *Congress & the Presidency* 35, no. 2 (Autumn 2008): 65–86.

————. "Principled Pragmatism: Abraham Lincoln's Method of Political Analysis." *Presidential Studies Quarterly* 34, no. 4 (December 2004): 804–27.

————. *Ratifying the Republic: Antifederalists and Federalists in Constitutional Time*. Stanford, CA: Stanford University Press, 2002.

Simonton, Dean Keith. *Why Presidents Succeed: A Political Psychology of Leadership*. New Haven, CT: Yale University Press, 1987.

Skowronek, Stephen. *The Politics Presidents Make: Leadership from John Adams to George Bush*. Cambridge, MA: Belknap Press of Harvard University Press, 1993.

Skyrms, Brian. *The Evolution of the Social Contract*. Cambridge: Cambridge University Press, 1996.

Sloan, Herbert. "The Earth Belongs in Usufruct to the Living." In *Jeffersonian Legacies*, ed. Peter S. Onuf, 281–315. Charlottesville: University of Virginia Press, 1993.

Smith, Adam. *Inquiry into the Nature and Causes of the Wealth of Nations*. New York: Alfred A. Knopf, 1991.

Stid, Daniel D. *The President as Statesman: Woodrow Wilson and the Constitution*. Lawrence: University Press of Kansas, 1998.

Storing, Herbert, ed. *The Complete Antifederalist*. 7 vols. Chicago: University of Chicago Press, 1981.

Strauss, Leo. *Thoughts on Machiavelli*. Glencoe, IL: Free Press, 1958.

Thompson, C. Bradley. "John Adams and the Science of Politics." In *John Adams and the Founding of the Republic*. Boston: Massachusetts Historical Society, 2001.

————. *John Adams and the Spirit of Liberty*. Lawrence: University Press of Kansas, 1998.

Thompson, Kenneth W. *The President and the Public Philosophy*. Baton Rouge: Louisiana State University Press, 1981.

Thorsen, Niels Aage. *The Political Thought of Woodrow Wilson, 1875–1910*. Princeton, NJ: Princeton University Press, 1988.

Tocqueville, Alexis de. *Democracy in America*. Trans. and ed. Richard D. Heffner. New York: Mentor, 1984.

Troy, Tevi. *Intellectuals and the American Presidency: Philosophers, Jesters, or Technicians?* Lanham, MD: Rowman & Littlefield, 2002.

Tucker, Robert W., and David C. Hendrickson. *Empire of Liberty: The Statecraft of Thomas Jefferson*. Oxford: Oxford University Press, 1990.

Tugwell, Rexford G. *The Brains Trust*. New York: Viking, 1968.

————. *The Democratic Roosevelt: A Biography of Franklin D. Roosevelt*. Garden City, NY: Doubleday, 1957.

————. *Roosevelt's Revolution: The First Year, a Personal Perspective*. New York: Macmillan, 1977.

Urban, Hugh B. *The Secrets of the Kingdom: Religion and Concealment in the Bush Administration.* Lanham, MD: Rowman & Littlefield, 2007.

Waldman, Michael. *POTUS Speaks: Finding the Words that Defined the Clinton Presidency.* New York: Simon & Schuster, 2000.

Walzer, Michael. *Spheres of Justice: A Defense of Pluralism and Equality.* New York: Basic Books, 1983.

Wann, A. J. "The Development of Woodrow Wilson's Theory of the Presidency: Continuity and Change." In *The Philosophy and Policies of Woodrow Wilson.* Chicago: University of Chicago Press, 1958.

Ward, Geoffrey C. *Before the Trumpet: Young Franklin Roosevelt, 1882–1905.* New York: Harper & Row, 1985.

Warren, Mercy Otis. *History of the Rise, Progress and Termination of the American Revolution.* Indianapolis: Liberty Classics, 1988.

Wayland, Francis. *The Elements of Political Economy.* New York: Leavitt, Lord, 1837.

Weisberg, Jacob. *The Bush Tragedy.* New York: Random House, 2008.

White, Morton. *The Philosophy of the American Revolution.* Oxford: Oxford University Press, 1978.

Wills, Garry. *Inventing America: Jefferson's Declaration of Independence.* New York: Doubleday, 1978.

———. *James Madison.* New York: Times Books, 2002.

Will, George F. *Statecraft as Soulcraft: What Government Does.* New York: Simon & Schuster, 1983.

Wilson, Woodrow. *The Papers of Woodrow Wilson.* Ed. Arthur S. Link, David W. Hirst, and J. E. Little. 69 vols. Princeton, NJ: Princeton University Press, 1966–1994.

———. *The State: Elements of Historical and Practical Politics.* Boston: D. C. Heath, 1889.

———. *Woodrow Wilson: Essential Writings and Speeches of the Scholar-President.* Ed. Mario R. DiNunzio. New York: New York University Press, 2006.

Witte, Edwin E. *The Development of the Social Security Act.* Madison: University of Wisconsin Press, 1963.

Wolin, Sheldon S. *Politics and Vision: Continuity and Innovation in Western Political Thought.* Princeton, NJ: Princeton University Press, 2004.

Wright, Robert. *Nonzero: The Logic of Human Destiny.* New York: Vintage Books, 2000.

Zinn, Howard, ed. *New Deal Thought.* Indianapolis: Hackett, 1966.

Zuckert, Michael. "The Political Science of James Madison." In *History of American Political Thought,* 149–66. Lanham, MD: Lexington Books, 2003.

Index

236 Index

Louisiana, 64, 67, 71; military, 62–63;
Montesquieu, view of, 53–54; *Notes
on the State of Virginia,* 51, 60; Obama
and, xii; philosophes, 48, 61–62;
political economy, 50, 52; as political
philosopher, 54, 70, 73; political
theory, approach to, 12, 44, 46, 49–56,
182, 185, 186, 194; political theory,
tensions within, 70–71; as president,
64–70; presidency, conception of,
68–69; presidential rankings, 184;
racism, 50, 203–4n8; radicalism, 49,
61–62; reading habits, 47, 48–49, 53–
54, 56, 192, 204n12, 204n17; reason,
46, 48–51, 62; religion, 64, 68, 71, 88,
190; Republican Party, 69; "Saxon
myth," 58, 65; scholarly views of, 48;
science, 48, 51–52; second inaugural
address, 46, 48, 49, 52; "short-leash
republicanism," 86; taxes, 64–65.
See also happiness; Enlightenment;
Scottish Enlightenment
Jesus, 3–4, 195, 198n6
Johns Hopkins University, 112, 118
Judiciary Act of 1801, 40, 41–42
Justinian, 43

Kames, Lord, 56, 57, 58, 62, 90
Kant, Immanuel, 166
Ketcham, Ralph, 65, 83, 101, 208n28,
209n48
Kennedy, John F., 187
King, Larry, 156
King, Martin Luther, Jr., 195
King Lear, 54
Klein, Joe, 177
Knock, Thomas J., 125
Knox, General Henry, 199n6
Koch, Adrienne, 48
Kraig, Robert Alexander, 119

laissez-faire economics. *See* free market
economics
leadership, 107, 112, 115–16, 119–21,
124–25, 129. *See also* presidential
leadership
League of Nations, 120, 125–27, 150
Ledeen, Michael, 8
Leonard, Daniel (Tory pamphleteer), 22
Leopard incident. *See* HMS *Leopard*
Lewinsky scandal, 171, 172
Lewis, Bernard, 8
Lewis and Clark Expedition, 64, 67–68, 71

Library of Congress, 79
limited government, 12, 56, 61, 63–64,
67–68, 72, 86–87, 89, 98–99, 120
Lincoln, Abraham, 9–11, 104, 106–7,
110, 187, 194–95, 197n3, 217n6. *See
also* Euclid; Young Men's Lyceum
Address (Lincoln)
Link, Arthur S., 107, 128–29
Locke, John, 4, 9–10, 14, 194–95, 201n45,
208n28; Adams and, 34, 36; Bush
(George W.) and, 7–8; Clinton and,
158, 161, 163, 166; "Essay Concerning
Human Understanding," 51; Jefferson
and, 51, 55, 57–58, 63–64, 69, 205n36;
labor theory of value, 69; Madison
and, 86–88; natural rights, 88; Obama
and, ix, xii; property rights, 69, 88,
205n36; religious toleration, 64, 68,
88, 99, 205n43; revolution, 34, 61–62,
63; *Second Treatise,* ix, 7, 14, 34, 63, 69;
separation of powers, 29–30, 85; social
contract, 86–88, 158, 161, 163, 166,
218n33; as suggested reading, 194
logic, 10–11, 187
Lolme, Jean Louis De, 30, 32
Louisiana Purchase, 40, 64, 67, 71, 97
Lycurgus, 29

Mably, Abbe de, 36, 82, 201n47
Macaulay, Thomas Babington, 142–43;
and Burke, 214n6; FDR distances
himself from, 138, 144; as influence
on FDR, 13, 133–34, 142–46, 149, 152,
183, 189; Theodore Roosevelt and,
144–45, 215n37
Machiavelli, Niccolo, 5, 8, 9, 10,
27, 73, 194; Adams and, 22, 25,
26–27, 33; Clinton and, 155–58,
177, 217n4; human nature, 33;
mixed constitution, 30, 85; political
development and, 33, 84; Wilson and,
110, 127
Macon, Nathaniel, 93–94
Madison, James: Adams and, 22, 76; "An
Examination of the British Doctrine,"
65–66, 80, 92; Antifederalists,
response to, 80–82; as political
theorist, 74, 75, 76, 100–103, 206–7n2;
as president, 92–101; assessments of
presidency, 17–18, 100–101, 184; Bill
of Rights, 74–75, 87, 208n26; Britain
and, 65–66, 72, 92–94, 98; Canada,
96, 97–98, 100; characteristics, 83,

About the Author

Photo by Dylan Stolley

David J. Siemers is Associate Professor of Political Science at the University of Wisconsin–Oshkosh and author of *The Antifederalists: Men of Great Faith and Forbearance* and *Ratifying the Republic: Antifederalists and Federalists in Constitutional Time.*